3/11/15

parents aren't supposed to like it

volume 1

parents aren't supposed to like it

Rock & Other Pop Musicians of the 1990s

David P. Bianco, Editor

AN IMPRINT OF GALE

Detroit · New York · Toronto · London

Parents aren't Supposed to Like It

Rock & Other Pop Musicians of the 1990s

David P. Bianco, Editor

Staff

Sonia Benson, U·X·L Senior Editor
Carol DeKane Nagel, U·X·L Managing Editor
Thomas L. Romig, U·X·L Publisher

Mary Beth Trimper, Production Director
Evi Seoud, Assistant Production Manager
Shanna Heilveil, Production Associate

Cynthia Baldwin, Product Design Manager
Barbara Yarrow, Graphic Services Director
Michelle DiMercurio, Art Director
Jessica L. Ulrich, Permissions Assistant
Marco Di Vita, Graphix Group, Typesetter

Library of Congress Cataloging-in-Publication Data
Bianco, David P., 1947-
      Parents aren't supposed to like it: rock and other pop musicians of the 1990s/David P. Bianco
      p. cm.
    Includes bibliographical references, discographies, and index.
    Summary: Profiles over 100 contemporary musicians and bands in the categories of alternative rock, rap, folk music, and others..
    ISBN 0-7876-1731-8 (alk. paper).—ISBN 0-7876-1732-6 (alk. paper).—ISBN 0-7876-1733-4 (alk. paper).—0-7876-1734-2
      1.Musicians—Biography—Dictionaries, Juvenile. 2. Musical groups—Dictionaries, Juvenile. 3. Popular music—Dictionaries, Juvenile. [1. Musicians.] I. Title.
    ML3929.B5 1997
781.66'0922--dc21
[B]
                                             97-34040
                                               CIP
                                          AC MN

10 9 8 7 6 5 4 3

Printed in the United States of America

contents

VOLUME 1

Green Day

VOLUME 2

Reader's Guide

There's something for just about every young music fan in *Parents Aren't Supposed to Like It: Rock & Other Pop Musicians of the 1990s*. This comprehensive resource contains more than 135 biographical/critical entries on the hottest bands and musicians of the 1990s, from a wide range of musical tastes and genres, including grunge, rap, traditional rock and roll, folk, heavy metal, British pop, ska, art rock, techno, rhythm and blues, and much more.

Perfect for browsing or for research, the three volumes are arranged by general musical categories with an overview of each category preceding the alphabetically arranged profiles of musicians in that genre. Volume 1 is devoted entirely to alternative rock; volume 2 contains Brit pop, dance music, and hip-hop and rap; and volume 3 features folk and folk rock, heavy metal, rhythm and blues and urban soul, rock and roll, and singers/songwriters.

Portraits and other black-and-white photos of the musicians accompany most entries. Fun facts and fascinating anecdotes ap-

k. d. lang

pear in sidebars throughout the volumes, and pertinent quotes by and about the musicians begin each entry and can be found highlighted within the text. The entries conclude with sections listing awards, selected discographies, further reading sources, and contact information, with web sites for nearly all the musicians. Along with a thorough subject index for the three-volume set, there are three tables of contents to aid the reader, listing entries in the order in which they appear, in alphabetical order by musician, and in a breakdown by specific genres.

Scope

All of the bands and artists selected for inclusion are relevant to current popular music of the late 1990s. Most sold a lot of records in the 1990s, are on the cutting edge of a musical trend, or have been highly influential to music of the 1990s. The bands featured in *Parents* provide a representative cross-section of different styles of pop music, reflecting the wide variety of tastes exhibited by the record-buying public. The musicians included differ greatly not only in musical style, but in attitude, image, political messages, belief systems, and lifestyles.

Placing musicians in general genre sections provides a unique opportunity to compare the stories and experiences of artists with those of their peers. With overviews introducing these sections, a reader can quickly come up with an overall picture of the particular musical scene in which their favorite bands participate. Many modern musicians, of course, play in several genres, or have combined genres for new sounds. The editors of *Parents* have made an effort to place musicians in the category they are generally associated with, knowing that in many cases the musicians could easily fit well into another category. The tables of contents are provided in order to facilitate quick reference.

The profiles in *Parents* present the stories of the lives and careers of the featured artists, revealing childhood and family life and the inspirations and obstacles involved in the rise to stardom. Descriptions of the artists' recorded music and live performances are provided along with views of the critical and commercial response to their work. Beyond this, the entries contextualize the musical scene and the pop music business in the various genres as they relate to the musicians' experiences. Music festivals, major and independent record labels, innovative producers, musical technology, social and political controversy, and many other behind-the-scene aspects of pop music are brought out in the context of the musicians' life stories.

About the Contributors

David P. Bianco, editor of *Parents Aren't Supposed to Like It,* is a freelance writer, editor, and publishing consultant. His longstanding interest in popular music has resulted in the publication of two previous music reference books, *Who's New Wave in Music: An Illustrated Encyclopedia, 1976-1982, The First Wave* and *Heat Wave: The Motown Fact Book.* Other contributors are listed on the following page:

Kathy Bilitzke: freelance writer.

Charity Anne Dorgan: writer and editor with thirteen reference books to her credit, and a classically trained amateur singer and harpist.

Brian Escamilla: former editor of *Contemporary Musicians,* a biographical reference series, and a freelance writer.

Jo-Ann Greene: contributor to a wide variety of music publications in both the United States and the United Kingdom, including *Hits, Goldmine, CMJ Monthly, Alternative Press,* and *NME: New Musical Express.* She is also the author of *The Cure* and co-author of *U2: A Visual Documentary.*

Jill Hamilton: contributor to *Rolling Stone, Entertainment Weekly,* and *Playgirl.* Winner of 1996 award from the National Society of Newspaper Columnists.

Ralph Heibutzki: contributor to *Goldmine, DISCoveries, Bass Player* and *Guitar Player,* among other publications. Author of liner notes for Rhino's *Sugar Hill* CD boxed set and for the *Dub Chill Out* compilation by Music Collectors International.

Tim James: cofounder and active member of the non-profit Detroit Musicians Alliance (DMA). Promoter of music festivals and concerts; manager of several Detroit-area bands. Contributor to *Jam Rag* magazine and *Musiczine,* the newsletter of DMA.

Allison Jones: freelance writer and contributor to various music publications, including *Contemporary Musicians* and *Canadian Newsmakers.*

Peter Schorn: multiple-award winning and nominated record producer, songwriter, guitarist, and performer with the band Red September. A founder and past president of the Detroit Musicians Alliance (DMA), he has worked to educate musicians and promote quality music in southeast Michigan. He is a columnist and reviewer for *Musiczine,* the newsletter of the DMA.

Sue Summers: cofounder and vice president of the Detroit Musicians Alliance (DMA); freelance writer for *Musiczine,* the fanzine of the DMA; manager of the independent label Static Records; music promoter and band manager.

Dave Thompson: author of more than sixty rock books, including biographies of Kurt Cobain, Depeche Mode, Red Hot Chili Peppers, Perry Farrell, and U2; regular contributor to *Alternative Press* and *Goldmine* magazines.

Patricia Whipple: co-owner of recording studio; manager, booking agent, and critic in music industry; freelance music writer.

Suggestions

We welcome any comments or suggestions on *Parents Aren't Supposed to Like It: Rock and Other Pop Musicians of the 1990s.* Please write: Editors, *Parents Aren't Supposed to Like It,* U•X•L, Gale Research, 835 Penobscot Bldg., Detroit, Michigan 48226-4094; call toll-free: 800-877-4235; or fax to 313-961-6348.

ALPHABETICAL LISTING OF MUSICIANS

(Boldface numeral indicates volume number, which is followed by page number.)

Tupac Shakur

musicians by genre

(Boldface numeral indicates volume number, which is followed by page number.)

Sheryl Crow

Picture Credits

The photographs appearing in *Parents Aren't Supposed to Like It: Rock & Other Pop Musicians of the 1990s* were received from the following sources:

Cover: Grant Lee Phillips of Grant Lee Buffalo: © **Ken Settle. Reproduced by permission.**

AP/Wide World Photos. Reproduced by permission: pp. 1, 5, 24, 57, 60, 78, 93, 138, 164, 174, 219, 220, 230, 241, 249, 310, 330, 344, 368, 378, 387, 418, 420, 439, 451, 473, 542, 574, 585, 588, 594, 597, 611, 621, 626, 627, 630, 643, 644; © **Larry Hulst/Michael Ochs Archives/Venice, CA. Reproduced by permission:** pp. 4, 27, 75, 584; **Archive Photos. Reproduced by permission:** pp. 6, 178, 180, 257, 314, 468, 504; ©**Ken Settle. Reproduced by permission:** pp. 7, 12, 16, 37, 43, 45, 50, 61, 69, 89, 96, 110, 130, 134, 145, 148, 160, 163, 169, 172, 190, 199, 231, 237, 248, 266, 267, 277, 284, 350, 382, 412, 454, 461, 465, 479, 482, 485, 545, 548, 552, 565, 572, 576, 579, 606, 613, 618, 636, 639, 653; **Photograph by Danny Clinch. Columbia, Sony Music. Reproduced by permission:**

The Fugees

p. 11; © Denise Sofranko/Michael Ochs Archives/Venice, CA. Reproduced by permission: pp. 20, 511; Photograph by Rafael Fuchs. Matador Records. Reproduced by permssion: p. 30; Photograph by Christine Alicino. Corbis. Reproduced by permission: p. 33; Photograph by Tim Mosenfelder. Corbis. Reproduced by permission: pp. 34, 182, 253, 254; Photograph by Timothy White. Arista Records. Reproduced by permission: p. 42; Photograph by Frank Ockenfels. Outline Press Syndicate. Reproduced by permission: p. 46; Photograph by Jeff Christensen. Archive Photos/ Reuters. Reproduced by permission: pp. 49, 53, 322; Photograph by Tina Paul. Archive Photos. Reproduced by permission: p. 65; Photograph by Jon Hammer. Archive Photos. Reproduced by permission: p. 70, 196, 222, 270; Photograph by Pauline St. Denis. Courtesy of Rykodisc: p. 81; Photograph by Tibor Bozi. Corbis. Reproduced by permission: p. 84, 291, 443; Michael Ochs Archives/Venice, CA. Reproduced by permission: p. 87, 355, 366, 382, 383, 622; Photograph by Scott Harrison. Archive Photos. Reproduced by permission: pp. 101, 153, 187, 559; Photograph by Sin/Tony Mott. Corbis. Reproduced by permission: pp. 105, 123, 497; Photograph by Scope/John Wallace. Corbis. Reproduced by permission: p. 106; Photograph by James Smolka. Reproduced by permission: p. 111; © Anna Luken/Michael Ochs Archives/Venice, CA. Reproduced by permission: pp. 115, 155, 617; Photograph by Gary Hershorn. Reuters/Archive Photos. Reproduced by permission: p. 117; Photograph by Mike Hashimoti. Corbis. Reproduced by permission: p. 124; Photograph by Lance Mercer. Columbia Records. Reproduced by permission: p. 127; © Joe Hughes/Michael Ochs Archives/Venice, CA. Reproduced by permission: pp. 150, 312; Photograph by Richard Drew. AP/Wide World. Reproduced by permission: p. 192; Photograph by Henry Diltz. Corbis. Reproduced by permission: p. 203; Photograph by Paul Banks. Corbis. Reproduced by permission: pp. 223, 224; Archive Photos/Popperfoto. Reproduced by permission: pp. 227, 516, 541, 634; Archive Photos/Big Pictures. Reproduced by permission: p. 228; Photograph by Mike Segar. Archive Photos/Reuters. Reproduced by permission: pp. 238, 265; © Waring Abbott/Michael Ochs/Archives/Venice, CA. Reproduced by permission: pp. 275, 287, 403, 405, 458, 528; Photograph by Tom Gates. Archive Photos. Reproduced by permission: p. 283; Corbis-Bettmann. Reproduced by permission: 303, 317, 343, 362, 376, 392, 403, 410, 446, 50, 5241, 655; © Al Pereira/Michael Ochs Archives/Venice, CA. Reproduced by permission: pp. 306, 360, 399, 520; © Raymond Boyd/Michael Ochs Archives, Venice, CA. Reproduced by permission: pp. 321, 340, 372, 424, 525; Photograph by Bob Grant. Fotos international/Archive Photos. Reproduced by permission: p. 326; Ruthless Records. Reproduced by permission: p. 338; Photograph by Miranda Shen. Fotos international/Archive Photos. Reproduced by permission: **p. 415**; Photograph by Sin/Roy Tee. Corbis. Reproduced by permission: **p. 441**; Photograph by Michael Miller. Eastwest Records. Reproduced by permission: **p. 490**; ©David Corio/ Michael Ochs Archive, Venice, CA. Reproduced by permission: **p. 493**; Photograph by Fred Prouser. Archive Photos. Reproduced by permission **p. 506**; Photograph by Adam Nadel. AP/Wide World Photos. Reproduced by permission: **p. 535**; © 1996 Rick Olivier. All Rights Reserved. Reproduced by permission: **p. 591**; Photograph by Ken Franckling. Corbis. Reproduced by permission: **p. 603**; Photograph by Ian Waldie. Archive Photos/Reuters. Reproduced by permission: **p. 647**; Photograph by Stephen Apicella-Hitchcock. Atlantic Records. Reproduced by permission: **p. 650.**

parents aren't supposed to like it

ALTERNAtive aND POP ROCK

From punk to grunge in fifteen years

In historical terms, alternative pop/rock has its beginnings in punk rock, the eruption of aggressive, speed-whipped music that emerged in Britain around the mid-1970s, and quickly established itself as both a social and a musical force. In England, groups like the Sex Pistols, Siouxsie and the Banshees, the Clash, the Vibrators, and the Stranglers, among others, with their short, sharp guitar-driven songs and politically aware lyrics, redesigned rock'n'roll from the basement up. Soon British new wave artists such as Elvis Costello, Nick Lowe, and the Jam were combining punk and pop sensibilities in innovative, challenging ways. (See volume 2 for more on British alternative/pop.) In the United States, groups like the **Ramones** (see entry), the Talking Heads, and Television were challenging established musical tastes. The music and the attitudes it conveyed were powerful and challenging to the existing rock establishment.

Overnight, such long-running, rock establishment-type bands as Genesis, the Rolling Stones, and Electric Light Orchestra

Sex Pistols leader, Johnny Rotten

were classified as dinosaurs—"Boring Old Farts" in the words of Sex Pistols singer Johnny Rotten—and though two decades have passed since then, this division in rock music between the new and the established still exists.

The original punk movement thrived in the late 1970s and 1980s, often without the acceptance of major record labels and mainstream radio. But the original movement eventually waned, leaving behind vast influences in music and style that were to be picked up again in the 1990s. No musical movement since then has ever had the impact of punk.

There are a variety of styles and musical categories in modern rock, but they seem to rise and fall with the changing seasons. Punk was—and is—more than that. It not only changed the sound of the music and how it was played, but also the business side: how the music would be made, marketed, packaged, and distributed. Virtually everything that has happened in music since then owes something to punk's impact.

New punk and alternative

The new punk that emerged in the 1990s—as well as other alternative forms of music—was very concerned about keeping their music "pure," which was hard, if not impossible, for groups on major labels. (Labels often dictated style and sounds to musicians.) Because punk rock had always rejected the idea of being "corporate" and "commercial," many of these groups couldn't handle success and burned out quickly.

While MTV and new "modern rock" radio stations helped many a British "alternative" band (the **Cure**, [see entry] Culture Club, A Flock of Seagulls, New Order, Soft Cell) achieve stardom, some U.S. bands who never sold many records turned out to be very influential. Los Angeles punk and post-punk groups like X (who would influence alternative rock and alternative country acts), The Minutemen (featuring bassist Mike Watt, who would later become a godfather of alternative rock) ruled the underground but never hit the big time. Minneapolis's The Replacements—which mixed pop and punk and boasted superb songwriter Paul Westerberg—didn't score big hits, though **Soul Asylum,** who came from the same town and were on the same indie label in their early years, broke through with a smash album in 1992. The alternative rock movement that exploded in Nirvana's wake was filled with acts who drew on the work of these less successful trailblazers.

By 1991 new music fans were buying certain kinds of records in vast quantities, including dozens of different styles, from the grunge of **Nirvana** and **Pearl Jam** (see entries) to the alternative pop /rock of **R.E.M.** and **Elvis Costello** (see entries) to the hardcore punk of **Green Day,** the rock/metal of **Soundgarden** and the heavy metal of **Living Colour** (see entries). The media promptly christened all of this music "alternative."

The Lollapalooza culture

The early 1990s also saw Perry Farrell (**Jane's Addiction** and **Porno for Py-**

ros) create Lollapalooza, a travelling alternative music festival. The event was inspired by the popularity of similar events in Europe, and was one of the most successful tours of 1991. Touring twenty-one cities, the festival played to nearly half a million people that summer. Since that time, Lollapalooza has become an annual event, highlighting mostly alternative bands but also including heavy metal and rap. In 1992 a second stage was added to feature lesser-known alternative groups. The day-long events helped spread alternative culture through more than just concerts; booths were set up to send a variety of social and political messages to the festival's young visitors.

Rapper **Ice-T** (see entry), one of the artists involved in the first Lollapalooza, offered a summary of what the tour and its music were all about: "This is a very pioneering tour. All the groups in their own way have pioneered a certain form of music, and none of us get played on the radio." Siouxsie and the Banshees, **Nine Inch Nails** (see entry), the **Butthole Surfers** (see entry), and the Rollins Band completed the 1991 line-up, and Ice-T was right. They had all pioneered something you would not be likely to hear on the radio, yet.

Pioneering in music continued. The influence of "electronica," hip-hop, and other recent forms began to appear in alternative rock during the 1990s as well. After scoring a hit with the alterna-anthem "Loser," Beck escaped being a one-hit wonder and stunned the music world with his award-winning second album, *Odelay*. He combined pop, rap, folk, and virtually every other imaginable style in the blender of his imagination, added surreal (folk-singer Bob) Dylan-inspired lyrics, and came up with music that sounded way-out and catchy, familiar and totally new all at the same time. Like other artists of this period, he mixed samples with live instruments and ended up with music that was impossible to pin down. Acts as diverse as **Garbage** (see entry), Sneaker Pimps, Forest for the Trees, Stereolab, Portishead, and Tricky achieved success with "trip-hop" and other hybrid (combined) styles.

The rise of the indies (independent record companies)

For many groups, getting a major record deal was an impossible dream. As the 1980s progressed, major multi-national corporations began buying up all the smaller record companies. By the mid-1990s, there were just six major labels left in America, each one operating a host of smaller subsidiaries. Their ideas of what would and would not sell excluded many of the new musicians who didn't fit into old molds.

Often if a band wished to make a recording, the only way to go was to form their own label. By the mid-1980s, independent labels like Alternative Tentacles, Slash, and Twin Tone were already well established. Once alternative music did break into the mainstream, it would be the independent labels that led the way: Sub Pop, with their stable of Seattle grunge groups; Epitaph, with

Perry Farrell

their Southern California punk and ska groups; Wax Trax, the home of industrial music, and so on. Most of the bands these labels brought to fame had already been rejected by the majors.

With local labels to release the music, local city scenes became underground obsessions. Athens, Georgia, the home of R.E.M. and the B-52s, enjoyed a moment in the spotlight; so did Chapel Hill, North Carolina, following the emergence of Swervedriver. The late 1980s saw the English city of Manchester rechristened "Madchester," after the Stone Roses and the Happy Mondays led a new charge of trippy dance bands into the spotlight.

Seattle becomes the center of alternative music

But few of these scenes stuck for any amount of time. Instead, one or two-off hits were the order of the day. Alternative bands that had worthwhile follow-up material were unable to get their songs played on American radio and television, at that time the supreme arbiters of record-buying taste.

Seattle at the time was bursting with new music, a local scene that was drawing a following without the support of commercial interests. And then Nirvana broke through in the fall of 1991 with *Nevermind,* and suddenly everybody was talking about alternative. Groups and artists who would once have been happy simply to register on the "alternative" charts were now getting phone calls from their record labels, outlining massive marketing campaigns and sales projections. Others, who had never even dreamed of catering to an "alternative" audience, were out having their hair restyled and redefining their sound.

The city of Seattle, Washington, led the charge. Bands that had been kicking around the city for years were suddenly thrust into the spotlight; groups long resigned to spending their careers on indie labels were suddenly being signed to the majors. "Grunge," the term the media applied to every scruffy-looking guitar band in the country, was out of the clubs and into the stadia; out of the wardrobe closet and into department stores.

Record companies opened offices in the city, all the better to scour the clubs in search of the next Nirvana. Musicians followed from all around the country, dragging their families across the country in search of the big break which had eluded them in their hometown. "I felt like one of those women you read about in the history books," one rock'n'roll widow said afterwards, "following my man to the gold rush. And when we didn't find it, he was out like a rat off a sinking ship."

The marketing men move in

Even before Nirvana released their long awaited third album, 1993's *In Utero*, Seattle was emptying out again, and bored journalists were already proclaiming that "grunge was over." Many alternative musicians objected strongly to the ease with which the media could come in and take a local musical fashion and turn it into a shortlived national fad.

Outraged at the media's inability to distinguish between Nirvana and Pearl Jam, for instance, Nirvana bassist Kris Novoselic laid it firmly on the line: "Bands who, previously, would have been considered heavy metal or soft rock or jazz or whatever, are being marketed as 'alternative' because that's what record companies believe they can sell."

Later in the 1990s, ska became a similarly abused term. In 1997, Dickie Barrett, vocalist with the Mighty Mighty Bosstones, complained, "Record companies put together bands all the time. There's 'ska' bands being constructed right now, by some marketing genius and record label weasels that are gonna try and cash in on the music's success."

Nirvana

Why can't music just be music again?

As long ago as 1977, **Iggy Pop** (see entry) swore at an English journalist who insisted on calling him a punk rocker: "I'm not a punk, I'm a ... man." And TV Smith (ex-Adverts), one of the artists signed to Henry Rollins' 2.13.61. label, made a similar statement when he insisted, "I'm so sick of all these divisions. Why can't music just go back to being music again?"

Nowhere is this more likely than when a new female vocalist is launched. All-girl bands like L7 and **Babes in Toyland** (see entry) rock as hard as men,

Eddie Vedder of Pearl Jam

1970s, **David Bowie** (see entry) openly acknowledged he was bisexual; in 1977, a singer named Tom Robinson had a British hit called "Glad To be Gay." Cross-dressing is also a long-standing rock tradition.

Mainstream/alternative

A lot of this is simply about an alternative external image to be portrayed to the public. And alternative music clearly has much to do with alternative images as well as alternative sound. There is, of course, no real meaning left to the term alternative music. When the major record labels and a huge listening public chose alternative for their own it became a buzzword used by radio stations and labels for marketing their products.

Further Reading

Garr, Gillian A., *She's A Rebel: The History of Women in Rock & Roll,* Seal Press, 1992.

Juno, Andrea, editor, *Angry Women in Rock,* Juno Books, 1997.

Murray, Charles S., *Shots from the Hip,* Viking Penguin, 1992.

Peterson, Charles, *Screaming Life: A Chronicle of the Seattle Music Scene,* HarperCollinsWest, 1995.

Raphael, Amy, *Grrrls: Viva Rock Divas,* St. Martin's Griffin, 1995.

Robbins, Ira, *Trouser Press Guide to '90s Alternative Rock & Roll,* Simon & Schuster Trade, 1997.

Rolling Stone Book of Women in Rock, Random House, 1997 (forthcoming).

Savage, Jon, *England's Dreaming,* St Martin's Press, 1992.

equalizing the playing field. **Hole's** Courtney Love and P. J. Harvey express very non-conventional and often shocking images about their gender in their songs. Other alternative bands in which women play an important role, such as **Veruca Salt** (see entry), play music that is not dependent on gender stereotypes.

Gender stereotypes have also been exploded by musicians who deliberately disguise either their sex, or their sexuality. Homosexuality has long been accepted in the music industry; far more so than in many other areas of society. In the early

Afghan Whigs

American alternative pop/rock band

Formed 1987 in Hamilton, Ohio, near Cincinnati

There can't be many bands who can claim they met in prison, but that's exactly how it happened for the Afghan Whigs. As the story goes, on Halloween 1986 in an Athens, Ohio, police cell, vocalist Greg Dulli was cooling off after running away with a policeman's hat; guitarist Rick McCollum was locked up with him, and having whiled away their captivity playing cards, they stuck together when they got out.

Took their name from a motorcycle gang

Over the next few months they worked hard to form a band. By spring 1987 they had not only found a rhythm section, bassist John Curley and drummer Steve Earle, they also had a name: the Afghan Whigs was a motorcycle gang from Florida. Within a year the Whigs had released their first album, *Big Top Halloween*, in 1988.

A powerful mix of 1970s rock and 1980s "indy" (independent label) sound of Dulli's own favorite bands, Dream Syndicate

"I want to experience something, feel something. I want to be taken places ... I want to travel in my head. That's what I try to do as a performer: lift people from their everyday lives, and take them to a place they've never been before." —Greg Dulli (vocals, guitar)

Greg Dulli

and Husker Du, only 2,000 copies of *Big Top Halloween* were released on the tiny Ultrasuede label.

Littered with Dulli originals, but highlighted by "Priscilla's Wedding Day" and "Doughboy," it was this album's success that brought the Whigs to the attention of Sub Pop, the Seattle-based grunge label. But if anybody thought they were simply going to fall in line with the label's other signings, the Afghan Whigs had no intention of simply copying **Mudhoney** (see entry) or **Nirvana** (see entry).

Rock and soul together

Dulli loved rock and roll, but he was also a big fan of soul music, and it did not take long for this influence to make itself heard. The Afghan Whigs' second album, 1990's *Up in It,* is just as energetic as *Big Top Halloween,* but it is a lot more varied as well. Dulli's voice slides easily from a whisper to a scream, while behind him the group proved itself equally able to change mood and style. Tender and terrifying, and sometimes both at the same time, *Up in It* was the sort of record that nails your ears to attention and never lets them go.

"I got hipped to the black music that white people didn't listen to when I was a kid," Dulli explained. "But I liked rock, too. All we've tried to do as a band is shove them together." The group's 1993 EP, *Uptown Avondale,* is the perfect example of this, with the group trying their hand at a couple of great soul oldies, including Freda Payne's "Band of Gold" and the Supremes' "Come See About

Me." Earlier in the year they also released their version of Diana Ross's "My World Is Empty Without You."

They sound like they want to kill each other

This same solid blend of classic soul moments and spontaneous rock-and-roll mayhem would become even louder on the Afghan Whigs' third album, 1992's *Congregation.* Only now the band sounded even more aggressive. Even their cover of "The Temple" from the rock opera *Jesus Christ Superstar* seemed dangerous. One English reviewer summed it up best when he said *Congregation* sounded like everybody involved wanted to kill each other.

"I got hipped to the black music that white people didn't listen to when I was a kid. But I liked rock, too. All we've tried to do as a band is shove them together."

It was after the band left Sub Pop for Elektra that people really started paying attention. *Gentlemen* was the group's major label debut in 1993, and Dulli explained, "when we began working on *Gentlemen,* I started thinking the songs might be too personal. This might be my own trip, and I don't wanna bring three of my friends into my own melodrama. So I said, 'look, let's scrap this, and I'll clear my head out,' and they were like, 'no man, we'll help you.'" By the time the album was completed, they had created what *USA Today* would call "a sly concept album."

The result was an explosion of emotion, a collection of songs that were alternately sad, bleak, and raw, and a long way from the wall of noise that made *Congregation* such a great record. It also proved that Dulli's love of soul went beyond simply liking the music; it proved he understood it as well. "There is no more emotional music that I've ever heard," he said. "Even the restraint in soul music feels like it's ready to burst at the seams, and when it does, you know exactly what that person is feeling." He injected this same honesty into his writing.

Changing drummers

The group spent a year touring after *Gentlemen* was released, watching while it became their first British hit record. They came off the road in the summer of 1995 just as drummer Steve Earle left the group. He was replaced by Paul Buchignani; he himself would leave the group after recording their next album.

"It was a personal thing and a musical thing," John Curley said of Earle's departure, although Dulli was less polite. When a heckler shouted out, "Where's Steve?" at a gig in 1996, Dulli replied, "Probably drunk." Then he dedicated a song about suicide, "Crime Scene Part One," to the drummer.

"Crime Scene" was one of the standout tracks on the Afghan Whigs' 1996 album, *Black Love,* an album so good that critics compared it with the Beatles' *White Album.* In an interesting break from tradition, the group wrote the songs and toured with them before they began recording the album. "We wanted to see what would happen to them," Dulli explained, adding that he wanted the songs to "unravel cinematically [as in a movie]. The music is more important than it used to be, the lyrics are less direct, less aggressive. We had to grow up and learn before we could do something like this."

I'm not depressed

The record was no less personal for that. While "Blame, Etc." was composed as a eulogy for the late David Ruffin, the Temptations vocalist who was one of Dulli's idols, other cuts—"Double Day," documenting the end of a relationship, and "Going to Town," about a pyromaniac—celebrate emotional extremes. Even the group's cover of "If I Only Had a Heart," from *The Wizard of Oz,* is somehow frightening.

In fact, it was a very dark album, but Dulli insists he can't help it. "Manic depression runs in my family," he laughs. "But I'm not depressed. I just use songwriting as a way to deal with my unhappiness."

Selected Discography

Big Top Halloween (Ultrasuede), 1988.

Up in It (Sub Pop), 1990.

Congregation (Sub Pop), 1992.

Uptown Avondale (Sub Pop), 1993 (EP).

Gentlemen (Elektra), 1993.

Black Love (Elektra), 1996.

Further Reading

Azerrad, Michael, "Whigging Out: Afghan Whigs Join Sub Pop Alumni with a Major Label Debut, 'Gentlemen,'" *Rolling Stone,* December 9, 1993, p. 21.

Norris, Chris, "Black Love," *New York,* April 22, 1996, p. 60.

Strauss, Neil, "Black Love," *Rolling Stone,* March 21, 1996, p. 95.

Wiederhorn, Jon, "The Notorious W.H.I.G.S.," *Entertainment Weekly,* March 15, 1996, p. 61.

Contact Information

Afghan Whigs Fan Club
PO Box 19700
Seattle, WA 98109

Web Site

http://elektra.com/alternative_club/
    afghanwhigs/

ALICE IN CHAINS

American alternative/heavy metal band

Formed 1987 in Seattle, Washington

Alice in Chains has always had a strange relationship with grunge, a guitar-heavy style with lyrics typically about despair and hopelessness. For one, the band was never originally planned as a grunge group; they started as a glam-heavy metal outfit. (Glam-metal is a performance style and involves wearing lots of make-up, having outrageous hair, and wearing spandex costumes.) Then, once grunge started hitting, the band was slow to start playing it. But by 1997, when most people thought of grunge as being over, Alice in Chains was one of the last grunge bands around.

Like any proper grunge outfit, Alice in Chains is big on angst (a feeling of anxiety or insecurity). Several of the members are deeply troubled and write about their problems in their music. The *New York Times* called their music "unremittingly bleak," saying "(Jerry) Cantrell's guitar riffs go nowhere, churning and pounding without resolution; (Layne) Staley's voice is utterly joyless."

The band sees music as a way of trying to handle their problems. Cantrell said about their 1992 record *Dirt* in *Guitar,* "*Dirt* is

"Our music's kind of about taking something ugly and making it beautiful."—Alice in Chain's Jerry Cantrell in *Rolling Stone*

Clockwise from top: Sean Kinney, Jerry Cantrell, Layne Staley, Mike Inez

Layne Staley performing

to vocals. "For Staley, music provided an escape from the monotony of school and the frustration of being unpopular," analyzed *Rolling Stone*.

Meanwhile, Jerry Cantrell was also having tough times. He and his younger sister and older brother were being raised by his mother, an amateur organist, while his father was off serving in the Vietnam War. "One of the first memories I have was my dad coming back from Vietnam in his uniform when I was three years old and my mom telling me that he was my dad," said Cantrell in *Rolling Stone*.

Cantrell's father had been badly affected by the war, and Cantrell's parents were divorced when he was seven. The rest of the family moved to Tacoma, Washington, to live with his grandmother. "We were on welfare and food stamps," said Cantrell in *Rolling Stone*. Like Staley, Cantrell decided early that his escape would be music. When Cantrell was little he wrote that he wanted to be a rock star in his Dr. Seuss book, *My Book about Me*.

Cantrell would need an escape, because bad things kept happening. He was a bad kid who got into trouble. His grandmother died of cancer. Cantrell got in a fight with his uncle and got kicked out of the house. Then his mother died of cancer. Because he wasn't allowed in the house; he didn't get to see her in her final days.

He moved to a place called the Music Bank, a place to stay and play music, and there he met Staley. Cantrell invited Staley to join a hard-rock band he had formed with drummer Sean Kinney and

not about us getting on some gloom wagon. It's meant to be a positive release for us so you don't wind up keeping these things stuck inside you. For us, it's definitely a form of therapy."

The problems start

Layne Staley was born in 1967 in Kirkland, Washington. He was a middle-class kid with two sisters. His first stab at music was when he was five, and he joined a preschool rhythm group. His parents divorced when he was ten, and his mother remarried, giving Staley a stepbrother. At twelve Staley started playing drums and in high school switched

bassist Mike Starr, but Staley wanted to work on his own funk band. The two compromised, each agreeing to play in the other's band.

From Alice 'N' Chains to Alice in Chains

The original Alice in Chains was a joke band Staley played in called Alice 'N' Chains. When the band broke up Staley gave the name to his new band with Cantrell. They gigged around the Pacific Northwest for over a year. Although they had more of a metal sound than a grunge sound, when record companies rushed to Seattle to sign grunge groups, Alice in Chains got swept up in the rush.

They distributed a free promotional EP, *We Die Young,* to record companies to get attention for their band. They toured with the heavy metal band Poison, then put out their debut, *Facelift.* They promoted the record with some high profile gigs, including a stint on the Clash of the Titans tour with Anthrax, **Megadeth** (see entry), and **Slayer** (see entry), plus a tour with Van Halen. But *Facelift* didn't really hit until Beavis and Butt-head made the song "Man in the Box" one of their anthems on their show on MTV.

A weird move, then success

Instead of coming back with a noisy metal record, Alice in Chains released an EP *Sap* in 1991. The record was low-key and acoustic. They said they gave it that name because of a dream Kinney had. He dreamt he was at a press conference

telling the press that the name of their new album was *Sap.*

The band got a big break playing a local grunge band in the Seattle-based movie *Singles.* The song they played, "Would?," became an international hit.

The next record, *Dirt,* was dark and harsh, with lyrics about drug addiction and abusive relationships. The record got good reviews. *Entertainment Weekly* gave it an "A" and called it "somber psychedelia." The *Los Angeles Daily News* called it "one of the year's most remarkable records."

Cantrell worried that fans might take the drug-oriented song as an endorsement of drugs. "That would be my worst fear," he said in *Guitar.* In *Rolling Stone* Staley agreed, saying having fans think he was saying drugs are cool was "exactly what I didn't want to happen."

The band's music has actually helped some people, acting as a negative example. In *Guitar,* Cantrell says that a fan told him that the song "Real Thing" helped him quit drugs. "That really meant a lot to me," said Cantrell. "We were really happy about that."

The song "Rooster" on *Dirt* helped Cantrell's relationship with his father. At one show that his father attended, the band played the song, which is about Cantrell's father. "He's a total Oklahoma man—at the end, he took his hat off and just held it in the air. And he was crying the whole time," said Cantrell in *Guitar.* "This song means a lot to me. A lot."

Trouble

After the success of *Dirt*, the band released the EP *Jar of Flies*. The record entered the charts at number one and was the first EP ever to hit number one. But the band began to fall apart. Starr quit and was replaced by Mike Inez. "We'd been going full force, just running at top speed with our eyes closed," said Cantrell in *Rolling Stone*. "We had been way too close for too long, and we were suffocating. We were like four plants trying to grow in the same pot." The main problem, though, was that Staley couldn't get his life in order. One day, right after he had gone to drug rehab, he'd come to practice high. That day, Kinney and Cantrell quit the band. The band broke up, canceling their spot on the **Metallica** (see entry) tour.

During the breakup Staley made a record with Mad Season, a side project with members of Seattle bands **Pearl Jam** (see entry) and Screaming Trees. Inez worked with Slash's (of Guns 'n Roses) Snakepit. Cantrell worked on solo material. Eventually Cantrell asked Inez and Kinney to work on some of his material. Staley ended up back with the band, and Alice in Chains was reunited.

> **"We had been way too close for too long, and we were suffocating. We were like four plants trying to grow in the same pot."**

The result was the album *Alice in Chains*. "If *Dirt* was a diary of pain and animosity (ill will) caused by addiction, betrayal and hypocrisy," said *Rolling Stone*, "*Alice in Chains* chronicles the bitter aftereffects of conflict, seeking to reassemble the shattered pieces." The record debuted at number one and a little over a month later, had sold a million copies in the United States.

No signs of improvement

The band followed *Alice in Chains* with a well-received appearance on *MTV Unplugged* and a record by the same name. No amount of success has seemed to help Staley deal with his problems, though. Which means the band is going to need to use music even more as musical therapy. "That's basically what we're trying to do in all our lyrics—clean stuff out and put it to rest," said Cantrell in *Guitar.* "And by somebody else picking up on that, maybe they can get a few things out of it for themselves at the same time."

Selected Awards

Nominated Favorite Heavy Metal Artist, American Music Awards, 1991.

Facelift, certified platinum, 1993.

MTV Video Music Award for Best Video from a Film, for "Would?," 1993.

Dirt, certified double platinum, 1993; triple platinum, 1995.

Sap, certified gold, 1994.

Jar of Flies, certified double platinum, 1995.

Alice in Chains, certified platinum, 1996.

Selected Discography

Facelift (Columbia), 1990.

Sap EP (Columbia), 1991.

Dirt (Columbia), 1992.

Jar of Flies EP, (Columbia), 1993.

Alice in Chains (Columbia), 1995.

MTV Unplugged (Columbia), 1996.

Further Reading

Abrahams, Andrew, "Alice in Chains," *People,* November 20, 1995, p. 23.

Darzin, Daina, "The Real Dirt," *Rolling Stone,* February 24, 1994, p. 18.

Resnicoff, Matt, "Chain smoking: Jerry Cantrell and Alice Grab Lightning," *Guitar Player,* March, 1996, p. 90.

Rotondi, James, "Lord of the Flies: Jerry Cantrell Unchains Alice," *Guitar Player,* March, 1994, p. 14.

Wiederhorn, Jon, "To Hell and Back," *Rolling Stone,* February 8, 1996.

Contact Information

Columbia
550 Madison Ave.
New York, NY 10022

Fan club e-mail address:

AICFC@speakeasy.org

Web Site

http://www.music.sony.com/Music/ ArtistInfo/AliceInChains/

BABES IN TOYLAND

American alternative pop/rock

Formed 1987 in Minneapolis, Minnesota

"Boys and girls are all babes in the universe." –Kat Bjelland, vocals/guitar

Babes in Toyland has made a career out of exploiting its "bad girl" image, from torn babydoll dresses and smeared lipstick to video appearances on MTV's *Beavis and Butt-head* and touring with Lollapalooza. The trio's aggressive, punk-inspired rock sound inspired the Riot Grrrls movement that sought to prove to the world that women could rock as hard as men. Their music is about as harsh as rock music gets: screaming vocals, thrashing guitar, and pounding bass and drums. It seemed like Babes in Toyland was angry at everything: the system, parents, men, gender stereotypes (especially Barbie dolls), and more.

Sugar baby doll

The Babes' lead vocalist, Katherine "Kat" Bjelland (sounds like Be-Yellin), was born in Salem, Oregon, and grew up there. During high school she became friends with a troubled California-transplant named Courtney Love, who later became famous as the leader of the band **Hole** (see entry) and wife of **Nirvana's** (see entry) Kurt Cobain. After high school graduation and a brief

Kat Bjelland

college stint, Bjelland and Love moved to San Francisco, California. At the time, they hadn't planned to form a band, though Bjelland had started teaching herself guitar when she was nineteen. But when Bjelland, Love, and their friend Jennifer Finch (of the band L7) saw an all-female punk band in a San Francisco club, they decided to form the band Sugar Baby Doll, which lasted only a short time until Bjelland and Love had a falling out.

Babes in Toyland formed in Minneapolis

With their on-again, off-again friendship back on, Bjelland and Love moved to Minneapolis, Minnesota, where they met a cocktail waitress named Lori Barbero who was a Minneapolis native. Bjelland convinced her that she could become a drummer. With Lori Barbero on the drums, Kat Bjelland singing and playing guitar, and Courtney Love on bass, the first version of Babes in Toyland appeared in 1987. Audiences must have been surprised at Bjelland's screaming vocals and thrashing guitar over the band's heavy rhythm section. After only a few months together, Bjelland once again kicked her long-time friend out of the band, and a nineteen-year-old named Michelle Leon replaced Love on bass.

The trio—Bjelland, Barbero, and Leon—grew so close that they thought of themselves as three sisters. They came to the attention of New York-based experimental rock band Sonic Youth, who brought them along on a European tour. In Minneapolis they played the club scene and released their first album, *Spanking Machine,* on the Minneapolis label Twin/Tone in 1990. Anticipating grunge's big breakthrough, the album was all bile and bite. It featured Bjelland's raw, thrashing guitar sound and angry songs like "Vomit Heart" and "Fork Down Throat." A follow-up EP, *To Mother,* was released in 1991.

Surprise signing to Warner Brothers/Reprise in 1991

Although not seeking a major label deal, Babes in Toyland signed with Warner Bros./Reprise Records in 1991 after performing in New York City. They spent most of the year touring. Just as they finished their tour and prepared to go into the studio to record their first album for Warner Brothers/Reprise, Michelle Leon decided to quit the band.

To keep the band's momentum going, Barbero and Bjelland recruited yet another bass player, Maureen Herman. Herman, who knew Bjelland and Barbero from Minneapolis, was playing bass for Chicago girl punk band Cherry Rodriguez. She also dabbled in film school and was planning to write for Chicago's comedy troupe, Second City. To solidify the new line-up, Babes in Toyland played more live shows before they went into the studio.

Just a few weeks before the release of the group's next album, Bjelland married Stuart Spasm from Australia's punk band Lubricated Goat. Then, *Fontanelle,* named after the soft spot of a baby's head, arrived in stores as the Babes' first major label release. The album's production, by Sonic Youth's Lee Ranaldo, was slicker than the Babes' independent releases. Some critics noted that the band's rage was toned down, but others felt the album made no "major label" concessions. By the end of 1992 *Spin* named *Fontanelle* one of the year's top twenty albums, and Jon Pareles of the *New York Times* listed Babes in Toyland among 1992's most notable groups.

More exposure for the Babes

In 1993 the Babes released an EP titled *Pain Killers,* which featured more of the band's intense, loud, punk rock. The EP included "Bruise Violet" as well as a 35-minute live performance of the songs from *Fontanelle.* MTV's hit show *Beavis and Butt-head* started playing the video for "Bruise Violet," which increased their exposure and rocketed album sales. Then in the summer of 1993, Babes in Toyland joined the renowned Lollapalooza summer festival tour.

The following year, the trio got a taste of the movies with a debut in *SFW* (which stands for Single Female White). They played themselves as bad girl punk rockers in the movie and recorded the title song. Soon after *SFW,* Babes in Toyland also recorded a cover of Little Richard's "The Girl Can't Help It" for the film soundtrack for *Reform School Girls.*

In yet another medium of exposure, Neal Karlen released his account of the band's career in the book *Babes in Toyland: The Making and Selling of a Rock and Roll Band* through New York Times Books in 1994. It was a book that the Babes didn't particularly like, and they've spent a lot of time "dissing" it.

Nemesister showed more controlled anger

In early 1995 Babes in Toyland released *Nemesister.* The album included the first single "Sweet 69" and covers of Sister Sledge's "We Are Family," Eric Carmen's 1975 hit "All By Myself," and Billie Holiday's "Deep Song." The album featured rhythmically and technically controlled songs, a change from the harsh punk rock of the band's previous recordings. The anger was still there, but it was expressed more subtly.

Before recording *Nemesister* Bjelland divorced Stuart Spasm and moved back to Minneapolis. Having been through many ups and downs, personnel changes, and broken friendships, the Babes felt strongly about their musical identity and partnership. "We are not regular musicians," Lori Barbero told *Billboard.* "We don't read and write music; we just do our own thing."

Selected Discography

Spanking Machine (Twin/Tone), 1990.

To Mother (Twin/Tone), 1991.

Fontanelle (Warner Bros./Reprise), 1992.

Pain Killers (Warner Bros./Reprise), 1993, EP.

Nemesister (Warner Bros./Reprise Records), 1995.

Further Reading

Evans, Paul, "Nemesisters," *Rolling Stone,* June 1, 1995, p. 64.

Karlen, Neal, "Babes in Boyland," *Mademoiselle,* October 1993, p. 180.

Mundy, Chris, "Kat Bjelland of Babes in Toyland Interview," *Rolling Stone,* May 18, 1995, p. 34.

Book:

Karlen, Neal, *Babes in Toyland: The Making and Selling of a Rock and Roll Band,* Times Books/Random House, 1994.

Contact Information

Reprise Records
3300 Warner Blvd.
Burbank, CA 91505-4694

Web Site

http://www.RepriseRec.com

Barenaked Ladies

Canadian alternative pop/rock band

Formed 1990 in
Toronto, Ontario, Canada

Barenaked Ladies makes sure its audience is having fun with the band. Adding humor to music, Barenaked Ladies jokes its way through every stage show, while using the recording studio as a means to express the band's musical ability.

Comic origins

Stephen Page (vocals, guitar) and Ed Robertson (guitar, vocals) grew up together in Toronto's suburbs. Before Barenaked Ladies, Page and Robertson started their careers in 1988 as a musical comedy act playing in Toronto clubs. Although opening only for minor acts, they began collecting fans. Joined in 1990 by brothers Jim Creeggan (bass), Andrew Creeggan (keyboards), and drummer Tyler Stewart, Barenaked Ladies (BNL) was born.

BNL's brilliance stems in part from their ability to combine just about every musical style with comedy. The band writes music blending pop, rock, jazz, rap, and almost every other genre into something original and fun. One is never sure whether the band cares more about comedy or music, both of which they handle equally well.

First release leads to contest win

Barenaked Ladies released a surprisingly successful independent cassette in 1990. They also released a cover of Bruce Cockburn's "Lovers in a Dangerous Time," which appeared on a tribute album. The success of those releases attracted attention, and Barenaked Ladies won a Toronto radio station's "Discovery-to-Disc" program. The award included money to record an album.

Debut album and record-breaking tour

Barenaked Ladies used the contest winnings to release *Gordon* in 1992 on the Sire/Reprise label. To promote *Gordon*, Barenaked Ladies went on tour. The tour set a record for the most sellouts in Canadian music history, as word spread of the group's highly energetic and entertaining performances.

Barenaked Ladies quickly gained a reputation as a must-see live act. They not only performed recorded songs, they ad-libbed (performed without preparation) and engaged in witty banter among themselves. Much of the audience's enjoyment comes from participating in the band's silly antics. For example, during the song "If I Had $1,000,000," when the band sings, "If I had a million dollars, we wouldn't have to eat Kraft Dinners / But we would still eat Kraft Dinners, right?," the audience throws boxes of macaroni-and-cheese at the stage. The

band tried to discourage this habit, asking audiences not to bring food into the auditorium, instead leaving it at the door to be distributed to homeless shelters. Of course, some boxes are left at the door, but the vast majority hit the stage.

When their cover of rap group **Public Enemy's** (see entry) "Fight the Power" was included on the soundtrack for the movie *Coneheads,* BNL achieved even more exposure.

But seriously

Breaking from the comedy that vitalized *Gordon,* Barenaked Ladies gave more attention to music on their second album *Maybe You Should Drive* in 1994. Even without as much of their comedic trademark, *Maybe You Should Drive* was well received. After noting that the record contained "more serious songs" than the band's first CD, critic Craig Tomashoff wrote in *People Weekly,* "The Ladies' melodies are still happy, full of Beatle-esque harmonies and easygoing, almost acoustic instrumentation. It's the sort of breezy material that blows around in your head for weeks after just one listen."

After recording *Maybe You Should Drive,* Andrew Creeggan left the band to continue his academic studies. A new keyboardist was recruited for the tour promoting the second album, but after the tour Barenaked Ladies became a quartet.

The 1996 release of Barenaked Ladies' third album, *Born on a Pirate Ship,* went further in showing off the band's musical abilities. Once again, the band gained critics' approval even as it explored new avenues. On this CD, a more mature BNL tackled adult concerns in country-flavored songs and acoustic rockers. Still, the album contained enough clever wordplay and humorous songs to satisfy fans and critics alike. *People Weekly* called it "a pure pop gem."

Live fun through multimedia

While recording serious albums Barenaked Ladies never lost their sense of humor during their live shows. *Rock Spectacle,* released in 1997, brought the fun of attending live shows to fans at home. Featuring live recordings from the group's seemingly endless 1996 tour of their native Canada, the United States, and the United Kingdom, the multimedia package includes such BNL staples as "Brian Wilson," "Jane," "If I Had $1,000,000," "The Old Apartment," and other songs spanning BNL's career. *Rock Spectacle* is not entirely music oriented, though, with twenty minutes of off-the-cuff comedy. It includes BNL-TV, a snippet of cable programming as imagined by the band, with such programs as "Ask Ed," a spoof on psychic hotlines; a sidesplitting sitcom called "Life in a Nutshell"; a home-shopping take-off titled "Shop Shop"; and a work-out program, "Sporto for Pirates."

In a record company press release Robertson explained the band's decision to release a live album. "It's just one more way to confuse people. All this new technology has really empowered us to goof around. At the same time, we've finally gotten it together to put out a live album, which is something our

fans have been requesting for a long time. There's been all sorts of bootlegs you can pick up on the Internet, so we decided it was time to do a semi-authorized version. Our live shows have always been far different from our records. People who have never seen us have only gotten part of the picture. We hope this will help fill them in."

The members of Barenaked Ladies have proven themselves to be versatile and serious musicians. However, their reputation has been based on the fun, and funny, side of the band. Tyler Stewart commented, "Humor is an important part of our performance, but that doesn't always come across on CD." *Rock Spectacle* solved that problem by combining the band's capacity for music with the wit and humor characteristic of their live performances.

Selected Discography

Gordon (Sire/Reprise), 1992.

Maybe You Should Drive (Sire/Reprise), 1994.

Born on a Pirate Ship (Sire/Reprise), 1994.

Rock Spectacle (Sire/Reprise), 1997.

Further Reading

Jennings, Nicholas, "Born on a Pirate Ship," *Maclean's,* April 8, 1996, p. 68.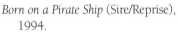

Jennings, Nicholas, "Naked Ambitions: The Barenaked Ladies Blend Rock and Satire," *Maclean's,* March 8, 1993, p. 54.

Jennings, Nicholas, "No More Class Clowns," *Maclean's,* August 22, 1994, p. 53.

Tomashoff, Craig, "Born on a Pirate Ship," *People Weekly,* April 8, 1996, p. 29.

Parents Aren't Supposed to Like It

Tomashoff, Craig, "Maybe You Should Drive,"
  People Weekly, October 3, 1994, p. 29.

Contact Information

Reprise Records
3300 Warner Boulevard
Burbank, CA, 91505-4694

Web Sites

http://www.repriserec.com/reprise_html_
  pages/bnlfolder/barenakedladies

http://www.fishertowne.com/barenaked

BECK

Alternative pop/rock singer and songwriter
Born Beck Hansen, July 8, 1970, in Los Angeles, California

"I don't think my music's weird. There's a fine line between being weird and trying to be weird. I just improvise and use the first thing that comes to mind." —Beck

In a period of less than three years Beck went from poster boy of the alternative slacker set to rock and roll's man of the year. Once dismissed as a novelty whose homemade song, "Loser," became a Top Forty hit and an MTV "Buzz Bin" regular, Beck silenced his critics with 1994's charming collection, *Mellow Gold.* He then stunned them into submission with 1996's *Odelay,* a swirling blend of hip-hop, acoustic shuffle, funky bottom, and assaultive guitar noise. *Rolling Stone* hailed it as their Album of the Year, Spin named Beck 1996 Artist of the Year, and Beck capped off the moment by taking home two Grammy awards. "It's pretty funny, if you ask me," Beck admitted to David Wild of *Rolling Stone* after the dizzying success of *Mellow Gold.* "It kinda seems like anybody can just get up and make a racket these days. Anything goes now, I guess."

Untypical childhood

Beck was born in Los Angeles, California, in 1970 to a bluegrass street musician father and an office-worker mother. His mother had once spent time working at pop artist Andy Warhol's Factory in New York. Beck's childhood was far from typical. Living initially in a rooming house in downtown Los Angeles, Beck and his family moved to Hollywood with their mother, just a few blocks from Hollywood Boulevard.

"Yeah, I spent my childhood watching the decline of Hollywood Boulevard," Beck told Mark Kemp of *Rolling Stone,* "watching the dying embers—the final light of the Hollywood era—fade into decay." Until the age of twelve, Beck would live off and on with his grandparents in Kansas—his grandfather was a Presbyterian minister—and spend time in Europe with his maternal grandfather, an avant-garde Fluxus artist named Al Hansen.

In the early 1980s Beck's parents split up, and Beck and his brother went to live full-time with their mother back in downtown Los Angeles in a Salvadoran neighborhood. "It wasn't the safest place, but it was definitely a community," he recalled to Kemp. "I remember walking to the bus in the morning to go to school, and there'd be roosters and chickens running though the street and mariachis [street musicians] passed out on the sidewalk. There was an anarchy [disorder] in the neighborhood, but still, it was a neighborhood." At Beck's house his mother would often let punk musicians who didn't have a place to stay crash in the living room.

Discovers the blues

Although Beck has admitted the first album he bought may have been the soundtrack to the Olivia Newton-John movie, *Xanadu,* his musical outlook changed forever when, at a friend's house, he found a copy of an album by bluesman Mississippi John Hurt. "It was shrink-wrapped, it hadn't even been opened," he told Mike Rubin of *Spin,* "and it was this insane close-up of his face, sweating, this old, wrinkled face, and I took it.... I loved the droning sound, the open tunings, the spare, beat-down tone. And his voice was so full." Inspired by his new find, Beck settled into his room with an old acoustic guitar that had been lying around the house and taught himself to finger-pick.

Feeling like an outcast and needing some time alone and away from the cramped apartment he shared with his mother, brother, and assorted punks, Beck quit school in the ninth grade. Spending most of the time practicing the guitar and working menial, low-paying jobs, Beck tried to overcome his shyness of playing in front of people by playing in the backs of the city buses of Los Angeles. There he'd play old blues tunes with improvised lyrics to a group of often disinterested passengers.

New York antifolk

In 1989 Beck took a Greyhound bus to New York where he worked a series of odd jobs, slept on people's couches, and stumbled onto the short-lived antifolk movement taking place on the city's Lower East Side. "That scene was the whole punk-rock thing, which was right on for me," Beck reminisced to Wild in *Rolling Stone.* "Punk was always sort of

The Dust Brothers

Part of the reason Beck's Odelay was such an astonishing success was due to the work of the album's producers, John King and Michael Simpson, a.k.a. the Dust Brothers. The two studio wizards have been working together since 1985. They first achieved success by producing rapper Tone-Loc's "Wild Thing" and other records for the Delicious Vinyl label. They then went on to hip-hop cult status with their innovative and detailed sampling work on the Beastie Boys' 1989 release, Paul's Boutique.

Digital sampling is a tape-looping technique that enables artists to lift or "sample" parts of other people's prerecorded material. Sampling came primarily from the pioneers in rap and hip-hop, who depended on recreating, remaking, and recycling other artists' material. Before sampling, rappers often relied on live bands, who rearranged popular hits. In the 1980s technology in the form of digital samplers made the live bands unnecessary.

Both King and Simpson were college DJ's when they met and teamed up to start what is thought to be Southern California's first radio rap show in 1985. Two years later, after scoring a hit with Tone-Loc's "Wild Thing," they were hired by Delicious Vinyl records to produce music by rappers Young M.C., Tone-Loc, and Def Jef. It was at Delicious Vinyl that they found their sound and name. "The current in hip-hop was very sparse and we were using all these textures, sampling and just layering sounds," Simpson explained to Sara Scribner of the Los Angeles Times. "People described it as being very 'dusted,' these multi-layered soundscapes, so we called ourselves the Dust Brothers."

The pair was soon sought out by the Beastie Boys, who enlisted them to help produce their 1989 psychedelic hip-hop classic, Paul's Boutique. More work on rap albums followed until 1995 when they were summoned by Beck to handle sampling and production duties for Odelay. The success of that record put the Dust Brothers on the A-list of producers for artists in need of a seamless groove. The Rolling Stones and Howard Stern are just two of the more recent clients of the Dust Brothers, and the two producers have launched their own independent label, Nickel Bag Records. In addition, Simpson was hired as an A&R executive and staff producer for the DreamWorks label, part of the DreamWorks mega-entertainment company headed by media moguls Jeffrey Katzenberg, David Geffen, and Steven Spielberg.

my favorite. But all I had was an acoustic guitar, and no one wanted to play with me. Here was a whole scene with just acoustic guitars punking out really hard." While playing in his new scene was fun, it was hardly a livelihood, and after a year Beck took the bus back to Los Angeles. "It was hard to be in New York with no money, no place, no honey, no thermostat, no spoons, no Cheerios," he admitted to Wild. "I kinda used up all the friends I had. Everyone on the scene got sick of me."

"Punk was always sort of my favorite. But all I had was an acoustic guitar, and no one wanted to play with me. Here was a whole scene with just acoustic guitars punking out really hard."

Back in Los Angeles, Beck got a job at a video store. At night he hopped on-stage in between bands at local clubs and coffeehouses. He also worked on making tapes of his songs, which by now combined the country blues he'd listened to in his teen years and the punk-folk from his time in New York, with the new addition of rap and hip-hop. At one show Tom Rothrock, co-owner of the independent label Bongload Records, saw Beck. "What hit me about Beck was that here was this self-contained folk artist who'd be great to make records with," Rothrock explained to Wild.

Beck performing: rock and roll's man of the year, 1996

"Loser"

Rothrock then put Beck in touch with hip-hop producer Karl Stephenson. One afternoon in 1992, Stephenson and Beck were messing around with some songs and a tape recorder in Stephenson's living room. One song featured a slide guitar lick by Beck that Stephenson recorded and looped over a hip-hop beat. Beck wrote some lyrics on the spot and tried to rap them in the style of **Public Enemy** (see entry) rapper Chuck D. After hearing the playback, Beck decided he was a terrible rapper, so when the song came to the chorus, he wrote some words to put himself down for the awful job he thought he'd done: "I'm a loser, baby / So why don't you kill me."

Bongload released the song over a year later, making only 500 copies for friends and college radio stations. By the fall of 1993, however, large commercial stations had gotten hold of the song and began to play it regularly. Unintentionally, the line Beck sang to make fun of himself was soon thought of as the motto of the slacker generation. "I didn't even connect it at all to that kind of message," Beck related to Rubin, "until they were playing it on the radio and I heard it, and they said 'This is the slacker anthem,' and immediately it just clicked and I thought, 'That sucks.'"

Major label, *Mellow Gold*

The success of the song prompted a bidding war by major record companies. Beck ended up with David Geffen's DGC label, signing a deal that gave him complete creative freedom and the ability to record and release other albums on independent labels. His first DGC effort, 1994's *Mellow Gold,* included the Top Ten hit, "Loser," a mix of hip-hop and folk. The album was recorded on an eight-track recorder in various living rooms. Wild of *Rolling Stone* described the album as "funny, folky, funky and freaky (often at the same time) ... a trip to a strange place where Woody Guthrie meets Woody Allen."

Beck released two more albums in 1994 on smaller independent labels. Naturally, they failed to get the promotional push afforded to *Mellow Gold.* While the major label release combined all of Beck's musical influences, the two smaller albums remained fairly consistent from track to track. *One Foot in the Grave,* on K Records, was a mostly acoustic album of country blues and folk, while *Stereopathic Soul Manure,* on Flipside Records, featured experimental, electric guitar noise.

Odelay produced by the Dust Brothers

In 1995 Beck was a featured performer on the Lollapalooza summer tour. He began to record his second album for DGC with the help of co-pro-

ducers the Dust Brothers, who produced the Beastie Boy's psychedelic hip-hop record *Paul's Boutique* and worked with rappers Young MC and Tone Loc. Beck set out to make a more finely crafted album than his previous efforts, if only to disprove the notion that he was only capable of "weird" music.

"I don't think my music's weird," Beck proclaimed to *Rolling Stone*'s Lorraine Ali, while recording what would become *Odelay.* "There's a fine line between being weird and trying to be weird. I just improvise and use the first thing that comes to mind.... Weird is happening in the 1990s. It's a genre. But the 1990s are getting too weird, so in the last two years I've been heading toward normal. That's gonna be the next radical thing."

Music's "Man of the Year"

Odelay was released in 1996 to much acclaim, with critics freely admitting the Beck was more than "Loser." Ken Miccalef of *Audio* said the album, "captivates with charismatic [charming] silliness while proving that Beck's phenomenal hit was no fluke," adding that Beck was a "golden-penned songwriting machine." Mark Kemp of *Rolling Stone* praised the album saying, "*Odelay* takes Beck's kitchen-sink approach to new extremes while also managing to remain a seamless whole; the songs flow together with intelligence and grace."

Beck soon found himself cradled in the arms of critics who hailed him as the biggest thing in contemporary music. Lavished by honors from *Rolling Stone* and *Spin,* he added three Grammy nominations to his list of achievements, taking home two. "I feel lucky," he told Kemp after winning. "I never had any expectations of winning a Grammy. It wasn't something I was set on, that I was hoping and praying and starving for. But it is incredible."

Selected Awards

Rolling Stone Album of the Year, for *Odelay,* 1996.

Spin Artist of the Year, 1996

Grammy Award for Best Male Rock Vocal Performance, for "Where It's At," 1997.

Grammy Award for Best Alternative Music Performance, for *Odelay,* 1997 (also nominated for Best Album of the Year).

Selected Discography

Mellow Gold (DGC Records), 1994.

One Foot in the Grave (K Records), 1994.

Stereopathic Soul Manure (Flipside Records), 1994.

Odelay (DGC Records), 1996.

Further Reading

Dunn, Jancee, "Beck: Resident Alien," *Rolling Stone,* July 11, 1996, p. 51.

Farley, Christopher John, "Beck to the Future," *Time,* January 20, 1997, p. 74.

Kemp, Mark, "Beck (interview)," *Rolling Stone,* April 17, 1997, p. 58.

Marzorati, Gerald, "Beck's Fugue," *The New York Times Magazine,* February 23, 1997, p. 32.

Micallef, Ken, "Odelay," *Audio,* November 1996, p. 106.

Wild, David, "Beck," *Rolling Stone,* April 21, 1994, p. 79.

Contact Information

DGC Records
9130 Sunset Blvd.
Los Angeles, CA 90069

Web Sites

http://www.rain.org/~truck/beck/

http://www.geffen.com/beck/

http://www.geocities.com/SunsetStrip/9294/beck.html

Bettie Serveert

Dutch alternative pop/rock band

Formed 1991 in Amsterdam,
The Netherlands

𝄞 "It's not always easy to explain a song. Some of them are like dreams. And when you dream, you make up your own language and symbols." —Carol van Dijk, lead singer/guitarist

Bettie Serveert is composed of singer/guitarist Carol van Dijk, guitarist Peter Visser, bassist Herman Bunskoeke, and drummer Berend Dubbe. The group developed out of the well-known underground Dutch band De Artsen (The Doctors), which broke up in 1990. Visser and Bunskoeke were members of De Artsen, van Dijk was the group's sound engineer on live dates, and Dubbe was the roadie. Visser was also an art school graduate who tried to make money painting and selling shoes. Van Dijk worked as a colorist for an animation company, Bunskoeke was a nightclub disc jockey, and Dubbe did commercial voice-overs and worked as a pirate radio disc jockey.

When De Artsen broke up the four friends decided to form their own group. Actually, it was the second time around for Bettie Serveert. They had briefly existed as a band (for about maybe twenty minutes) in 1986, before De Artsen became too popular to allow time for side ventures. Bettie Serveert (sounds like "severe" with a "teh" at the end) translates as "Betty Serves," a reference to a book about tennis that one of the band members found amusing.

Signed with Matador Records in 1992

The new, reformed Bettie Serveert worked on playing songs that singer van Dijk had been writing. In 1992 they recorded a seven-song demo that came to the attention of the record executives at Matador Records in the United States, who were so interested in the group that they flew to Amsterdam to sign them as quickly as possible. Later that year Bettie Serveert released their first album, *Palomine,* on the Matador label.

Palomine

Palomine featured Van Dijk's intensely personal songs, delivered in her own individual way. Her songs are often difficult to interpret, and she has said, "It's not always easy to explain a song. Some of them are like dreams. And when you dream you make up your own language and symbols." The fact that her vocals sometimes sound over-pronounced and the rhythm of her language awkward may be due to her background. She was born in Vancouver, Canada, to Dutch parents and spoke English. She moved with her family to Amsterdam when she was seven. The move changed her from an outgoing child to a more withdrawn person who had trouble with the language. As a result, she developed her own unique accent and her own way of speaking both Dutch and English.

The fact that Bettie Serveert was a band with a female lead singer led critics to draw all sorts of comparisons to other female-led bands. In the end, though, it was clear that the group had an independent, alternative-pop sound. Van Rijk's distinctive vocals created moods, even if the lyrics were hard to decipher. Peter Vissar's strong Neil Young-influenced guitar, with its basic blues-rock progressions, provided the necessary hooks and melodies to counterbalance Carol's cool vocals. Behind them churned the rhythmic patterns of Bunskoeke's bass and Dubbe's drums.

Second album released in 1995

It was nearly three years before the second album, *Lamprey,* was released in January 1995. The band took their time with this record, initially going into the studio with only seven songs written. Once they were in the studio in Amsterdam, though, everything seemed to click. The album captures a more mature Bettie and a different Van Rijk, "cool and a bit dangerous, as though she's establishing a distance between herself and the listener," according to reviewer Terri Sutton of the *Village Voice.*

Dust Bunnies

The band's third album, *Dust Bunnies,* was released in March 1997. It was recorded at Bearsville Studios in scenic Woodstock, New York, and was the first Bettie Serveert disc that was recorded entirely within the United States. By recording in a fairly remote setting, the band was able to concentrate more on the recording process and less on the socializing aspects of making music. They went into the studio with fifteen songs completely written and arranged. They wrote only one other song while they were in the studio, where the album was produced under the direction of Matador's Bryce Goggin.

Spin Online praised *Dust Bunnies,* pointing out that Van Dijk's voice is "entirely distinct." In addition, producer Goggin helped the band achieve "newfound dynamics and finesse" in backing van Dijk. Overall, Spin's reviewer concluded, "Bettie Serveert aren't clever or extraordinary. But by choosing plainspeak over poetry, they do a first-rate job of conveying how it feels to be second-best." As far as seeing the band perform live, American audiences had to be content with a brief spring tour and the video of "Co-Coward" from the album.

Selected Discography

Palomine (Matador/Atlantic), 1992.

Lamprey (Matador/Atlantic), 1995.

Dust Bunnies (Matador/Capitol), 1997.

Further Reading

Ali, Lorraine, "Who's Bettie Serveert?," *Los Angeles Times,* January 22, 1995.

"Bettie Serveert: Dust Bunnies," Spin Online.

Micallef, Ken, "Bettie Serveert," *Alternative Press,* April 1995.

Sutton, Terri, "Go Fish," *Village Voice,* February 14, 1995.

Toliver, Chris, "Dutch Treat," *Mirabella,* March 1995.

Contact Information

Matador Records
676 Broadway
New York, NY 10012

Web Site

http://www.matador.com

THE BUTTHOLE SURFERS

American alternative pop/rock band

Formed in San Antonio, Texas, in 1981

What's in a name?

With a name like the Butthole Surfers, you just know that singer Gibby Haynes and guitarist Paul Leary formed their band with the intention of upsetting people. The pair met at Trinity University, in San Antonio, Texas, where neither really fit in. "Gibby was the weirdest guy at school," Leary remembers. "So, we fell in real well, we both liked horrible music. His accounting career wasn't blossoming, and it didn't look like I was going to be a very good stockbroker. So, we started a band, sold all our possessions, bought a van, and went out to California."

Alternative punks

At that time, in the early 1980s, hardcore bands like the Dead Kennedys were most kids' favorite music. In a way the Surfers fit right in, since they certainly had the right attitude. And the right name, even though neither newspapers nor radio stations would print or say it. Kids heard about them anyway, and they quickly

> "The Buttholes have been so cool for so long because their spaced-out bird-flippin' reads like a cut-and-paste ransom letter."
>
> — *Alternative Press*

The Butthole Surfers—music and lyrics designed to shock

became a popular live act. That's how the Dead Kennedys' singer, Jello Biafra, became a fan; he saw them onstage. Biafra had his own label, Alternative Tentacles, and quickly signed the Surfers.

Surfing records

In 1983 the group's first album, *The Butthole Surfers,* appeared. By then it was already clear that the group wasn't a true punk band. Punk was much too straightforward for them. Instead, they were really more art school aural (relating to the ear or hearing) terrorists, with a mission to shock. Their band name and unprintable song titles were merely the shock troops. It was their music that was

really revolutionary, colliding bits of country and western twang, psychedelic guitars, and rockabilly guitar riffs into hardcore punk.

The next year the Surfers released *Live PECP,* a raucous and outrageous record that almost captured the sheer anarchy of their live shows. The group then moved to the larger independent label, Touch & Go, for 1985's *Psychic ... Powerless ... Another Man's Sac.*

Recreating the past

That album began the next phase of the Surfers' musical career. Many bands have done cover songs of their favorite groups. Most try to do their heroes proud, but not the Surfers. What they wanted to do was twist, fold, and mutilate other people's songs and sounds. On *Psychic* it was classic rock bands like Black Sabbath, Led Zeppelin, and the Grateful Dead who fell under their knives.

The band continued down this musical path throughout the 1980s, reaching the heights on 1988's *Hairway to Steven*. The album title is a twisted take-off on Led Zeppelin's "Stairway to Heaven." The music itself was a kaleidoscope of musical styles from the past and present, all turned inside out.

We hate what we hear

"We still identify, and come from the same place of just hating what we heard," Leary explains, "and wanting to make something that was even worse, that people would hate even more, and somehow get paid for it. That's what we were trying to do; make the worst records possible." Some critics would agree that's exactly what they'd done, but the band's fans felt otherwise. They saw the Surfers as an exciting band doing something totally unique and cool. And their live shows were the equivalent of grown-up circuses, you never knew WHAT was going to happen onstage. Except that it would be something gross that no other group would dare do.

The big time

After having made some of the "worst records possible," the Surfers then released *Pioughd*, their most commercial album yet, in 1991. On it, the band did a cover of 1960s flower child

Donovon's simpering hippy song, "Hurdy Gurdy Man." Needless to say, their version was far from simpering, and it became the Surfers' first hit.

Soon after, the group moved up to the majors and signed with Capitol. Meanwhile, Haynes guested on the industrial group Ministry's first hit, "Jesus Built My Hotrod." A supercharged, drag-race of a song, Haynes' lyrics were "totally indecipherable." Ministry leader Al Jourgensen joked that he wanted to make a lyric sheet written phonetically. "Gibby really just invented his own language for the song, that's the only way to describe it!" Jourgensen said in awe.

Chainsaw massacre overload

During the summer of 1991 the Surfers played the annual touring festival, Lollapalooza, and then they went to work on their next album, *Independent Worm Saloon*. The record was produced by John Paul Jones, Led Zeppelin's bassist, which was a bit surprising after the Surfers treatment of Led Zep on *Hairway! Rolling Stone* called the album a "no-holds-barred chain-saw-massacre overload. Few records can beat it for sheer guitar-choking feedback ecstasy."

"We still identify, and come from the same place of just hating what we heard and wanting to make something that was even worse, that people would hate even more...."

After its release and a tour, the Surfers took time off to pursue their own projects. Drummer King Coffey spent time with his independent label, Trance Syndicate. Leary moved into producing, and worked with indie bands like the Meat Puppets and the Supersuckers. Haynes, in contrast, still couldn't mention his band's name on the radio, but he could now DJ all the same.

Slamabama Punk Rock

In 1996 the Surfers released *Electriclarryland*. The album "divides its time between slamabama punk rock and the Texas band's patented mix of strange psychedelia, spacey drum sounds, and bits of rockabilly," *Request* explained. It was nowhere near as shocking as some of their older albums, but the Surfers still knew how to shake up people's ideas of what music should sound like. "The Buttholes have been so cool for so long because their spaced-out bird-flippin' reads like a cut-and-paste ransom letter," raved *Alternative Press*. And that pretty much sums up the Surfers to a tee.

Selected Discography

Hairway to Steven (Touch & Go), 1988.

Pioughd (Touch & Go), 1991.

Independent Worm Saloon (Capitol), 1993.

Electriclarryland (Capitol), 1994.

Further Reading

Cohen, Jason, "In Through the Back Door," *Rolling Stone,* June 24, 1993.

Dunn, Jancee, "Gibby Haynes," *Rolling Stone,* May 2, 1996.

Merson, Marcia, "World in Reverse Is the Lesser Evil," *B-Side,* October, 1993.

Young, Charles M, "Where Would the Beatles be Today if They Had Called Themselves the Butthole Surfers?" *Rolling Stone,* January, 1996.

Contact Information

Capitol Records
1750 N. Vine St.
Hollywood, CA 90028

Website

http://buttholesurfers.com/

THE CRAN-BERRIES

Irish alternative pop/rock band
Formed 1989 in Limerick, Ireland

usic has become a staple export for Ireland in the last part of the twentieth century. There may be any number of reasons for the success of Irish talent in the 1990s—like the appeal of a national heritage rich with storytellers, emotion, and imagination—but the popularity of The Cranberries is due to something more. According to Polygram Ireland's Paul Keogh, "The Cranberries sell because it's good music, not because it's Irish."

Beginnings

The Cranberries formed in 1989 in Limerick, Ireland. Noel and Mike Hogan (descendants of the noted, nineteenth-century Irish poet Michael Hogan, the Bard of Thomond), Feargal Lawler, and Niall Quinn gathered as the group Cranberry Saw Us (pronounced quickly as "cranberry sauce"). When Quinn left the group in 1990, Dolores O'Riordan joined as the vocalist and Noel Hogan's songwriting partner. The band then changed its name to The Cranberries.

"Sometimes there's so much emphasis on image, but we were always under the impression that the music would say who and what we are." —Noel Hogan, guitarist

Dolores O'Riordan

Dolores O'Riordan was born in 1971, the youngest of seven children. She started singing at age five and won numerous awards at music festivals. By age twelve, O'Riordan was writing songs. Though her mother asked her not to join a rock and roll band until she finished high school, O'Riordan auditioned for and accepted a job with The Cranberries before graduating. Her beautiful, versatile voice became the trademark sound of The Cranberries, and her songwriting crafted the messages the group's music sends.

Overall, The Cranberries enjoyed a quick rise to stardom. They were superstars within three years. The group's folk-pop style—the melodies, the guitars, and especially Dolores O'Riordan's voice—created a graceful, quiet sound just right for songs of family, love, and death. Yet their music was also emotionally vibrant, revealing its rock and roll roots. The Cranberries' innocent, polite stage manner also enchanted audiences. By 1994, their world tour averaged 13,500 in attendance at each performance. Nick Rowe of Island Records observed to *Billboard:* "They're quite unusual, because they're almost in the Simply Red/Enya league of positioning to an older audience, but through their gigs they connect to quite a vibey audience as well."

The struggle to succeed

Success for The Cranberries did not come without heartache, though. Disagreements between band members and their manager, Pearse Gilmore, intensified as they began recording their first album in 1992 for Island Records. The Cranberries eventually fired Gilmore. With Gilmore gone and the album abandoned, The Cranberries began recording again with Stephen Street as producer.

The media, too, sent mixed signals regarding The Cranberries. Initially, the European press received the band well, but then it turned cool toward the group's first single "Uncertain." Upon its release, the group's first album was virtually ignored in the United Kingdom. Journalists also began to portray the band members in an unflattering light—as bumpkins—because of their naive manner.

Without support of the media, their debut album, *Everybody Else Is Doing It, So Why Can't We?*, stayed on British charts only one week, so The Cranberries concentrated on American tours. U.S. audiences loved the group. In fact, The Cranberries became a big hit in America owing to MTV's and college radio's play of "Linger," the dreamy single release from the album. The group also enjoyed a big following during its tours. Thousands attended even their early concerts in America. Performances were added to meet ticket demands. While touring as the opening act for British pop band **Suede** (see entry), billing was reversed for some engagements, making The Cranberries the headlining act.

"We've been through so much together as a band, I think everybody's decided to keep their heads together and follow their hearts."

When *Everybody Else Is Doing It, So Why Can't We?* returned to the United Kingdom charts after the group's three U.S. tours, it was number one. The European press was forced then to reevaluate The Cranberries. Commenting to *Rolling Stone,* O'Riordan said, "I think the more the press stays away from us, the better we are. The American press is slightly more mature, but the British press is a very small group of people and they all jump on the same band at once, and they jump off the same band at once."

Big sellers

Everybody Else Is Doing It, So Why Can't We? soon earned platinum record status by selling more than one million copies. "It soon became very clear," Jonas Nachsin of Polygram recalled in *Billboard,* "that wherever the Cranberries' music was played, there was an immediate and explosive reaction at retail." *Everybody Else Is Doing It, So Why Can't We?* went on to sell 2.8 million copies worldwide, plus an additional 1.7 million in the United States, giving The Cranberries the distinction of being the first Irish band to sell more than three million copies of a debut album. "They made exactly the kind of album they wanted to make," said Geoff Travis of Rough Trade Records, "and it sold. They've got a canny sense of the commercial."

The Cranberries' second album, *No Need to Argue,* was released in 1994 and continued the group's commercial success, selling five million copies. It achieved gold or platinum status in twenty-five countries. This second al-bum was more experimental and out-spoken. "By the time we came to do this album, we knew what we were capable of. We're really happy with it," Noel Hogan told *Billboard.* "We did it the way we wanted to do it. It is what it's meant to be." The hallmark song from *No Need to Argue* was "Zombie." This composition by O'Riordan and Hogan gave voice to the long history of violence in Northern Ireland, showing it as part of Irish consciousness. "Zombie" was later named Song of the Year at the MTV Europe Music Awards.

Continued success

In May 1996 The Cranberries released a third album, *To the Faithful Departed.* Less personal and more political, this album had a tougher edge compared to the dreamy sound of its predecessors. "Hollywood," for example, commented on the immorality of that city, "War Child" reflected suffering of children, and "Bosnia" the sadness of war. The album was well received nevertheless, proving the constancy of the band's followers.

The cranberry flavor

O'Riordan's voice can be soothing or growling. In one *Melody Maker* review, Jennifer Nine observed that "like many small things, Dolores's voice is neither as simple nor as frail as it seems, there's a world of headstrong energy inside it." The singer, for example, waxed wistful on "Linger," but showed her strident side for "Zombie." According to *People Weekly's* Michael Small, "O'Riordan's intense delivery [of 'Zombie'] brings out a slight tartness—which, of course, is the mark of a truly good cranberry."

Whether tender or howling, O'Riordan's voice is always emotionally dramatic, particularly when singing songs with political or social commentary. Songs like "Zombie," "War Child," and "Bosnia" are outspoken—tough—and O'Riordan's delivery matches the mood. Yet her skill and musicality are not lost in the growl. As *Time*'s Christopher John Farley commented: "O'Riordan remains a terrific crafter of melodies, and a prettiness sparkles beneath the surface of her most raucous songs."

That The Craberries' songs have become more political and less dreamy marks them as refreshing changes in contemporary music. As Farley noted, commentary "can add an invigorating edge to pop music." O'Riordan, however, sees herself as more caring than political. "I'm more into the humanitarian aspect," she explained in *Seventeen,* "I don't care who wins or who rules, but if I see children suffering, it bums me out."

This attitude gives the band's compositions and singing an intensity typical of Celts and an assertiveness common among feminists. Because of this, O'Riordan has been called the voice of contemporary Ireland's women—rich with history but remarkably feminist and modern. In another *Time* article, Farley noted that O'Riordan's contemporary sound is so connected to Ireland's past that she, like singers Sinead O'Connor and Katell Keineg, creates "pop music that's stirring and new and also beautifully traditional."

Melody Maker's Andrew Mueller concurred. O'Riordan's voice, he said, "can sound both young and ancient simultaneously. It can span the ages. It's so filled with emotion, it will break your heart with the merest slipped quaver."

The Cranberries' continued success came from all its members' determination. "The Cranberries have been focused from day one," their manager Lewis Kovac told *Billboard* in 1995. "They just wanted to tour, write, and perform, and they've done nothing but that for the past three years." Despite their achievements and the pressures associated with success, The Cranberries remain a happy and close group. "We've been through so much together as a band," O'Riordan revealed in a *Billboard* interview. "I think everybody's decided to keep their heads together and follow their hearts."

Selected Awards

Melody Maker, Single of the Week for "Dreams," 1992.

Irish Recorded Music Awards, Best Irish Act, 1995.

MTV Europe Music Awards, Song of the Year Award for "Zombie," 1995.

Juno Awards, Best Selling Album (Foreign or Domestic) Award for *No Need to Argue,* 1996.

Selected Discography

Everybody Else Is Doing It, So Why Can't We? (Island), 1993.

No Need to Argue (Island), 1994.

To the Faithful Departed (Island), 1996.

Further Reading

Duffy, Thom, "Island's Cranberries Hope Hits Linger," *Billboard,* August 20, 1994, p. 1.

Farley, Christopher John, "Singing to a Silent Harp," *Time,* November 7, 1994, p. 87.

Sexton, Paul, "Cranberries Are the Pick of Island's International Group," *Billboard,* September 30, 1995, p. 1.

Talkington, Amy, "Dolores O'Riordan," *Seventeen,* November 1996, p. 104.

White, Timothy, "Cranberries' Hymns To the Faithful'," *Billboard,* March 23, 1996, p. 3.

Book:

Carran, Mick, *The Cranberries,* Omnibus Press, 1995.

Contact Information

Island Records
825 Eighth Ave.
New York, NY 10019

Web Site

www.polygram.com\doors\homefaith.html

CRASH TEST DUMMIES

Canadian alternative pop/rock band

Formed mid-1980s in Winnipeg, Canada

If nothing else, Crash Test Dummies "Mmm Mmm Mmm Mmm" was the strangest hit of 1994. In the song, singer Brad Roberts tells stories about young, oddly afflicted kids in a croaking deep baritone. That the song became a surprise hit was about as lucky and unplanned as the rest of the band's career. After all, Crash Test Dummies had never been planned as anything more than a way to pass the time and avoid the cold weather in the band's native Winnipeg, Canada.

Cold start

In the mid-1980s Roberts had his life all planned out. He was about to graduate from the University of Winnipeg with an honors degree in English literature and philosophy, and was planning on getting his Ph.D. and becoming a professor. "At the time I was going to university. I was a total geek. I didn't do any socializing and I was really very compelled by all the reading I was doing," said Roberts in *Rolling Stone*.

Around the same time, Roberts and his younger brother Dan decided to start a loosely organized band including Dan on bass, Benjamin Darvill on harmonica, and Ellen Reid on keyboards. At first they had no drummer and Brad played guitar, thinking he had a bad singing voice. Brad didn't start singing until a singing teacher told him he had a perfect bass-baritone voice.

"My plans to do the master's degree receded as I got sucked into the vortex of the music industry."

The band played informal gigs at an after-hours club in Winnipeg, playing "ridiculous cover tunes, everything from cheesy Irish traditionals to TV theme songs to acoustic versions of Alice Cooper hits," said Roberts in *Rolling Stone*. (Brad Roberts says he does all the band's interviews because his bandmates would "rather be out walking around.") The group called themselves many names, including the Chemotherapists and Skin Graft. Eventually they stuck with one favorite, Crash Test Dummies.

The band put out a lo-fi acoustic demo tape and sent it around to Canadian music festivals. Eventually some record company executives heard it, setting off a bidding war for the band. "My plans to do the master's degree receded as I got sucked into the vortex of the music industry," said Roberts in *Rolling Stone*.

Their 1991 debut *The Ghosts that Haunt Me* had a hit song, "Superman's Song," and the record went number one in Canada. In the United States, the

Brad Roberts, the deep-voiced lead singer of the Crash Test Dummies

band didn't get much attention except for a little bit of college radio play.

Mmm Mmm good

The band got ex-Talking Heads member Jerry Harrison to produce their second record, *God Shuffled His Feet*, released in 1993. At first marketing their new single "Mmm Mmm Mmm Mmm" was tough. "When we put out the record, the reaction was 'What is this? This is too weird.' It was an uphill battle to convince radio to play the damn thing," said Roberts in *Rolling Stone*.

Radio stations near the U.S.-Canada border started playing "Mmm Mmm

Mmm Mmm;" then influential Los Angeles station KROQ picked up the song. Soon Howard Stern became a fan and plugged the song a lot on his radio show.

The rest of the record was just as quirky, especially the words. In "How Does a Duck?" Roberts sang "How does a duck know what direction south is? / And how to tell his wife from all the other ducks?" *People Weekly* called the record an "improvement" over the debut, saying the record was "filled with songs that sound like nothing you've heard before yet are completely hummable from first listening." The reviewer also compared Roberts' voice to a "Bea Arthur [the deep voiced 'Golden Girl'] recording played back at slow speed."

It's A Worm's Life

The band came back in 1996 with *A Worm's Life*. The band could still write witty lyrics—like "I sit and concentrate and try hard not to hate my enemies / I try to picture them dressed up as furry little bunnies" on "My Enemies"—but the record had no "Mmm Mmm Mmm Mmm." *Entertainment Weekly* gave the record a C-grade, criticizing the records' "self-consciously clever lyrics and watery pop melodies." *People Weekly* was kinder, complimenting the band's "startling, stimulating tunes." But the record-buying public agreed more with *Entertainment Weekly* and *A Worm's Life* was a stiff.

Selected Awards

God Shuffled His Feet, certified double platinum.

Juno Awards, Group of the Year, 1992.

MTV's European Music Awards, Breakthrough Artist, 1994.

Selected Discography

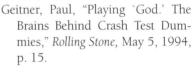

A Worm's Life (Arista), 1996.

God Shuffled His Feet (Arista), 1993.

The Ghosts That Haunt Me (Arista), 1991.

Further Reading

Geitner, Paul, "Playing 'God.' The Brains Behind Crash Test Dummies," *Rolling Stone,* May 5, 1994, p. 15.

Hajari, Nisid, "Crashing into the Top 10," *Entertainment Weekly,* April 29, 1994.

Ostick, Stephen, *Superman's Song: The Story of Crash Test Dummies,* Quarry Press, 1995.

Popper, Tracey, "A Worm's Life," *Entertainment Weekly,* October 11, 1996, p. 92.

Tomashoff, Craig, "A Worm's Life," *People Weekly,* October 7, 1996, p. 28.

Tomashoff, Craig, "God Shuffled His Feet," *People Weekly,* January 10, 1994.

Contact Information

Arista Records
6 West 57th Street
New York, NY 10019

Fan club:

Dummyheads
Box 370
Oakbank, Manitoba
Canada R0E 1J0

Web Site

http://www.crashtestdummies.com/ aboutband.html

Dinosaur Jr.

American alternative pop/rock band

Formed in Amherst, Massachusetts, in 1984

Dinosaur Jr. has become nearly as famous for fuzzy guitar rock as for "J Mascis' budding rep as a weirdo," according to *Rolling Stone.* In a 1994 interview with Dinosaur Jr.'s frontman Mascis, *Entertainment Weekly* agreed, saying Mascis has "developed a reputation—one built on maddeningly comatose interviews, navel-gazing live performances, and his refusal to move out of his parents' house until last year—as somewhat of a wuss."

J Mascis, the unkempt, lackadaisical "couch potato of epic stature," was the right man at the right time, though. "J Mascis' lethargic vocals and sprawling rhythms predated slacker culture," said Spin Online. *Rolling Stone* called him a "underground noise-guitar guru" and "slacker guru."

"I ... am usually not too enthusiastic." –
Dinosaur Jr.'s J Mascis

Golf and drums

J Mascis grew up in Amherst, Massachusetts, and was the son of a dentist. As a boy, Mascis developed a legendary interest in

J Mascis

Dinosaur Jr., a tribute to slacker culture

golf. When he was about nine he won the trophy for his age group at the Amherst Country Club. "There weren't that many people in my flight, but I felt like I was at the top of my game. I still have the trophy," he said in a press release for *Without a Sound.*

Mascis started thinking that music might be as interesting as golf. He played drums in the Amherst Youth Orchestra, then started a hardcore punk band, Deep Wound, with guitarist Lou Barlow. "There was nothing else to do. All those people with no friends tried to make a punk scene in Amherst, but it really didn't work," Mascis said later to *Rolling Stone*. For a new band they called Dinosaur, Barlow switched to bass, Mascis to guitar, and they got Mascis' friend Murph (Emmett Murphy) to take over on drums.

New name

By the time Dinosaur had put out 1987's *You're Living All Over Me* and had attracted enough attention to get an opening spot on a Sonic Youth tour, they had to change their name to Dinosaur Jr. It was to avoid possibly being sued by a band called the Dinosaurs, formed by members of 1960s bands Country Joe and the Fish and Quicksilver Messenger Service.

College radio and infighting

A cover version of the Cure's "Just Like Heaven" helped make 1988's *Bug* a college radio success for Dinosaur Jr. But the band wasn't getting along. "We'd go on ten-hour trips in the van and no one would say a word," said Murph to *Rolling Stone*. When Mascis and Murphy wanted Barlow out of the band, they took the wimpy route; they told him the band had broken up when it really hadn't. Barlow started his own band, Sebadoh.

On Dinosaur Jr.'s major label debut *Green Mind,* Mascis pretty much took over the band. He recorded the album almost completely by himself, only having musicians come in later to fill in parts. This set the cycle for the future of the band. The not-so-secret secret about Dinosaur Jr. is that it is basically a J Mascis solo project.

More fame, more infamy

Dinosaur Jr. became more known for its feedback-heavy music and Mascis's sleepy vocals with the next records. "*Where You Been* orchestrates feedbacking chaos and emotional confusion into more recognizable forms," said *Rolling Stone*. Mascis also became more known for his subdued, un-rock-star-like behavior on stage. "Mascis has become legendary for hiding behind a Cousin It-like mane of hair, even on 1993's Lollapalooza Main Stage," reported *Entertainment Weekly*. "I'm more nervous than guys like Mick Jagger. I'm fine when I'm playing, but in between songs, I can't think of anything to say," Mascis said to *Entertainment Weekly*.

Mascis' record company, Sire/Reprise, tried to push the 1994 record *Without A Sound* to mainstream success. Mascis made a video for "Feel the Pain" featuring him playing golf. The video was played a lot, but the song topped out at #44 on the U.S. charts. Spin Online later said, "Even when he tried to enter the mainstream with blatant pop songs ... his misanthropic demeanor, cracked and whiny voice, and overzealous guitar noodling kept him on the outside." Mascis came back with an acoustic solo record called *Martin and Me*. "Self-indulgent," wrote Jason Adams, a contributing editor to *Might*.

Redeemed

With Dinosaur Jr.'s 1997 release *Hand It Over,* J. Mascis is back where he started—playing loud guitar over songs about failed relationships, getting critical acclaim, and being generally ignored by the mainstream. "Mascis has finally stopped crafting what he thinks people want to hear and returned to following his own self-indulgent muse," said Spin Online.

Selected Discography

Dinosaur (Homestead), 1985.

You're Living All Over Me (SST), 1987.

Bug (SST), 1988.

Fossils (SST), 1991.

Green Mind (Sire/Warner Bros.), 1991.

Where You Been (Sire/Warner Bros.), 1993.

Without a Sound (Sire/Reprise), 1994.

Hand It Over (Reprise), 1997.

Solo:

J Mascis, *Martin and Me* (Reprise), 1996.

Further Reading

Coleman, Mark, "Monster Magnetism," *Rolling Stone,* May 13, 1993, p. 17.

Diehl, Matt, "Dinosaur Jr.: Without a Sound," *Rolling Stone,* October 6, 1994, p. 90.

Hajari, Nisid, "Dinosaur Jr's Dude Emeritus Grows Up—Kind Of," *Entertainment Weekly,* September 9, 1994, p. 55.

Rotondi, James, "Smokin' J," *Guitar Player,* October, 1994, p. 88.

Wiederhorn, Jon, "Hand It Over," Spin Online.

Contact Information

Reprise Records
3300 Warner Blvd.
Burbank, CA 91505-4694

Web Site

http://www.iuma.com/Warner/html/ Dinosaur,Jr.html

THE FOO FIGHTERS

American alternative pop/rock band

Formed in 1995 in Seattle, Washington

"I've got no voice and I need to pee." So said Dave Grohl, returning to a Seattle stage in March 1995 for the first time since the end of **Nirvana** (see entry). His new band, the Foo Fighters, had been together less than a month and had played just one show before the Seattle gig, in neighboring Portland the night before.

The line outside the Velvet Elvis club began forming hours before the so-called secret show began. The fact that nobody knew what to expect only added to the excitement. The group was named after the UFOs American airmen reported sighting and fighting during World War II. As the audience waited for Grohl to take the stage, these new Foo Fighters were just as mysterious.

Life after Kurt Cobain

Grohl had not been idle since the death of Nirvana frontman Kurt Cobain. He toured with Tom Petty's band and was offered the job full time. He also played on the soundtrack to the movie *Backbeat*. He did not want to become known simply as a drum-

"Sometimes I think ... sometimes, I just don't think." —Dave Grohl (vocals, guitar)

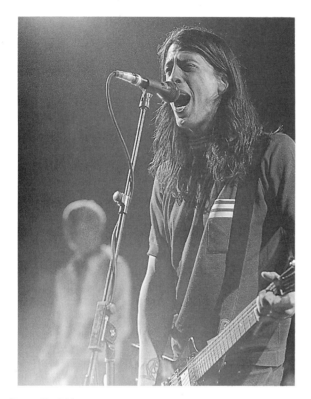

Dave Grohl in concert

Nate Mendel of the Seattle group Sunny Day Real Estate, and lead guitarist Pat Smear, who himself had toured with Nirvana towards the end of their career. The band kicked up a rocking roar, "a cross," one reviewer wrote, "between Nirvana, Grohl's last band Scream, and Britain's Catherine Wheel."

All my own work

These impressions carried over to the Foo Fighters' debut album, released on the band's own Roswell label later in the year (Roswell is the New Mexico research laboratory famous for a UFO crash in the late 1940s). Although Grohl would later complain that some of his lyrics were trivial—"absolute nonsense" were his exact words—there was also a lot for him to be proud of. For instance, *Foo Fighters* was credited to the entire band, but in reality, the multitalented Grohl recorded the entire album himself (the only other featured musician was Greg Dulli of the **Afghan Whigs** [see entry]).

"I had no intention of it being anything but this tape I could do in five days," he admitted later. He made 100 copies of the tape, which he passed around to friends and interested record companies, and once he had formed the group, he did think about rerecording it. In the end, however, there wasn't time. The Foo Fighters' first album, therefore, is also Dave Grohl's demo tape!

A lot of the album was very personal. Several of the songs, including the band's first single, "This Is A Call," and "I'll Stick Around," were influenced by Kurt Cobain's suicide, with "I'll Stick

mer for hire. Grohl had, after all, already shown himself to be a capable songwriter; the tiny Simple Machines label had already released an album-length cassette of his own songs, while Nirvana had recorded his "Marigold," for the b-side of the "Heart Shaped Box" single. Producer Steve Albini raved, 'Marigold' was really outstanding. Of all the `pop' songs we recorded, `Marigold' was an obvious stand-out."

There would be no space for "Marigold" in the Foo Fighters' live show. Grohl stepped out from behind the drums for this new band. He played rhythm guitar and sang, accompanied by drummer William Goldsmith, bassist

Around" also answering the fans who insisted that the Foo Fighters simply pick up where Nirvana left off. "I don't owe you anything," Grohl roared in the chorus, while the band punked out behind him, and that was a shock as well, just how powerfully he could sing.

An instant hit

Other songs rocketed off in new directions, musically and lyrically. Although the overall feel of the record was very punk and grunge influenced, it ended up sounding considerably more diverse than anybody ever expected. A mix that proved so successful on the American and European charts that Foo Fighters would spend much of the next year on the road. The work paid off as well. In March 1996, a full year after the band's first show, they scored their first hit single, "Big Me."

Work began on the Foo Fighters' second album in mid-1996, and if anything, the songs Grohl was writing were even more private than those on his first album. Having reached new heights of fame with his own band, he had also seen his marriage to his high school sweetheart collapse. He would later agree, "A lot has happened and it's made its way into the songs."

Their second album

This would be proven in May 1997, when *The Color and the Shape* was released. Grohl had been faced with two choices when the group started work on the record, either to sing about the things that mattered most to him—like

Cobain's death and his own divorce—"or I could do the same thing as the last record and deny everything all over again." He chose the first course. With the band helping to write the songs, Grohl was able to let his emotions out without being too personal. He also brought in an outside producer for the first time, choosing Gil Norton—whose past work included Catherine Wheel.

The result was a far noisier record than *Foo Fighters,* but a far deeper one. A year spent touring had turned the group into a tightly coiled spring of punk energy and pop madness, with Grohl's own thoughts and passions firmly bound up inside. At least one song, the call and response "Hey Johnny Park" addressed Kurt Cobain, while another, "Monkey Wrench," mourned the loss of youth: "what have we done with innocence?" Grohl sang. "It disappeared, it never made much sense."

The high energy of these songs was balanced by three beautiful ballads, "February Stars," "Up in Arms," and "Walking After You." Reviews of the album reckoned that any one of these five deserved to go straight to number one. Another brilliant track was the group's cover of British new wave artist Gary Numan's "Down in the Park," which they gave to the television series *The X Files.*

A new drummer

Drummer William Goldsmith left the Foo Fighters shortly after the album was completed, on March 4, 1997. He was replaced by Taylor Hawkins of Alanis Morisette's band, and with *The Color* and the Shape still warm on the shelves, the Foo Fighters set off on another solid bout of touring. Before they started, though, they went back into the studio and proved that they were not afraid of hard work.

"We knocked out five songs in one day," Grohl said happily. "If we recorded five songs in a day, and we're only going to put thirteen songs on an album, we can finish an album in a week." Clearly, the Foo Fighters are going to be buzzing around for a long time to come.

Selected Discography

Foo Fighters (Roswell/Capitol), 1995.

The Color and the Shape (Roswell/ Capitol), 1997.

Further Information

Cross, Charles, "The Truth Is Still Out There," *The Big O*, May 1997, p. 35.

Daley, David, "Foo For Thought," *Alternative Press*, June 1997, p. 18.

Diehl, Matt, "Foo Fighters," *New York Times*, July 9, 1995, p. 29.

Mundy, Chris, "It's a Band, Damn It (And Don't Mention the "N" Word)," *Rolling Stone*, October 5, 1995, p. 40.

Rosen, Craig, "Modern Rock Fans Await Capitol's Foo Fighters' Album," *Billboard*, June 24, 1995.

Web Sites

http://www.foofighters.com/foo/

http://www.nol.net/-dfx/foo/html

Garbage

American alternative pop/rock band

Formed in Madison, Wisconsin, in 1994

Garbage began in 1993 as an experimental rock band formed by three producer-musicians in Madison, Wisconsin. They were Brian "Butch" Vig (lead producer/drums), Steve Marker (guitars/bass/samples), and Duke Erikson (guitars/keyboards). They had played in bands together for years, and Vig and Marker were partners in Smart Studios, which was founded in 1984.

Their music, which employed tape loops and samples in addition to guitars and drums, was so bad their friends called it garbage, so that's what they called their band. After adding Scottish singer Shirley Manson in 1994, Garbage released a series of singles and a self-titled debut album in 1995. Their popularity grew on the strength of songs like "Supervixen," "Only Happy When It Rains," "Stupid Girl," and "Queer." "Stupid Girl" won a Grammy nomination in 1997 for Best Rock Performance by a Duo or Group.

Different backgrounds

The members of Garbage came from vastly different backgrounds. Shirley Manson grew up in Edinburgh, Scotland. Her

"We let it go as far as we can. Then, out of the racket, we pick what we like." —Duke Erikson

"There are no rules, but if the choice is to do less or to do more, usually the answer is more."
—Butch Vig

"The strong overpowers the weak. But when it sounds too clean, we mess it up." —Steve Marker

"Weirdness lurks in the most unlikely corners." —Shirley Manson

Shirley Manson

father was a professor of animal genetics and poultry breeding; her mother was a former big band singer. She described her childhood as "desperately unhappy, despite a perfect upbringing. I was convinced I was the ugliest creature that ever lived, that everybody hated me, and the only way to deal with it was to be as unpleasant as possible."

As a child Manson learned to play violin, clarinet, and piano. She joined her first rock band at sixteen and dropped out of school. As she told *People Weekly,* "The only reason I was ever in a band was because it was the antithesis of humdrum, nine-to-five reality." Manson was in two Scottish bands, Goodbye Mr. MacKenzie and Angelfish, before hooking up with the men of Garbage late in 1994.

Manson's background contrasted sharply with the Midwestern upbringing of the other band members. Brian "Butch" Vig, for example, was raised in the small dairy farm community of Viroqua, Wisconsin. His mother was a music teacher, his dad the town doctor. Though he studied piano until the sixth grade and then the drums, when he enrolled at the University of Wisconsin in Madison he was presumably headed to medical school. Two years later he dropped out and joined the band Spooner as its drummer.

Smart Studios established in Madison

Vig met Erikson, who grew up in rural Nebraska, in Spooner; Erikson was Spooner's guitarist and singer. Vig returned to college to study filmmaking while playing with Spooner. It was his interest in making soundtracks to his experimental films that led to dabbling with synthesizers in an electronic music studio and catching the production bug.

Vig and Marker established Smart Studios by taking out a loan together to buy an eight-track and rent warehouse space, sticking egg cartons on the walls for better acoustics. They produced records for local punk bands. "Forced to work with severe limitations and not knowing the correct way, we had to figure it out as we went along," Vig recalled in his record label biography.

Spooner recorded three albums of garage rock, then became Firetown. Firetown's albums, recorded on Smart's meager eight-track, helped the studio break through on the indie scene. Vig went on to produce albums with such bands as Killdozer, the **Smashing Pumpkins** (see entry), and Sonic Youth, as well as other bands for labels such as Sub Pop, Touch and Go, Slash, and Twin Tone.

It was **Nirvana's** (see entry) 1991 album *Nevermind,* whose demos were done at Smart, for which Vig is most remembered as a producer. He never expected it to become a milestone and prefers not to dwell on its enormous success. "It affected so many people and changed the music business, but I don't want to get caught up in that. To try to put a perspective on it is scary."

Manson met the men from Madison in 1994

By 1994, Vig, Marker, and Erikson were looking for a female singer to front the noise, tape-loop, and sampling experiments that was Garbage. After they saw the video of Shirley Manson fronting her group Angelfish on MTV, they decided she was the one. "It was the way she sang," Vig recalled for *People Weekly,* "low and dark and really cool." They contacted her from Wisconsin by phone at her home in Edinburgh and talked her into meeting them in London. After auditioning for the group, she came to Madison and spent six months recording songs for Garbage's self-titled debut album.

Three singles preceded debut album

Garbage's early songs were written at a fishing cabin in the north woods of Wisconsin and recorded back at the studio. At first the group wanted to use the latest in expensive digital gear, but they finally went with outdated analog equipment: a 1965 Epiphone guitar and a monophonic synthesizer of unknown age. The melody of one song was inspired by an unplanned sample of a digital tape deck in its death throes, and another opened with the sound of Vig accidentally wiring the mixing desk into the air conditioning system. "But," says Erikson, "whatever weird sounds there are have to serve the song. Whatever takes away from it is out. The song is what's important."

Before they had enough material for an album, Garbage released its first single, "Vow," a song Manson called "a vengeful little ditty." Attempting to appeal to record collectors as well as music fans, the single was released in limited quantities with special packaging in the United States and Great Britain. The follow-up single, "Subhuman," was "a dark, but spirited piece of Gothic grunge," according to Gavin Stoker of *Rock: The Rough Guide.* With their third release in mid-1995, "Only Happy When it Rains," Garbage cracked the Top 40 in England with a poppier sound.

Garbage released their self-titled first album in August 1995. The album's twelve songs combined strong guitar and drum sounds with Manson's vocals. Writing in *Entertainment Weekly,* Steven Mirkin described the album's "menacing sexuality, sonic playfulness, inventive guitar treatments, and cool vocals by Shirley Manson."

Gradually the band gained in popularity through 1995 and 1996. The band's singles, "Only Happy When it Rains," followed by "Stupid Girl," gained considerable airplay on college and alternative radio stations. Toward the end of 1996 the band received more recognition with nominations for Best New Act and the Breakthrough award for "Stupid Girl" at the MTV Video Awards. "Stupid Girl" was also nominated for a Grammy.

Selected Awards

MTV Video Award nominations for Best New Artist and for the Breakthrough award, for "Stupid Girl," 1996.

Grammy nomination for Best Rock Performance by a Duo or Group, for "Stupid Girl," 1997.

Grammy nomination for Best New Artist, 1997.

Selected Discography

Garbage (Almo Sounds/Geffen), 1995.

Further Reading

Aaron, Charles, "Garbage: Talking Trash with Shirley Manson," *Spin,* June 1997, p. 56.

Chrisman, Kimberly, "Top of the Heap," *People Weekly,* September 9, 1996, p. 109.

Dunn, Janice, "Work in Progress," *Rolling Stone,* October 17, 1996, p. 76.

Mirkin, Steven, "Garbage," *Entertainment Weekly,* August 11, 1995, p. 52.

Schoemer, Karen, "Skanks, but No Skanks," *Newsweek,* January 13, 1997, p. 72.

Willman, Chris, "Top of the Heap," *Entertainment Weekly,* June 7, 1996, p. 26.

Contact Information

Garbage
P.O. Box 3282
Madison, WI 53704

Record company:

Geffen Records
9130 Sunset Blvd.
Los Angeles, CA 90069

Web Site

http://www.geffen.com/almo/garbage/

GOO GOO DOLLS

American alternative pop/rock band

Formed in Buffalo, New York, in 1986

Johnny Rzeznik, singer and guitarist for the Goo Goo Dolls, claims he's happy his band found success so late. "If it would've happened when I was nineteen, when I started the band, I probably would've been dead," he said in *Rolling Stone*. When the band finally scored a hit with the ballad, "Name," the Goo Goo Dolls had pretty much given up on success. They'd put out record after record for nine years and only gotten some critical success and a cult following.

"We stopped operating under the illusion that we were going to change the world and sell millions of records when we were eighteen," said Rzeznik in *Rolling Stone*. They were wrong. After "Name" hit in 1995, the Goo Goo Dolls have sold millions of records. Becoming known only for "Name" doesn't bother the band because the song got them some attention from new fans. "If 'Name' was the bait to lure them in, great," said Rzeznik in *Billboard*.

"What do you say to him? I'm kind of intimidated by him. He's a legend." —the Goo Goo Dolls' Johnny Rzeznik on working with his hero Paul Westerberg of the Replacements

Johnny Rzeznik, left, and Robby Takac, right

Hard beginning

Rzeznik and guitarist/singer Robby Takac grew up in the blue-collar town of Buffalo, New York. Rzeznik was in vocational school studying to be a plumber. He also got beat up a lot. When Rzeznik was fifteen, his father died of alcoholism. His mother died less than a year later. He met Takac and original drummer George Tutuska, and they named themselves the Goo Goo Dolls.

At first Rzeznik was too shy to sing but has said that Takac "made" him. "I couldn't even talk to people without putting my hand over my mouth," he said in *Rolling Stone*. The band didn't fit in with the Buffalo music scene and had to rent out halls just to get gigs. After finally getting a deal with a tiny label and releasing a self-titled record, they got noticed by a better indie label, Metal Blade, and released *Jed* in 1988. Some good things began to happen for the band. They had a song on the soundtrack for the film *Nightmare on Elm Street 6,* and their label made a distribution deal with Warner Bros. This meant better visibility for the band. Still, most people didn't know who the Goo Goo Dolls were.

Massive touring

The Goo Goo Dolls dealt with their slow career and lack of money by touring and perfecting their live show. Live, they went wild. "The stocking-footed and beer-bellied Takac was in constant motion, running from side to side, goofing with the crowd and meeting Rzeznik center stage to mug," said *Rolling Stone,* describing one show.

They toured and made more records. *Rolling Stone* called 1990's *Hold Me Up* "a throwback to the glory days of postpunk heroes like the Replacements and Husker Du." The magazine praised the "slovenly majesty" of 1993's *Superstar Car Wash.* However, the band's deliberately sloppy rock sound and their blue collar Buffalo image wasn't attracting many fans. Tutuska and the other guys fought over money and Tutuska was replaced by drummer Mike Malinin.

A band with a "Name"

At first it looked like the Goo Goo Dolls' record, *A Boy Named Goo,* was going to go the way of their last records—basically nowhere. Two singles, "Only One" and "Flat Top," were released but failed to do much. Then a DJ at the influential alternative rock station KROQ in Los Angeles decided to start playing the slower song, "Name." Other stations started playing it too. The song shot to number one, and suddenly the Goo Goo Dolls sold their million records.

An appearance on *Beverly Hills 90210* and the gentle sounds of "Name" have had many new fans thinking the Goo Goo Dolls are "lite" rockers. "It's not hard to tell the people who haven't seen us before, since they're the ones who are standing in the front looking at us like this," said Takac, imitating a shocked grimace to *Rolling Stone.*

"Name" might be a good indication of where the band is headed sound-wise, but not because the band wants to cash in—just because they're getting older. "It's never been my goal to be famous," said Rzeznik in *Rolling Stone.* "It's just that your mind works differently when you're twenty-nine than it did when you were nineteen."

Selected Awards

A Boy Named Goo, certified platinum.

Selected Discography

Hold Me Up (Warner Bros.), 1990.

Superstar Car Wash (Warner Bros.), 1993.

A Boy Named Goo (Warner Bros.), 1995.

Further Reading

Borzillo, Carrie, "Goo Goo Dolls Get a 'Name,'" *Billboard,* October 7, 1995, p. 1.

Mundy, Chris, "Volley of the Dolls," *Rolling Stone,* April 1, 1993, p. 23.

Mundy, Chris, "Goo Goo Dolls," *Rolling Stone,* March 21, 1991, p. 24.

Reece, Douglas, "Wal-Mart Halts 'A Boy Named Goo' Reorders," *Billboard,* June 29, 1996, p. 64.

Sprague, David, "What's in a 'Name?'" *Rolling Stone,* December 14, 1995, p. 36.

Contact Information

Goo Goo Dolls Fan Club
P.O. Box 234
Niagara Square Station
Buffalo, NY 14201-0234

Record company:

Warner Bros. Records
3300 Warner Blvd.
Burbank, CA 91505

Web Site

http://www.wbr.com/googoodolls

Green Day

American alternative pop/rock band

Formed in San Francisco, California, in 1989

"I don't come from that world where you can afford to turn down cash." —Billie Joe Armstrong

If ever an alternative rock group epitomized modern punk, it would be Green Day. Influenced by groups like British punk rockers The Sex Pistols and The Clash as well as by the 1960s British Invasion pop group The Kinks, Green Day's Billie Joe Armstrong, Mike Dirnt, and Tre Cool built on the British punk sound of the 1970s to carve their own place in pop music history. Like their punk predecessors, Green Day showed commitment and passion in their songs while reveling in disorder with their outlandish stage theatrics.

Troubled Children

Green Day began in San Francisco, California, as an escape for two troubled teens: Michael Dirnt and Billie Joe Armstrong. Dirnt (born Michael Pritchard) was the son of a heroin-addicted mother. A Native American woman and her white husband adopted Dirnt, but they divorced when he was an adolescent. At that time, Dirnt returned to his birth mother, then left home at age fifteen, renting a room from the family of a school friend—Billie Joe Armstrong. (The friendship had solidified around the time of the death of Armstrong's father, when Billie Joe was about ten years old.) Dirnt and Armstrong eventually moved out on their own, inhabiting various basements throughout Berkeley, California, and frequenting the Gilman Street Project, a club.

In 1987 they formed the band Sweet Children with drummer Al Sobrante. In 1989, Sobrante left the group, and Sweet Children became Green Day, a name taken from a song about pot. Armstrong and Dirnt hired Jeff Kiftmeyer as the new drummer and began touring. Upon their return to California in 1990, Gilman Street Project regular Tre Cool replaced Kiftmeyer as drummer. This combination proved the formula for Green Day's success as the band tried to bring punk rock into the mainstream.

Armstrong and Green Day are known for punk energy and punk theatrics on stage

Three Minutes of Punk

In fact, the group is responsible for bringing the three-minute punk rock song to a much wider audience than before. Green Day is best known for short, fast songs with dynamic arrangements and varying rhythms. Most of their catchy tunes feature speedy guitar riffs and walloping drums. Their lyrics dwell on "hormone-related" issues such as alienation, resentment, disillusionment, hopelessness, and self-destruction. Typically punk, they preach redemption through realism. It is not surprising then that Green Day's material was once classified as "music for people with raging hormones and short attention spans."

Whoever their fans, Green Day has been embraced by the public. Two of the group's albums—*1039/Smoothed Out Slappy Hours* and *Kerplunk*—earned gold certifications from the Record Industry Association of America for sales in excess of 500,000 copies. Their 1995 album *Insomniac* received double platinum certification for selling more than two million copies. *Dookie*, released in 1994, sold ten million copies. After the first eight million, the album became the best-selling punk rock album ever in the United States.

Despite the limited air play of punk overseas, *Dookie* sold 50,000 copies in

Green Day and the Parental Advisory Labelling Investigation

Though regarded as one of the group's trademarks, the lyrics of Green Day's material came under close scrutiny in 1994 as the result of an obscenity lawsuit filed in Georgia. Since it is illegal in Georgia for a minor to purchase sexually explicit recordings without a parent's consent, Robert A. and Lorraine Hendricks decided to test the enforcement of the law by record stores. They had their ten-year-old son visit various record stores in Georgia without an adult escort to purchase albums that contained questionable lyrics, including Green Day's albums. The boy successfully purchased several albums, some of which were marked with parental-advisory stickers.

The Record Industry Association of America instituted a parental-advisory sticker program to signal material that may be considered unsuitable for minors in 1990. Participation in this program by record companies is voluntary. Green Day's record company had the option of placing advisory stickers on albums or not. Sometimes larger chains and retailers will not accept stickered material for sale in their stores, so record labels often refrain from adding parental-advisory stickers.

As Alan Levinson, president of retail music chain Backstage Music, observed: "Green Day is a best-selling record. But the labels aren't going to sticker it, because they want it in Kmart."

Although the Hendricks ultimately dropped the suit after proving the problem, the Douglas County, Georgia, district attorney promised to investigate retailers' sales of such material to minors, but changes in selling practices may be a long time coming since they could affect where albums are sold and therefore revenue.

Activists in the fight to moniter obscene, misogynist (hostile to women), or violent lyrics of music being sold to minors have arisen from a wide spectrum of backgrounds. Some of the best-known players in this confrontation are: C. Delores Tucker, an African American civil rights activist; William Bennett, a writer and philosopher known for his conservative and right-wing political thought; and Tipper Gore, wife of Democratic Vice President Al Gore.

Europe in 1994 and built a following for Green Day internationally. To heighten the group's impact, a forty-date tour of the world was planned to promote the album. The band performed in London, Holland, Germany, Belgium, Italy, Sweden, Denmark, and Spain, home to their largest number of international fans.

Moreover, critics lauded *Dookie* for its melodies and lyrics as well as for its controlled frenzy. In June 1994, *Time* reviewer Christopher John Farley even went so far as to declare the work the best rock CD of the year thus far. In 1995 *Dookie* won the prestigious Grammy Award for Best Alternative Music Performance. *Rolling Stone* Music Awards also recognized *Dookie* as the best album of the year and named Green Day the best band of 1995. "Longview" from *Dookie* also received two honors at *Billboard*'s Music Video Awards. It was MTV's constant playing of "Longview" that made the punk-pop song more than an alternative hit and Green Day a major crossover success with mainstream audiences.

"They're just a bunch of nice guys. They're polite. They never put holes in the wall. Never vomited on stage."

Similarly, Green Day's singles earned impressive credits. In 1995, for example, "When I Come Around" spent more than twenty weeks on *Billboard*'s Hot 100 Chart, eighteen weeks on the Modern Rock Tracks Chart, eleven weeks on the Hot 100 Recurrent Air Play List, and nine weeks on the Top 40 Air Play Chart. The next year "Geek Stink Breath" endured for eight weeks on *Billboard*'s Hot 100 Air Play Chart.

Bad Behavior

Green Day is as well known for its punk theatrics as for its music. Their antics during performances earned them a reputation for anti-establishment behavior. For example, band members engaged in a mud fight at Woodstock II in 1994. Billie Joe Armstrong once performed naked for a New York City concert, and bass player Mike Dirnt regularly jumps into mosh pits. Another notable incident involved Armstrong mooning an audience in Wisconsin. He

was promptly arrested and charged more than $140 in fines for indecent exposure. The punishment, however, did not deter him or other band members from future theatrics.

The tomfoolery is all part of the act, though. "They're just a bunch of nice guys," noted a club booker from Berkeley, California, in *People Weekly*. "They're polite. They never put holes in the wall. Never vomited on stage."

Whether drawn to the on-stage antics or the music, listeners responded to Green Day. Audiences purchased unprecedented numbers of their records and flocked to their concerts worldwide. Both critics and music industry organizations have lauded Green Day with honors and praise for their music and lyrics. It is their overall "punkness" that is most appealing, for—as Steve Masters, a San Francisco radio personality, explained to *People Weekly*—"They have that awesome punk rock energy that makes me want to smash beer bottles on my head."

Selected Awards

Billboard Music Video Awards, Maximum Vision and Best New Alternative/Modern Rock Clip Awards for "Longview," 1994.

Blockbuster Entertainment Awards, Top Modern Rock Band Award, 1995.

Grammy Awards, Best Alternative Music Performance Award for *Dookie*, 1995.

Rolling Stone Music Awards, Best New Band, Best New Male Singer for Billie Joe Armstrong, Best Album for *Dookie*, and Best Album Cover Awards, 1995.

Rolling Stone Critics' Picks Awards, Best New Band Award, 1995.

Selected Discography

1000 Hours (Lookout Records), 1989.

1039/Smoothed Out Slappy Hours (Lookout Records), 1990.

Kerplunk (Lookout Records), 1992.

Dookie (Reprise), 1994.

Insomniac (Reprise), 1995.

Further Reading

Dougherty, Steve, and Michael Small, "Pop Go the Punks," *People Weekly,* March 20, 1995, p. 94.

Farber, Jim, "Billie Joe," *Seventeen,* April 1996, p. 103.

Farley, Christopher John, "Green Day: Dookie," *Time,* June 27, 1994, p. 72.

Fitzpatrick, Eileen, "Georgia D.A. Issues Warning about Explicit-Music Sale," *Billboard,* January 21, 1995, p. 5.

Pareles, Jon, "Green Day: Insomniac," *New York Times,* October 8, 1995, sec. 2, p. 34+.

Contact Information

Reprise Records
3300 Warner Blvd.
Burbank, CA 91505-4694

Web Site

www.repriserec.com/GreenDay

HOLE

American alternative pop/rock band

Formed in Los Angeles, California, in 1989

The band Hole has become synonymous with its lead singer, Courtney Love. A controversial and multitalented figure, Love's off-stage antics have overshadowed the band's grungy and abrasive music. Perhaps known best as the widow of Kurt Cobain, Love has overcome a troubled childhood and other adversities—such as her well-publicized heroin addiction and Cobain's suicide—to leave an indelible mark on the history of women in rock.

"I wanna be the girl with the most cake." —from "Doll Parts"

Troubled beginnings

Courtney Love was born Love Michelle Harrison on July 9, 1965, in San Francisco, California, to hippie therapist mother, Linda Carroll and writer, entrepreneur, and one-time Grateful Dead associate father Hank Harrison (the Dead's Phil Lesh is Love's godfather). Her parents separated when she was just one year old. In her mother's custody, she had her name changed to Courtney Michelle Harrison. Part of her childhood was spent commuting from New Zealand to Eugene, Oregon, with her mother.

Courtney Love

Eventually Love was sent away to boarding schools. After being caught stealing a Kiss t-shirt, she spent time in and out of juvenile and foster homes. By her mid-teens, Love was legally on her own. With the help of a trust fund and money earned as a part-time stripper, she began a traveling odyssey through America, Europe, and Asia, hanging out with several rock bands while in England. She had a couple of minor acting roles followed by very brief stints performing with an early version of girl punk band **Babes in Toyland** (see entry) and alternative rockers Faith No More. Love ended up back in Los Angeles, California, in 1989, where she decided to form her own band.

Making 'Hole' happen

Through an ad in a local paper, Love found guitarist Eric Erlandson, drummer Caroline Rue, and bassist Jill Emery, and Hole was formed. (The name "Hole" is reportedly derived from Euripides' Greek play entitled *Medea*.) 1989 also found Love marrying Los Angeles transvestite punk rocker James Moreland, only to divorce him a year later. Hole's early releases, "Retard Girl" and "Dicknail," along with the band's outrageous live performances, helped create quite a buzz in the U.S. music underground.

Sonic Youth's Kim Gordon and Gumball's Don Fleming co-produced Hole's 1991 Caroline Records debut album, *Pretty on the Inside*. Soon after *Pretty*'s release, Hole toured England and quickly became the darlings of the British music press, although some crit-

ics thought the band's recording was a bit too raw. *Entertainment Weekly* writer, David Browne, noted that the CD "seemed mostly an excuse for Love to throw a musical temper tantrum."

The sum of the parts is greater than the Hole

Love ran into an old acquaintance, Kurt Cobain, in 1991 at the Los Angeles Palladium. She had met Cobain, **Nirvana's** (see entry) frontman, two years earlier in Seattle, Washington. The couple quickly became an item and got married in Hawaii in February 1992, just as Nirvana was exploding to the top. The pair suddenly found themselves wearing the title of the new king and queen of rock. (Coincidentally, for the many critics who claimed Love only married Cobain to capitalize on his band's success, Hole's debut album, *Pretty on the Inside,* was outselling Nirvana's *Bleach* album two to one when they started dating.)

Love eventually gave birth to the couple's healthy daughter, Frances Bean Cobain, in August 1992, while speculation continued that she had been using heroin during the pregnancy. Love strongly denied the allegations at first, then later admitted to *Chicago Sun-Times* reporter Jim DeRogatis that she had used a small amount in the very beginning of her pregnancy.

Tragedy vs. success

With Hole looking for a new rhythm section, they added drummer Patty Schemel and bassist Kristen M. Pfaff in 1993. Meanwhile, Love and guitarist

Eric Erlandson were busy finalizing the details of their lucrative new major label contract with Geffen Records subsidiary, DGC Records.

Hole was now ready to release their next album, the more radio-friendly *Live Through This*, but tragedy would interrupt not only the album's release, but also its subsequent success. Just days before the album's April 1994 release, Cobain was found dead in his and Love's Seattle home with a self-inflicted gunshot wound. Love took heavy criticism for her perceived role in the self destruction of her late husband. At the same time, *Live Through This* was winning rave reviews from music critics, finally being named "album of the year" by *Rolling Stone, Spin,* and *The Village Voice.*

Only two months after the album's release, new bassist Pfaff was found dead in her bathroom of a heroin overdose. Melissa Auf Der Maur took over bass duties for the group and they resumed touring. *Live Through This* was steadily climbing on the charts, eventually hitting #52 and going platinum one year after being released. Two singles from the album, "Doll Parts" and "Miss World," received significant radio airplay.

Love, however, continued fighting personal demons while on tour. First she was arrested in Australia for abusing a flight attendant, then she had misdemeanor charges brought against her for assault in the United States. Eventually she was hospitalized for reportedly taking too much prescription medicine.

Tough act to follow

Hole became a headlining and headline-making act on the Lollapalooza '95 tour. With the tour only a few hours old, Love managed to engage in a brief backstage fist fight with Bikini Kill's singer Kathleen Hanna, who filed assault charges. Love eventually received a one-year suspended sentence for the incident, but didn't hesitate to continue verbally abusing the fans throughout the tour. Love, who insiders consider a cunning and calculating individual, may have just been preparing for her next big career move, acting.

After Hole's tour ended, Love earned a starring role along side Keanu Reeves in the movie *Feeling Minnesota,* to better-than-expected reviews. Love then went on to star in *The People vs. Larry Flynt* with Woody Harrelson. Her performance was so strong that it earned her a Golden Globe Award nomination for best dramatic actress. Love's sudden move from rock's bad girl to a respected actress is one that even pop diva Madonna couldn't top. Following Love's big screen successes and her band's critically acclaimed last CD, music critics were awaiting Hole's next release, tentatively titled *Celebrity Skin,* with high expectations.

Selected Discography

Pretty on the Inside (Caroline), 1991.

Live Through This (DGC), 1994.

Further Reading

"A False Spring," *People Weekly,* May 2, 1994, p. 72.

Browne, David, "Live Through This," *Entertainment Weekly,* April 15, 1994, p. 56.

"Courtney Love: Punk Provocateur," *Time,* June 17, 1996, p. 68.

Dougherty, Steve, "In Like Flynt," *People Weekly,* February 24, 1997, p. 61.

Karlen, Neal, "Love Hurts," *Playboy,* February 1996, p. 104.

Raphael, Amy, *GRRRLS: Viva Rock Divas,* St. Martin's Griffin, 1996; (contains a chapter on Courtney Love).

Rolling Stone, December 23, 1993; April 21, 1994; June 2, 1994; August 11, 1994; November 3, 1994; December 15, 1994.

Schoemer, Karen, "Playing the Game of Love," *Newsweek,* February 6, 1995, p. 56.

Contact Information

DGC
9130 Sunset Blvd.
Los Angeles, CA 90069

Web Site

http://www.geffen.com/hole/

Iggy Pop

Punk rock musician

Born James Jewell Osterberg, April 21, 1947,
in Ypsilanti, Michigan

Down on the streets of Detroit, Michigan, a new sound was rising up from the ashes of Motown in the late 1960s. A revolutionary, punk-spirited movement was breaking through the barriers of music and culture. The battle cries of the MC5 and other Detroit-area bands were shouting to be heard, and the loudest screamer of them all was Iggy Pop. The sonic assault and sheer raw power of these bands shook the underground music world and brought the wild man into the limelight. Three decades later, Iggy remains the original madman of the Motor City and the appointed "Godfather of Punk."

Real wild child

James Jewel Osterberg, later known as Iggy Pop, was hatched in 1947 at a mobile home trailer park in the small train depot town of Ypsilanti, Michigan. He was a loner, and the isolated simple life of his hometown gave him the ability to concentrate and imagine.

"It was about loud and annoying, the more annoying and loud the better." —Iggy Pop

Iggy Pop in concert, Berkeley, California, 1977

to Succeed." His musical desire soon overwhelmed him. "Music is the only place to hide, the refuge, really," Iggy recalled in his book *I Need More.*

Osterberg started a high school rock band, The Iguanas, where he played the drums and sang. On and off jobs drumming for the likes of blues singers Junior Wells and Buddy Guy and girl group the Shangri-La's followed. The Iguanas released a cover of Bo Diddley's "Mona" and got a house gig playing five sets a night, six nights a week for $50 a week. It was a job playing music away from home, so Osterberg grew his hair out, dyed it platinum, got arrested, and got fired.

"The sort of music I do is very aggressive and intoxicating, and after a few songs I enter another state. Probably an adrenal overload of some kind. I believe I can do just about anything."

While still at school, he would watch the kids hanging out in the coffee shop after school, observing their social patterns. The observations would later become material for future songs. In 1966, he dropped out of the University of Michigan to pursue his rock n' roll interests full time. "So, I decided to gamble with music. It was the only thing that was really fun to do," he said later. He changed his name to Iggy Pop and the rest is history.

Iggy and the (Psychedelic) Stooges

Inspired by 1960s progressive rock bands the Doors and the Velvet Underground, Iggy formed a new band. The

Turning his Lincoln Logs into drumsticks at the age of five was his first musical step. Three years later he heard Frank Sinatra and discovered his desire to sing. Known as the "Atomic Brain" in high school, he was voted "Most Likely

Parents Aren't Supposed to Like It

Psychedelic Stooges came together when Iggy found two fellow high school dropouts, the Asheton brothers (Ron, guitar, and Scott, drums) on a street corner in the college town of Ann Arbor, Michigan.

Iggy and the Psychedelic Stooges made their debut at a house party on Halloween night, 1967. Their early audiences were made up of "disaffected high school kids and mentally deranged people," according to Pop. Their first real gig was on March 3, 1968, opening for Blood, Sweat & Tears at Detroit's historic Grande Ballroom.

The sound and fury of the Stooges ("Psychedelic" was dropped from the band's name somewhere along the line) took Detroit by storm. Their electrifying performances and abrasive dangerous music, fronted by the psychotic stage antics of Iggy, became legendary. "The sort of music I do is very aggressive and intoxicating, and after a few songs I enter another state. Probably an adrenal overload of some kind. I believe I can do just about anything."

Iggy and the Stooges on record

Iggy and the Stooges obtained a recording contract with Elektra in 1969 when the label's talent scout was in Detroit to sign the MC5. With Dave Alexander joining the band on bass, the band's raw debut album, *The Stooges,* was recorded in four days and produced by the Velvet Underground's John Cale. Their rage was captured in songs like

Iggy's stage antics

When Iggy Pop unleashed his self-destructive behavior onstage, the madman within escaped. Onstage, he's rolled around in broken glass (that the audience kindly provided), hung from the ceiling, taken off his clothes, smeared peanut butter on himself (once), and self-mutilated his body. Challenging resistant audiences, he'd take the show to them. He refused to be ignored, so "I'd do what little kids would do to get attention, lose my clothes, nick myself with a drumstick, fall into the crowd, go out and find the prettiest girl and seize her. It was a great way to meet girls," Iggy would say about his early intense performances.

"1969," "I Wanna Be Your Dog," and "No Fun."

The Stooges' hypnotic second release, *Funhouse,* was a musical carnival ride that carried the listener through a maze of aggressive psychedelic rock to sleazy deranged blues. The album featured an expanded line-up with Steve Mackay on sax, Bill Cheatham on guitar, and James Williamson on guitar.

Raw power

The band was slowly disintegrating, but they returned in savage form with *Raw Power.* Released in 1973, *Raw Power* was produced by **David Bowie** (see entry). It featured the primal screams of the title track and the Iggy classic "Search & Destroy," an angry, self-immortalizing anthem. "I am the world's forgotten boy / The one who searches only to destroy," said it all.

Unfortunately, the excesses of the rock and roll lifestyle disrupted the band and the Stooges went out in a blaze of glory. "We got so good, we had to die," Iggy said of the Stooges. A live (unofficial) album, *Metallic KO* became their grand finale. Capturing the Stooges last-ever gig, it was recorded on a cassette machine at the Michigan Palace in 1973. Included on the album were the sound of bottles breaking onstage and Iggy egging on the hecklers in the audience. It was a fitting farewell from the world's most dangerous band. Iggy Pop quit the band in 1974.

Picking up where the Stooges left off, Iggy recorded the "Kill City" sessions with guitarist James Williamson in 1975. The album, not released until 1978, marked Iggy's transition from the Stooges to the artist known as Iggy Pop.

The idiot: the Berlin years (1976-79)

Iggy Pop and David Bowie began working on Pop's first solo album in 1976, first in France, then in West Berlin, Germany. The two collaborated on writing songs, and the album became 1977's *The Idiot*. The new "mature" Iggy sang more easy listening fare, including the first version of future Bowie hit "China Girl." The album contained a new electronic mixture of "Sister Midnight" and "Nightclubbing." Only "Funtime" recalled the Stooge within.

Bowie also produced Pop's next album, *Lust for Life*. Released later in 1977, it was recorded and mixed in thirteen days. From his smiling mug on the cover to the catchy songs inside, it was clear that Iggy was having fun again.

Although their creative partnership lasted for only two albums, Iggy Pop and David Bowie remained friends. They both lived in West Berlin for about three years in the late 1970s. After Bowie produced Iggy's first two solo albums, Iggy later returned the favor and appeared on Bowie's "Station to Station" tour. Iggy was also featured on Bowie's 1977 album, *Low*.

Punk loves (Iggy) pop

In 1977, the music world finally caught up to Iggy Pop. "Punk" before the term was even invented, Iggy was later dubbed "The Godfather of Punk" by the new generation of punk rockers that burst forth from England and New York. Many punk bands would cover his songs and make them their own. Iggy's bizarre stage antics were adopted by punk vocalists everywhere in tribute to their leader. The brutal high energy shows left their mark on many of punk rock's finest.

"New Wave," a safer, cleaner version of punk rock, entered the airwaves in 1979, just as Pop's new album *New Values* appeared. The song, "Five Foot One," got him his first-ever radio hit and music video. A new Iggy was revealed in the three albums that took him into the 1980s, *Soldier, Party,* and *Zombie Birdhouse*. They showed the dual nature of his music personality—raw rocker and sleazy crooner.

Blah! Blah! Blah!

After a brief disappearance from music, Iggy resurfaced in 1986 with *Blah! Blah! Blah!* It was his slickest, most commercial record to date, with Bowie coproducing the album along with Dave Richards. It included Pop's first major single success, "Real Wild Child," which reached number ten in Great Britain while failing to chart in the United States. Although the album was a disappointment to some of his fans, he still held his own during his live shows.

Instinct, released in 1988, featured guest guitarist Steve Jones, formerly of British punk band the Sex Pistols. Despite the ultimate punk influence, it was more of a heavy metal sound for Iggy. The album did receive a Grammy nomination in the "Best Heavy Metal" category, which Pop lost to Jethro Tull that year.

Pop's first (and only) taste of Top 40 success in the United States was "Candy," a duet with Kate Pierson of the B-52s. The album *Brick by Brick,* was released in 1990 and was produced by Don Was. It earned Iggy a unique award, an induction into the National Association of Brick Distributors "Brick Hall of Fame." He received a trophy, made of brick, of course.

American Caesar, 1990s style

Iggy got down and dirty again for his next two releases. It was a welcome step backward for his old fans, who didn't want to see a kinder, gentler Iggy. *American Caesar* (1993) and *Naughty Lit-*

Iggy Pop in Hollywood

In the 1980s and 1990s Iggy took up acting. He found many quirky parts in films by independent film directors, such as Crybaby, Tank Girl, The Crow: City of Angels, Dead Man, and Coffee & Cigarettes, a short film. He did a few cameos in The Color of Money and Sid & Nancy, a film about punk rock star Sid Vicious of the Sex Pistols and his girlfriend.

His TV appearances included small roles in Miami Vice and Tales of the Crypt. He was cast as Mr. Mechlanburg in the children's show Adventures of Pete & Pete. The thought of Mr. Pop in a children's TV show boggles one's mind.

---

tle Doggie (1996) crushed the facade as Iggy returned to his bad boy roots.

The Iggy of the 1990s is getting more exposure than ever. At the Rock and Roll Hall of Fame Dedication concert he performed "Back Door Man" (made famous by Jim Morrison and the Doors) and "I Wanna Be Your Dog" (from the Stooges first album) with **Soul Asylum** (see entry) as his backup band. When he licensed his 1973 composition "Search & Destroy" to Nike shoes for their 1996 Olympic advertising campaign, the sound of Iggy Pop invaded family living rooms everywhere.

In 1997, Pop's autobiography, *I Need More,* was re-released. The book is life philosophy according to Iggy Pop. Virgin released an overview of Iggy's music career on *Nude & Rude: The Best of Iggy Pop.* Iggy also headlined the ROAR Tour in 1997, a music festival of new alternative acts.

With the 30-year mark of the Stooges debut gig coming in 1997, there have been countless rumors of a reunion in the works. Nothing has been planned or announced, or will it be another surprise attack from Iggy? From his not-so-humble beginnings with the Stooges, Iggy Pop, the world's unforgotten boy, is still in the spotlight, withs many wondering what he'll do next.

Selected Awards

Rolling Stone Critics Poll, "Comeback of the Year," 1977.

Inducted into "Brick Hall of Fame," for *Brick by Brick*, 1991.

Selected Discography:

With the Stooges:

The Stooges (Elektra), 1969.

Fun House (Elektra), 1970.

Raw Power (Elektra), 1973.

Solo (as Iggy Pop):

The Idiot (RCA), 1977.

Lust for Life (RCA), 1977.

T. V. Eye (RCA), 1978.

New Values (Arista), 1979.

Soldier (Arista), 1980.

Zombie Birdhouse (Animal), 1982.

Blah-Blah-Blah (A&M), 1986.

Instinct (A&M), 1988.

Brick by Brick (Virgin), 1990.

American Caesar (Virgin), 1993.

Naughty Little Doggie (Virgin), 1996.

Nude & Rude: The Best of Iggy Pop (Virgin), 1996.

Further Reading

Castro, Peter, "Talking with Iggy Pop," *People Weekly,* May 6, 1996, p. 29.

Fricke, David, "Naughty Little Doggie," *Rolling Stone,* February 22, 1996, p. 62.

Schoemer, Karen, "Still Wild at Heart," *Newsweek,* October 28, 1996, p. 70.

Sinclair, Tom, "Still a Modern Guy," *Entertainment Weekly,* September 13, 1996, p. 113.

Books:

Kent, Nick, *The Dark Stuff,* Da Capo Press, 1995.

Pop, Iggy, *I Need More,* 2/13/61 Publishing, 1996 (originally published 1982).

Contact Information

Virgin Records
1790 Broadway, 20th Fl.
New York, NY 10019

Web Site

http://www.virginrecords.com/iggy_pop

Jane's Addiction

American alternative pop/rock band

Formed in Los Angeles, California, in 1986
Disbanded 1991-92; "relapsed" 1997

A controversial band led by eccentric and outspoken frontman Perry Farrell, Jane's Addiction released only two albums on their major label—Warner Brothers. However, their unique blend of rock, metal, jazz, punk, and folk—which was accented by Farrell's high pitched and quirky (some say annoying) voice—would ultimately have a big influence on contemporary music audiences everywhere. With their colorful and outrageous live stage shows and their "in-your-face" attitude, Jane's Addiction helped pave the way for other "art-rock" performers such as **Nine Inch Nails** (see entry) and **Marilyn Manson** (see entry). Jane's Addiction eventually broke up at the pinnacle of their success, which only served to perpetuate the mystique and unpredictability of the group, but the call of fans everywhere brought them back together six years after they disbanded.

Jane says, "Change is good"

In 1986, after his gothic sounding band Psi Com had built a small local following on the Los Angeles club scene, Perry Farrell

"The aural equivalent of a psychopath's nightmare, Jane's Addiction set about their mission to corrupt and enlighten with refreshing honesty, shaped by Farrell's perverse and arrogant artistic sensibilities, and superlative all-around musicianship." —Essi Berelian, music critic

Perry Farrell

(born Perry Bernstein, he changed his last name to his brother's first name, Farrell, trying to create a play on the word "peripheral") was ready for something different. When Farrell was introduced to bass player Eric Avery that year by a mutual friend, he decided to form a new band. After recruiting old school pals Dave Navarro on guitar and Stephen Perkins on drums, Farrell's new band, Jane's Addiction, was prepared to take the L.A. club scene by storm.

Talk of the town

Farrell's exotic stage appearance (thick black eye make-up, neon dreadlocks, a black vinyl bodysuit, and dayglo girdles) combined with the band's abrasive and ominous sound (often compared to Led Zeppelin), soon made Jane's Addiction the one of the most talked about groups on the scene. They released a self-titled live album recorded at the Roxy in Hollywood on the indie label Triple X in 1987. Interest in the band from the major record companies built to a frenzy at this point. Warner Brothers won the bidding war that followed and immediately put the band in the studio to record their Warner's debut album.

Shock value works

In October 1988, *Nothing's Shocking* (complete with controversial cover artwork featuring a Farrell sculpture of a pair of Siamese twins with their hair on fire) was released, and Jane's Addiction went on the road to help promote sales of the CD, opening up for Detroit punk rock legend **Iggy Pop** (see entry). With a foundation of diverse songs like "Jane Says," "Idiots Rule," and "Ocean Sized," and the energy of the album's blistering guitars, hypnotic rhythms, and Farrell's trademark voice, *Nothing's Shocking* has been called by some music critics one of the most important rock albums of its era.

More controversy, more success

The band's second major label album, *Ritual De Lo Habitual,* had even more provocative artwork (another Farrell sculpture) than the first. Upon its 1990 release, it was banned from several large American record chains. Eventually Farrell designed an ironic substitute cover for the album about freedom of speech, a plain white cover with the First Amendment of the Bill of Rights printed on it.

Critics gave *Ritual De Lo Habitual* better marks overall than the band's fine first effort. With a maturity in songwriting and production, the CD has several notable tracks, including the fiery "Ain't No Right" and the majestic "Classic Girl." The catchy single "Been Caught Stealing," helped the album explode up to #19 on the U.S. charts. In fact, first week sales of *Ritual* topped the entire sales figures of the first album.

More success, more problems

Unfortunately, the band wasn't doing as well as their album was. Internal disputes within the band were straining relationships. Excessive drug use had become a big problem. Farrell took a break to finish his film, *The Gift,* and begin organizing his latest brain-child, an alternative music festival with a circus atmosphere he called Lollapalooza (a term coined by the Three Stooges meaning a real whopper of a scam).

After the very successful Lollapalooza '91 tour, the members of Jane's Addiction continued having problems that were capped by Farrell's October 16 arrest on drug charges. Then in 1992, to the shock of fans and critics alike, the band announced their breakup. Farrell formed a new group, **Porno for Pyros** (see entry), with Jane's Addiction's old drummer Steve Perkins. Guitarist Dave Navarro and bassist Eric Avery joined the band Deconstruction for a brief period, before Navarro moved on to play guitar for the **Red Hot Chili Peppers** (see entry).

In 1997 Jane's Addiction once again surprised the music world by announcing their "relapse" (as opposed to a reunion). Re-formed with a lineup of Perry Farrell, Steve Perkins, Dave Navarro, and friend Flea (both Navarro and Flea from the Red Hot Chili Peppers), the band released an album called *Kettle Whistle* in November and started a 23-date Relapse Tour at the end of October.

Selected Awards

Ritual De Lo Habitual, certified platinum, 1991.

MTV Video Music Awards, Best Alternative Music Video, for "Been Caught Stealing," 1991.

Lollapalooza

Featuring a diverse line-up of acts such as rapper Ice-T and the dream pop of Siouxsie & the Banshees, along with Farrell's own Jane's Addiction, the travelling tour Lollapalooza became one of the hottest selling concert tickets during its first tour in the summer of 1991. Farrell would continue working on the annual alternative music festival until 1996, when he disassociated himself from it, even though he still held a significant financial interest in the event. By 1997, though, Farrell was once again involved in directing the event.

Selected Discography

Jane's Addiction (Triple X), 1987.

Nothing's Shocking (Warner Bros.), 1988.

Ritual De Lo Habitual (Warner Bros.), 1990.

Further Reading

Guitar Player, December 1988; January 1991, March 1991.

Musician Magazine, August 1988.

Rolling Stone, October 20, 1988; February 9, 1989; October 18, 1990; September 9, 1991.

Spin, June 1991.

Contact Information

Warner Bros.
3300 Warner Blvd.
Burbank, CA 91505

Web Site

http://www.cacamerica.com/user/bin/tkk/ja.html

marilyn manson

Alternative pop/rock

Formed in 1990 in
Fort Lauderdale, Florida

"Music is one of the only things that matters. I don't even think kids care who the president is ... I think if someone like Adolf Hitler or Charles Manson were going today, they would be rock stars" —Marilyn Manson

Combining shock-rock theatrics with a soundtrack of aggressive industrial metal, Marilyn Manson has provoked the establishment by forcing the taboo subjects of sex, death, violence, and Satan onto alternative audiences, making parents cringe and drawing a following of young fans. The band was discovered in 1990 by fellow music madman, Trent Reznor of **Nine Inch Nails** (see entry). He signed them to be the first act on his new record label, Nothing Records.

While rock and roll spectacles are nothing new, Marilyn Manson takes it to the limit. The band tries and succeeds in being as offensive as possible. Unlike the forefathers of shock rock from whom he conveniently borrows, lead singer/songwriter Marilyn Manson claims to live the life he sings about. Looking like a cross between Alice Cooper and Vampira, he is difficult to ignore.

Every parent's nightmare

"I think I've grown to become all the things that tormented and terrorized me as a child," Marilyn Manson, formerly known as Brian Warner, said to *Alternative Press*. He says he was raised on caffeine, sugar, violence, and drugs in Canton, Ohio. At age eighteen he left town to study journalism in Fort Lauderdale, Florida.

It was there where he met guitarist Daisy Berkowitz, and the two created Marilyn Manson and the Spooky Kids, a four-piece performance art group. When the Nine Inch Nails tour made a stop in Florida, Marilyn interviewed Trent Reznor for his college newspaper. The bond was formed, and soon after Manson's band was opening for Nine Inch Nails. A demo tape and phone call later came Marilyn Manson's big break.

The beautiful people

Members of the band, Marilyn Manson, have adopted stage names that combine the first name of a well-known star with the last name of a serial killer or mass murderer. The band's lineup includes Marilyn Manson (vocalist), Twiggy Ramirez (bassist), Ginger Fish (drummer), Madonna Wayne Gacy (keyboardist), and Zim Zum (guitarist). "I think the rock star today is dead. My stage persona is closer to who I am than my true identity," bassist Twiggy Ramirez stated in *Alternative Press*.

Beyond the death makeup, the gender-crossing costumes, and the rockstar lifestyle they project, lies the music. Borrowing from glam, goth, punk, death metal, and industrial sounds, Manson admitted, "We're probably somewhere between the Village People [disco] and [heavy metal band] **Slayer** (see entry)."

Marilyn Manson and Satanism

The self-proclaimed "All-American Antichrist" says he developed his vision by absorbing modern American culture and TV. Capitalism, Christianity, hypocrisy, moral values, individuality, sex, violence, and devil worship all find a place in the songs of Marilyn Manson. On the subject of Satanism, Marilyn Manson practices what he preaches; he is an ordained reverend in Anton Lavey's Church of Satan. His call is for kids to reject Christianity and "be their own gods." He believes his fans are "selling their souls to themselves, forming their own values and their own morals based on what makes them happy, not what makes their parents happy."

Marilyn Manson has enraged many people and organizations from any number of standpoints. C. Delores Tucker and Bill Bennett, activists who have been attempting to monitor and label music that they feel is too provocative for minors, accused the band's distributor, MCA, of "peddling filth for profits." Even the British Parliament tried to ban their debut album *Portrait of an American Family*, calling it "an outrage against society."

Bomb threats and protesters have picketed venues, touting the evilness of the band. Meanwhile, Marilyn Manson leads his fanatical followings with a chorus of "We hate love. We love hate!" and urges the crowd into chanting "Hate! Hate! Hate!" after city officials in Virginia attempted to cancel an upcoming show. Officials backed down after the band fought back and threatened them with a lawsuit by the American Civil Liberties Union. The show went on as scheduled.

His favorite record is **David Bowie's** (see entry) apocalyptic album, *Diamond Dogs,* which he plays often as an introduction to his shows. His idols include Alice Cooper, whose horror themes, ghoulish looks, and rock and roll dictatorship are inspirations, and **Iggy Pop.**

"What I've always wanted to do was find a happy medium and create powerful music that says something to a lot of people. Then it actually makes a difference. I think to not do that is to sell out. For me, to become part of the mainstream is the most subversive thing I can do," Manson told *Scene* magazine.

The band has released three albums of musical madness. An EP entitled *Smells Like Children* features a Mansonized version of "Sweet Dreams (Are Made Of This)" (originally by the 1980s pop group Eurythmics), and a concept album *Antichrist Superstar,* that casts Manson as a misfit who turns into a rock n' roll antichrist and destroys the world.

"For me, to become part of the mainstream is the most subversive thing I can do."

It was this album that arrived on the Billboard Top 200 chart at number three and propelled the band into the mainstream. They now attract legions of fans that call themselves "Spooky Kids," who dress like their favorite band member, recalling memories of the Kiss era. The music media loves Manson for the controversy that follows the band. The band's frightening image often appears on MTV, and Marilyn himself played a porno star in David Lynch's film *Lost Highway.* With all this exposure, Marilyn Manson is quickly turning into the cultural icon he resented in the first place. Whether he's a genius or a madman, parents everywhere should be worried.

Selected Discography

Portrait of an American Family (Nothing Records), 1993.

Smells Like Children (Nothing Records), 1995.

Antichrist Superstar (Nothing Records), 1996.

Further Reading

Batten, Steve, "Diary of a Madman; Marilyn Manson's Message for the Masses," *Scene,* April 1997.

Pecorelli, Johnny, "Marilyn Manson Family Values," *Alternative Press,* April 1996.

Rotter, Jeffrey, "Our Little Satan," *Spin,* March 1997.

Straus, Neil, "Sympathy for the Devil," *Rolling Stone,* January 23, 1997, p. 48.

Thigpen, David E., "Satan's Little Helpers," *Time,* February 24, 1997, p. 68.

Contact Information

Nothing Records
75 Rockefeller Plaza
New York, NY 10019

Web Site

http://www.marilyn-manson.com

http://geocities.com/Sunset Strip/Towers/4568/

morphine

American alternative pop/rock band

Formed 1992 in Boston,
Massachusetts

orphine, a guitarless alternative pop/rock trio, employs the unusual instrumentation of a baritone saxophone, a unique two-string bass, and drums to achieve a bottom-heavy rocking sound. Fronted by bassist, vocalist, and principal songwriter Mark Sandman, Morphine's sound is the perfect complement to Sandman's smoky vocals and dark, intriguing lyrics. Through extensive touring since their first album was released in 1992, the band has built a reputation as an exciting live act. With four albums released through 1997 and a deal with mega-conglomerate DreamWorks (the media company founded by film and record industry moguls David Geffen, Steven Spielberg, and Jeffrey Katzenberg), Morphine has also developed an audience for its recordings.

Morphine began as an experiment

Morphine began as an experimental project for Mark Sandman and saxophonist Dana Colley, who both continued to be involved with other Boston-area bands while developing the Mor-

"We're trying to keep
the definition of
'what's a Morphine
song?' pretty flexible."

—Mark Sandman,

vocalist/bassist/songwriter

phine concept. Sandman was experimenting at the time with playing one- and two-stringed basses and using a slide to achieve a unique sound. The two developed an unusual rhythm and bass sound by pairing Sandman's slide bass with Colley's baritone sax behind Sandman's vocals. Their first live performances with jazz-rock drummer Jerome Deupree were well received, proving there was an audience for the group's music. An independent album titled *Good* was released in 1992. Some of it was recorded at Sandman's low-tech home studio. Of the sound, Sandman told *Pulse!* "It just seems like the guitars are there. They're just sort of imaginary."

Signed with Rykodisc in 1993

Morphine's debut album was promising enough for Rykodisc to sign the band and rerelease *Good.* A second album, *Cure for Pain,* was released in 1993 to acclaim from critics and underground music fans. Billy Conway became the group's permanent drummer, replacing Deupree on the album. According to *Rolling Stone,* "Morphine evoke the zonked swing of lounge jazz and the grind of dirty blues while maintaining rock & roll convictions."

Morphine toured for thirteen consecutive months in support of *Cure for Pain.* They went to more than a dozen countries and were featured in nine European festivals. Finding themselves in the midst of the massive Los Angeles earthquake of January 1994, Morphine broke the citywide curfew and played a show there the next night.

yes revealed Morphine's commercial potential

Morphine released their third album, *yes,* in 1995. It debuted at the top position on the *Billboard* Heatseekers album chart and stayed on the chart for months. The album received rave reviews, and a single, "Honey White," was released. Critic Phil Gallo of *Daily Variety* marveled at Morphine's impact, "There's no compromise within Morphine's daringly original songs that challenge notions of rhythm, melody and even the use of instrumentation as the band bounces off tuneful skeletons from the closets of rockabilly, improvisational jazz, punk and blues."

"It just seems like the guitars are there. They're just sort of imaginary."

No strangers to touring, Morphine joined the H.O.R.D.E. tour in the summer of 1995.

New album and deal with DreamWorks for 1997

Morphine's fourth album, *Like Swimming,* was released in April 1997. It was the first under an agreement between DreamWorks and Rykodisc and featured a new DreamWorks logo with a photo of the band on the label. The album marked no new musical direction for Morphine. Ben Edmonds of the *Detroit Metro Times* commented, "That is precisely its strength. It's a reassuring work, almost as if the group is saying 'the logo may have changed but the music remains.'"

The music that remained continued to reflect Sandman's lyric preoccupation with dark incidents, twisted plots, and wordplay inspired by his reading of mystery thrillers by authors such as Raymond Chandler and James Ellroy.

Selected Awards

Boston Music Awards, Independent Album of the Year, for *Good,* 1992.

Boston Music Awards, Act of the Year and Outstanding Rock Band, 1996.

Selected Discography

Good (Accurate/Distortion; rereleased by Rykodisc), 1992.

Cure for Pain (Rykodisc), 1993.

yes (Rykodisc), 1995.

Like Swimming (DreamWorks), 1997.

Further Reading

Colapinto, John, "Just Say 'Yes,'" *Rolling Stone,* June 29, 1995, p. 20.

Daily Variety, April 3, 1995.

Edmonds, Ben, "Offbeat Excellence," *Detroit Metro Times,* April 2-8, 1997, p. 22.

Gardiner, Jeff, "Mr. Sandman, Sing Me a Song," *Entertainment Weekly,* August 25, 1995, p. 112.

Gulla, Bob, "Morphine," *Option,* March-April, 1995.

"Morphine's Potent Formula," *USA Today,* April 8, 1997, p. 4D.

Contact Information

Rykodisc
Shetland Park
27 Congress St.
Salem, MA 01970

MUDHONEY

American alternative pop/rock band
Formed in 1988 in Seattle, Washington

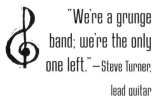

"We're a grunge band; we're the only one left." —Steve Turner, lead guitar

Mudhoney is one of those bands who seem destined to struggle in relative obscurity. Though they played a central role in the development of the "Seattle scene" in the mid-to late 1980s, they ended up being overshadowed by other Seattle grunge bands like **Nirvana** (see entry), **Pearl Jam** (see entry), and **Soundgarden** (see entry).

Mudhoney has been referred to as the "Grizzled Grandpappies of Grunge." Though not as well-known as Nirvana, Pearl Jam, or Soundgarden, Mudhoney actually launched the "Seattle Invasion" with their first single, "Touch Me, I'm Sick," in August 1988. Mudhoney was pushing the guitar-heavy, distortion-pedaled sound in a blend of garage rock and early 1980s punk that would become grunge well before Nirvana or Pearl Jam became known outside of Seattle. Noted for their low production sound and their refusal to compromise, Mudhoney kept the pure grunge sound alive—tattered and with an attitude—for nearly a decade.

From one band came two

Mudhoney was formed from the remains of one of Seattle's first grunge bands, Green River, in 1988. After being together for about three years, Green River members split to form Mudhoney, on the one hand, and Mother Love Bone, which would later develop into Pearl Jam. Mark Arm, rhythm guitarist and lead singer, hooked up with singer and lead guitarist, Steve Turner. Turner was in college studying anthropology; Arm had received his degree in English. Turner and Arm had both played in Green River. Bassist Matt Lukin, formerly with perhaps the grungiest of all Seattle bands, the Melvins, soon joined the band, followed by journeyman drummer Dan Peters. Turner later claimed in *Musician,* "We never meant to make an album."

"Touch Me, I'm Sick"

Mudhoney's first single, "Touch Me, I'm Sick," set the buzz in motion about Seattle bands and the guitar-heavy grunge sound when it was released in August 1988. Featuring Mark Arm's howling vocals over fuzz-guitar riffs and a heavy rhythm section, the single sold out through each of three releases.

The band quickly followed with an EP (extended play) on Seattle's premier grunge label, Sub Pop, called *Superfuzz Bigmuff,* which also came out in 1988. *Rolling Stone* described Mudhoney's early sound as "'70s metal riffing and a no-frills punk sensibility ... dense, sloppy, distorted and full of dissatisfaction."

While the underground took notice, the mainstream was put off. Jon Regardie of *Detour* suggested that "Mudhoney's oceans of feedback and distorted wah-wah mess have never produced the ... pop hooks that canonized [made famous or glorified] Nirvana." But the album was on the British charts for a year, and *Superfuzz Bigmuff* can be said to have set the stage for the "grunge revolution."

Mudhoney released their self-titled debut album in 1989, again on independent label Sub Pop. Still an "indie" band, they nevertheless were gaining popularity. With the release of their next album *Every Good Boy Deserves Fudge* in 1991, the band began looking for a bigger record deal.

Mudhoney signs with Reprise

With the promise of grunge in full force, Mudhoney signed with Reprise Records in 1992. Shortly afterwards they released *Piece of Cake.* James Rotondi in *Guitar Player* declared that the album preserved "the sick sludge factor of previous efforts." *Rolling Stone* writer Trent Hill found the effort a cross between "formulaic rock that nobody believes in anymore" and capable "reworkings of the band's signature sound." Perhaps the band says it best on the song "Acetone": "Oh lord, what have we become / We're not fooling anyone."

The "death" of grunge

Mudhoney's most celebrated release came in 1995, in the form of *My Brother the Cow.* Despite the fact that grunge was officially dead, Mudhoney produced what critics said would put them on the same playing field as Pearl Jam. Full of "punk rage and fury," the album was described as "commercially viable" by *People Weekly* reviewer Andrew Abrahams. Abrahams wrote that the album delivered "pure grunge—messy music that casts a powerful spell." *Rolling Stone's* Grant Alden called it "stunning," with "elegant structures, led by Steve Turner's guitar lines." Calling Mudhoney the first great grunge band, Alden added that the band had put together a collection of songs "that matter."

Rolling Stone writer Daina Darzin described *My Brother the Cow* as a "powerful blast of noise and attitude." And that is exactly what the band has always delivered, whether from a neighborhood garage, local club, indie label, or corporate record company. They have consistently "got by for years on just a riff or a phrase, delivered with piercing intensity." And while they have made the corporate leap, they have demonstrated their commitment to a sound no classically trained musician would ever play.

Selected Discography

Super Fuzz Bigmuff (Sub Pop), 1988.

Mudhoney (Sub Pop), 1989.

Every Good Boy Deserves Fudge (Sub Pop), 1991.

Today's Stars (Caroline), 1993.

Five Dollar Bob's Mock Cooter Stew (Reprise), 1993.

My Brother the Cow (Reprise), 1995.

Further Reading

Abrahams, Andrew, "My Brother the Cow," *People Weekly,* May 8, 1995, p. 31.

Alden, Grant, "Mudhoney: My Brother the Cow," *Rolling Stone,* April 6, 1995, p. 64.

Darzin, Daina, "Mudhoney: The First Great Seattle Band of the '80s Has the Last Laugh of the '90s," *Rolling Stone,* June 1, 1995, p. 46.

Hill, Trent, "Mudhoney: Piece of Cake," *Rolling Stone,* January 7, 1993, p. 46.

Musician, January 1993; June 1995.

Rigardie, John, *Detour Magazine,* March 1995.

Rotondi, James, "Piece of Cake," *Guitar Player,* January 1993, p. 116.

Rolling Stone, August 20, 1992; January 7, 1993; January 21, 1993; January 26, 1995.

Contact Information

Reprise Records
3300 Warner Blvd.
Burbank, CA 91505-4694

Web Site

http://www.repriserec.com

NiNE INCH NaiLS

American alternative pop/rock band

Formed in 1988 in Cleveland, Ohio

In 1989, Nine Inch Nails brought industrial music into the mainstream, launching a more listenable, danceable version of this type of electronic music for pop music fans. The mastermind behind the band is Trent Reznor, who essentially *is* Nine Inch Nails. Combining distorted guitars, rapid fire beats, and electronic collages with dark, tormented lyrics, he creates a sonic landscape that has become life's soundtrack for many alienated youths.

Capturing the first Lollapalooza audiences with their assault on the ears and brutal performances in 1991, Nine Inch Nails broke through the guitar grunge period and helped to make electronic music become the music of the future. Earlier 1980's industrial acts like Skinny Puppy, Ministry, and KMFDM failed to make this commercial breakthrough. Drawing upon those influences, Nine Inch Nails opened up the airwaves to this harsh, relentless music, spawning a new era of electro-industrial madness. The band later seized the attention of the masses at Woodstock II in 1994, winning over the crowd with the most intense perfor-

"The point is just to bring people out of complacency, sonically and lyrically–Your parents should hate it." –

Trent Reznor/Nine Inch Nails.

mance of the festival when Reznor covered himself with mud.

The becoming

Reznor was born in rural Mercer, Pennsylvania, on May 17, 1965. Forced into taking piano lessons at the age of five, the shy, quiet Reznor quickly gained confidence playing music since it came naturally to him. At age fifteen he was told by his music teacher that he could be a concert pianist if he applied himself enough. He studied trumpet and saxophone, joining the marching band at Mercer High School. "Growing up I so wanted to get out of where I was, away from the mediocrity and mundaneness [ordinariness] of rural life. Anything extreme caught my attention," Trent Reznor recalled for *Spin*.

It was the band Kiss who changed his world. Evil and scary, they were the symbol of rebelliousness at the time. He picked up the guitar, taking lessons from his father who bought him his first electronic piano and urged him to play. He admits he was "never good at (playing guitar) and still isn't. I still only know two bar chords, but I don't care."

When the early 1980's synthesizer explosion hit, he begged his parents for a Moog synthesizer and turned his attention toward keyboard instruments. "The excitement of hearing a Human League [British new wave synth-pop band] track and thinking, 'that's all machines, there is no drummer,' that was my calling, it wasn't the Sex Pistols [British punk rock band]," Trent recalls.

One of his early band experiences was a high school cover band called Op-

tion Thirty, where he played keyboards and sang. The band only made $300 a week. After graduating from a local college where he studied computer engineering, he moved to Cleveland, Ohio. Other bands followed, but they went nowhere fast. By hanging out at a local music store, he landed a job there. His work allowed him a chance to sample all the latest high-tech synthesizers and sequencers on the market.

A coworker had an all-original synth-pop band called Exotic Birds. Trent joined them as a keyboardist and met future NIN bandmates Chris Vrenna and Richard Patrick (later with Filter) in the band. Exotic Birds released an EP (extended play) on the local Pleasureland label. Afterward Reznor joined various local bands, including Problems (who made an appearance in the movie *Light of Day*), Slam Bam Boo, and Lucky Pierre.

"The excitement of hearing a Human League track and thinking, 'that's all machines, there is no drummer,' that was my calling, it wasn't the Sex Pistols."

In 1988 he recorded a three-song demo tape for TVT Records at Right Track Studios, where he worked as a recording engineer.

Mr. Self-destruct

"One day I woke up and wondered what am I doing? And made a pact with myself. I'd been getting high a lot lately and was turning into what I never wanted to be. So I started this experiment. What would happen if every ounce of

Trent Reznor performing

energy went into something?" "Down in It" was the first song to come out of this self-realization. It was inspired by the musical forms of aggression and energy of the industrial/electronic bands, Skinny Puppy and Ministry.

Reznor's private anxiety had found its release as he spilled his guts out into the songs he was now writing. The lyrics were as angry as the music, and the songs became the album *Pretty Hate Machine,* released on TVT Records. Though not an instant hit, it charted in 1990 and stayed on the charts for years afterward, thanks to endless club play and MTV's repeated showings of the video "Hero Like a Hole," the album's first single.

After constant touring a sizable cult following developed around NIN, erupting after the first Lollapalooza tour in 1991. Lollapalooza, the multi-band alternative music festival, included acts as diverse as goth-punk Siouxsie and the Banshees, hardcore confrontationalist Henry Rollins, and gangsta rapper **Ice-T** (see entry). Nine Inch Nails stood out from the pack with their destructive music and raging performances, winning over new fans. Their merchandise outsold other, more established performers. Onstage, Reznor paid homage to 1980s British new wave singer Adam Ant, reviving the song "You're So Physical," a highlight of his set.

Reznor's Sound Tracks

Before the downward spiral began to swing upward, Reznor found himself branching out from Nine Inch Nails to do film soundtracks. Reflecting back on his youth, "My world was comic books, science fiction and scary movies, whatever I could absorb."

He recorded a cover of Joy Division's haunting "Dead Souls," that echoes the desolation of the original. His version appeared on the soundtrack to The Crow, a movie about a lost individual not unlike himself. In 1994, the film director Oliver Stone commissioned Reznor to produce the soundtrack for his movie Natural Born Killers, a story about two mass murderers that became media darlings. This soundtrack featured two Nine Inch Nails songs, "A Warm Place" and a remix of an early song, "Something I Can Never Have."

In early 1997, after relocating to New Orleans, Reznor completed another soundtrack. He provided abstract musical compositions for David Lynch's film Lost Highway. "The score here is tense and powerful and as inventive as the orchestration of the shower scene in Hitchcock's Psycho," wrote Rolling Stone. Also coordinating the other artists for the soundtrack album, Reznor can look forward to an extended music career as soundtrack and record producer.

Established Nothing Records in 1992

Legal problems with TVT Records delayed the release of a second album. To satisfy his new fans and not lose the momentum he had built up, Reznor released an EP in 1992. *Broken* was much harder in style than the first offering, but it debuted in the *Billboard* Top Ten. Around the same time as the breakdown of the relationship with the label, he decided to start his own, calling it Nothing Records. It became a vehicle for future NIN releases and acts of his liking. The first act to be signed to Nothing was shock rockers **Marilyn Manson** (see entry), followed by the U.K.'s Pop Will Eat Itself and Prick, former bandmate Kevin McMahon's project, which he also co-produced. The latest signing was true industrial pioneer band, Einsturzende Neubauten.

In November and December 1992, both *Pretty Hate Machine* and *Broken* were certified gold and platinum in sales. At the 1993 Grammy Awards, "Wish" was named Best Metal Performance. The next release, a remix of the *Broken* EP called *Fixed,* had him rearrange the songs into true industrial renderings, making them almost unlistenable. A much-needed break to write and record followed.

The downward spiral

Explaining NIN's three releases prior to 1994's *The Downward Spiral,* Reznor said, "The three albums have different focal points, *Pretty Hate Machine,* I'm depressed by everything around me, but I still like myself. *Broken's* theme is self-loathing, I've lost myself, nothing's better and I want to die. On *The Downward Spiral* I'm searching for some kind of self-awareness. I was searching for the core by stripping away all the different layers."

It took five years to create, but in 1994, Nine Inch Nails returned with the industrial concept album *The Downward Spiral*. Influenced by **David Bowie's** (see entry) *Low,* it featured ex-King Crimson and one-time Bowie guitarist Adrian Belew and **Porno for Pyros** (see entry) drummer Steve Perkins. The album was recorded in the Los Angeles house where Charles Manson's "family" of followers murdered actress Sharon Tate and her guests in the 1960s. At the time, Reznor denied he knew it was the house of horror. Considering that two song titles on the album are "Piggy" and "March of the Pigs," it's hard to believe he didn't know of the home's grisly origins, but it did bring much pre-publicity for the new album.

The Downward Spiral went on to reach platinum status with the charting singles "Hurt," "March of the Pigs," and the lyrically shocking, "Closer." Disturbing videos of the songs received the MTV Overkill designation for their shock value. Sold-out shows in eleven cities on the tour and a two-night stint at Madison Square Garden gained the band a strong foothold in the pop market. They were invited to play at Woodstock II, the Generation X version of the infamous 1960s concert.

Further downward

A follow-up EP of remixes called *Further Down the Spiral* was released in 1995, just as sales figures reached the two million mark for both *The Downward Spiral* and *Pretty Hate Machine*. In the fall of the same year, Reznor had a personal career dream fulfilled, touring with the legendary David Bowie on "The Outside Tour." The double bill of modern music's oldest and newest icons found the two sharing the stage for renditions of each other's songs. NIN picked up another Grammy Award in 1996 for Best Metal Performance for the song "Happiness in Slavery," which had appeared on the *Broken* EP of four years earlier.

Work in progress

As of this writing, Reznor is simultaneously working on two new albums. In March 1997, he told *Rolling Stone* about the upcoming works. "The new stuff I'm working on is even more disparate [different] than *The Downward Spiral*. I'm not afraid of trying things out. The next record will either be huge or a career stopper. It won't be safe, that's all."

Selected Awards

Pretty Hate Machine, certified gold, 1992; certified double platinum, 1995.

Broken, certified platinum, 1992.

Grammy Award, Best Metal Performance, for "Wish," 1993.

The Downward Spiral, certified platinum, 1994; double platinum, 1995.

Grammy Award, Best Metal Performance, for "Happiness in Slavery," 1996.

Selected Discography

Pretty Hate Machine (TVT), 1989.

Broken (Interscope), 1992.

Fixed (Nothing/Interscope), 1992.

The Downward Spiral (Nothing/Interscope), 1994.

Further Down the Spiral (Nothing/Interscope), 1995.

Further Reading

Dougherty, Steve, "The Music of Rage," *People Weekly,* February 6, 1995, p. 105.

Gilmore, Mikal, "The Lost Boys," *Rolling Stone,* March 1996, p. 36.

Hajari, Nisid, "Trent Reznor," *Entertainment Weekly,* December 30, 1994, p. 46.

Weisband, Eric, "Sympathy for the Devil," *Spin,* February 1996, p. 34.

Book:

Remington, Tuck, *Nine Inch Nails,* Omnibus, 1995.

Contact Information

Nothing Records
75 Rockefeller Plaza
New York, NY 10019

Web Site

http://www.nineinchnails.net

http://www.wallofsound.com/artists/nineinchnails/

nirvana

American alternative pop/rock band

Formed in Aberdeen, Washington, in 1987

Elvis Presley, the Beatles, the Sex Pistols, and Nirvana. Few pop stars have really changed the course of rock music history, but for millions of fans around the world, these bands not only changed history, they created it. Without Presley, rock and roll it-self might never have got off the ground. Without the Beatles, it could have faded away. Without the Pistols, it would have grown old and fat. And without Nirvana, commercial rock would still be where it was at the beginning of the 1990s, with nothing exciting happening at all.

Time for a change

Even the hottest selling new artists were old ones: **U2** (see entry), who'd been around for most of a decade; **R.E.M.** (see en-try), who were almost as old; and so on. Then Nirvana broke through, and things would never be the same again. That weird-est of all English singers, Robyn Hitchcock, looks back on the early 1990s and says, "it's very significant that my latest album, *Perspex Island,* was knocked off the top of the alternative charts

"I feel a duty to warn the kids about false music that's claiming to be underground or alternative. They're just jumping on the alternative bandwagon." —Kurt Cobain (vocals, guitar)

by Nirvana. I think all the bands who came through at the same time as us were just there to be scattered, and that included us. We were still there as an alternative act, but it had altered, it all became `rock' again, people were allowed to have long hair and punch the air again, buy pretzels and shout 'way to go.'" He laughs at the memory. "A lot of people were very surprised." And that included Nirvana themselves.

"We came along at a time of great change, politically and socially," Nirvana's bass player, Kris Novoselic, later explained. "Suddenly all the people who'd been waving yellow ribbons during the Gulf War [the 1991 conflict when the United States fought against Iraq] were wondering what it was for, how things had changed because of it. And when they found they couldn't answer those questions, they got angry." That anger found its outlet in Nirvana, a band whose rage had already dominated the American alternative scene for three years by the time they broke through.

A scruffy kid who was always in trouble

Nirvana was formed in 1987 by Kurt Cobain and Kris Novoselic. Novoselic was a Californian whose parents came to America from Croatia, then moved to Aberdeen, Washington, in 1979. Cobain was already well-known around town, a scruffy kid who was always getting into trouble of some sort, and whose home life was so unsettled that he spent his childhood moving from one parent's home to the other—his folks, Don and

Wendy Cobain, had divorced when he was seven. Since leaving home, he had played in a couple of bands with some of the guys from another local group, the Melvins: one band was called Fecal Matter, another was Brown Towel.

The new band would not keep Kurt out of trouble—shortly after he and Novoselic began playing together, Cobain was fined $180 for spray painting graffiti on the wall of a downtown bank—but it did help. He was writing songs at a furious rate, and spending almost as much time trying to come up with a name for the band. With a stream of friends passing through the group to accompany them, Cobain and Novoselic played their first live shows under such names as Ted Ed Fred, Throat Oyster, Pen Cap Chew, and Windowframe. Finally they reached Nirvana, and it stuck.

Punk meets heavy metal

The sound of early Nirvana was the sound of punk rock on the one hand, and heavy metal on the other. Aberdeen is a logging town several hours outside of Seattle; the brainless energy of metal rules there, in a way that city people could never understand. It was the soundtrack to drinking, to dancing, to all the things you do when you're trying to unwind after a busy day, and Cobain grew up with it pounding in his ears.

However, it was punk that excited him, even though it angered the metalheads around him. The mixture of the two was guaranteed to raise even the slowest tempers. As Nirvana took their first fragile steps towards fame, the audience's reaction was as important to them as the music.

Nirvana sign with Sub Pop

The group recorded its first songs, including "Downer," "Floyd the Barber," and "Paper Cuts," late in 1987. By now they had been joined by drummer Dale Crover (who would later join the Melvins), and they were playing regularly throughout the northwest. Local record labels were already paying attention. C/Z, in Seattle, included a Nirvana track, "Mexican Seafood," on the *Teriyaki Asthma* compilation album; across town Sub Pop offered them the chance to record a single.

Dale Crover left Nirvana in early 1988; he was replaced by Chad Channing, who would remain with the band for the next two years. The group also, briefly, got a second guitarist to allow Cobain to concentrate more on singing onstage. Jason Everman had played with another Seattle band, **Soundgarden** (see entry), before joining. After he left the group Nirvana became a trio again, before bringing in ex-Germs guitarist Pat Smear in 1993.

Nirvana's first single "Love Buzz" was a cover of a song by the Dutch pop group Shocking Blue, performed with an energy that matched both the band's enthusiasm and its inexperience. Like the album that followed it, 1989's *Bleach*, it is recognizable as Nirvana, but it still sounds a million miles away from the brilliance of *Nevermind*, their breakthrough record.

The birth of grunge

In America, *Bleach* was barely noticed by music critics outside of Seattle. In Britain, however, it was immediately recognized as one of the most exciting new albums in years. The British press was just as fast to pick up on the other Seattle-area bands breaking through at that time: **Mudhoney** (see entry), Soundgarden, the Melvins, and so on, and it was an English journalist who actually gave the movement a name. He called it grunge.

Nirvana toured almost constantly through 1990 and 1991. Chad Channing departed; he was replaced by Dan Peters (later of Mudhoney), who played on the band's next three singles, "Silver," "Molly's Lips," and a cover of the Velvet Underground's "Here She Comes Now." When he left, the band recruited Dave Grohl, of the Washington, D.C., hardcore group Scream. Around the same time, the group left Sub Pop and signed with Geffen. They began work on their second album.

An unexpected hit

A Geffen spokesman later admitted the label didn't expect to sell more than 250,000 copies of *Nevermind*. Nirvana was a respected, but largely unknown band; the company had far higher hopes for the new Sonic Youth album, *Dirt*. Sonic Youth's guitarist, Thurston Moore, admitted, "Everyone in the industry said we had a gold album. We had top priority at the label. But our [music's] not as fresh personality wise, and there's no secret weapon as universally rocking as

Kurt Cobain

Cobain's voice." From the moment the first copies of "Smells Like Teen Spirit" went out to radio, the excitement started growing. By the time the first reviews of *Nevermind* appeared in the music press, Nirvana was already on its way.

"Money, fame, groupies, the world at your feet. What they don't understand is the way it changed everything overnight."

"An album of almost breathtaking majesty, savage pop stranded so far out on the edge that the slightest push could propel it into legend," raved *Alternative Press*. By Christmas, just three months after its release, *Nevermind* was number one.

Knocking Michael Jackson off the top

"We never set out to knock Michael Jackson off the top of the chart," Cobain said later. "We just wanted something we could live with." Two years after Nirvana's second album reinvented rock and roll, Cobain continued, "there were all these bands we thought were cool. We hoped they would think what we did was cool as well."

Most of *Nevermind* was recorded within the space of one week, but it had taken two years to write. It was still punk rock, of course, but it had a much more pleasing melody than most people expected punk to have. Cobain's voice— a painful yell that started somewhere around his stomach then spent the rest of the song looking for the way out— was instantly recognizable as that of

frustrated youth, which is what punk was always about. What made it unique was the way it bridged the gap, as Cobain said, "between what people said was hip to listen to, and the kind of stuff which we all really listened to, Kiss, Black Sabbath and Cheap Trick."

Rumors of drug abuse

While *Nevermind* continued to sell through the ceiling, and three more singles, "Come As You Are," "Lithium," and "In Bloom," climbed charts around the world, Nirvana toured endlessly. Their faces stared out from every magazine on the stands; their every action was a headline story. When Kurt Cobain and Courtney Love (see entry on **Hole**) first started dating, they were instantly America's most photographed couple. When they married and had a child, daughter Frances Bean, they became the most famous parents in America, with every aspect of their life together going under the media microscope. Rumors of drug abuse and violence accompanied them everywhere.

It was barely any easier for Cobain's bandmates, but unlike other superstars they did not suffer in silence. "A lot of people look at us and wonder what we're complaining about," Grohl said. "Money, fame, groupies, the world at your feet. What they don't understand is the way it changed everything overnight." At the time, he continued, it felt as if Nirvana was the end of his life. "I could be 43 and an English teacher, and I'd still be known as Nirvana's drummer."

Nevermind was still high in the chart when Geffen released the next Nirvana album, a compilation of old singles and out-takes called *Incesticide,* in 1992. It was not essential listening, and certainly bore little resemblance to *Nevermind,* but it still became one of the big Christmas hits that year, and reduced the record collectors' demand for the original, and now very rare, releases. It also gave Nirvana more time to work on their real next album.

In the studio with Steve Albini

In Utero was recorded with underground producer Steve Albini. Cobain had already warned that the next album was going to be more abrasive than *Nevermind,* adding, "we have complete control over what we do and what we release, which literally means that if we handed in a sixty-minute tape of us defecating [discharging waste], Geffen would have to release it." No one expected that, but many outsiders felt that in choosing Albini, the band was deliberately going for a sound that would shock, and maybe scare away, much of the band's fame.

Of course they didn't. "I have too much respect for our fans to do that," Cobain insisted, and besides, the songs that made up *In Utero* were too good to be buried away like that. In fact, *In Utero* was in many ways an even better album than *Nevermind,* boasting far more variety, and more hooks than a pirate ship, a fact proven by "Heart Shaped Box," the first single from the album.

A triumph at MTV's *Unplugged*

In the fall of 1993, Nirvana played MTV's *Unplugged,* offering up a perfor-mance that proved just how strong Cobain's songs were. Even with the roar of electricity stripped away, songs from all three Nirvana albums were affectingly powerful, so much so that following Cobain's suicide, many writers claimed that the pain that led him to that final act was already visible in his face. It wasn't. He had been looking forward to the show for months. He had even introduced a short acoustic set into Nirvana's traditionally skull-crushing live show. "A lot of people miss the point, that not all our songs are shrieking punk rock monsters," he smiled. "'Unplugged' is something of a buzz word right now, but if you do it properly...." And Nirvana did it very properly indeed.

Kurt Cobain dead at 27

With Pat Smear on second guitar, the band toured America through the fall of 1993, then flew to Europe for the first months of 1994. It was there, in Rome at the end of March, that Cobain almost died following a drug overdose. He survived, but only for another week. On April 8, 1994, an electrician working at the Cobains' Seattle home discovered his body on the floor of a small apartment above the garage. The cause of death was a self inflicted gunshot wound to the head. The corpse had been lying there, the coroner later said, for two or three days.

Cobain's death was one of the those horrific events in rock history. Like John Lennon's murder, or Elvis Presley's fatal heart attack, the moment the news broke is burned into the memory of every member of his huge following who lived through it. For them, it was as senseless as it was tragic; still only 27, Cobain had so much more to give, musically and personally. And now it was all over.

Nirvana ceased to exist

Nirvana ceased to exist immediately. Dave Grohl and Pat Smear would reappear in the **Foo Fighters** (see entry); Kris Novoselic would go into local Seattle politics before reemerging with his own band, Sweet 75. Periodically, former band members would authorize a new Nirvana release, such as a recording of the MTV *Unplugged* broadcast in 1994 and a raging live compilation, *From the Muddy Banks of the Wishkah,* in 1996. Both present different aspects of Nirvana to the world; both are utterly essential reminders of the band that once ruled rock.

Selected Awards

Nevermind, certified platinum, 1991; triple platinum, 1992; U.S. sales of seven million copies, 1995.

"Smells Like Teen Spirit," certified platinum, 1992.

MTV Video Music Awards: 1) Best Alternative Music Video, and 2) Best New Artist Video, both for "Smells Like Teen Spirit," 1992.

BRIT Award, Best International Newcomer, 1993.

MTV Video Music Award, Best Alternative Video, for "In Bloom," 1993.

Rolling Stone's Music Awards Critics' Picks, Best Band and Best Album, for *In Utero,* 1994.

MTV Video Music Awards: 1) Best Alternative Video, and 2) Best Art Direction, both for "Heart Shaped Box," 1994.

MTV Unplugged In New York, certified triple platinum, 1995.

In Utero, certified quadruple platinum, 1995.

Insecticide, certified platinum, 1995.

Bleach, certified platinum, 1995.

American Music Award, Favorite Artist, Heavy Metal/Hard Rock, 1995.

Grammy Award, Best Alternative Music Performance, for *MTV Unplugged in New York,* 1996.

Selected Discography

Bleach (Sub Pop), 1989.

Nevermind (Geffen), 1991.

Incesticide (Geffen), 1992.

In Utero (Geffen), 1993.

MTV Unplugged In New York (Geffen), 1994.

From the Muddy Banks of the Wishkah (Geffen), 1996.

Further Reading

Fricke, David, "Kurt Cobain: The Rolling Stone Interview," *Rolling Stone,* January 27, 1994, p. 34.

Mundy, Chris, "Nirvana vs. Fame," *Rolling Stone,* January 23, 1992, p. 38.

Rolling Stone, June 2, 1994, (contains several articles).

Thompson, Dave, "The Boys Are Back In Town," *Alternative Press,* October, 1993, p. 49.

Books:

Arnold, Gina, *Route 666: On the Road to Nirvana,* St. Martin's Press, 1993.

Azerrad, Michael, *Come as You Are: The Story of Nirvana,* Main Street Books/Doubleday, 1994.

Editors of *Rolling Stone, Cobain,* Little Brown, 1996.

Sandford, Christopher, *Kurt Cobain,* Carroll and Graf, 1996.

Thompson, David, *Never Fade Away: A Biography of Kurt Cobain,* St. Martin's Press, 1994.

Web Sites

http://rgfn.epcc.edu/users/ao162/traderpg.html

http://www.sonicnet/%7etheruler/nirvana.html

NO DOUBT

American dance/pop band

Formed in Orange County, California, in 1986

Released in October 1995, No Doubt's *Tragic Kingdom* finally reached the top spot on *Billboard*'s album charts in December 1996. After conquering American audiences on the strength of singles like "Just a Girl" and "Don't Speak," the album was "warmly greeted worldwide as a record that speaks the international language of pop," according to *Rolling Stone*. Led by "pretty and petite" blond Gwen Stefani, who always seemed to be photographed with her midriff showing, No Doubt also won over audiences with its live performances.

On the other hand, the magazine also noted that No Doubt's brand of danceable ska-tinged pop "is frequently dismissed as meaningless, superficial pop." British music magazine *Kerrang!* for example, trashed No Doubt when reviewing their number one hit "Don't Speak" by writing, "Much like an anteater with a punctured snout, No Doubt suck badly."

"I'm just a girl, all pretty and petite / So don't let me have any rights." —from No Doubt's "Just a Girl."

Gwen Stefani

Another band from Orange County, California

Gwen Stefani's older brother Eric was the musician in the Italian family. He would play the piano or accordion and make his sister sing naughty songs with him. She told *Rolling Stone,* "Growing up, my brother was the one with all the talent and all the focus. I had him, so I didn't have to do anything, you know?" As teenagers, they were both fans of British ska groups Madness, the Specials, English Beat, and Selecter. For the school talent show, brother Eric made Gwen sing Selecter's "On the Radio."

At the end of 1986, Eric formed a real band that included a black punk singer named John Spence. The band, with Stefani singing backup vocals, was called No Doubt. In the spring of 1987 Tony Kanal, a sixteen-year-old Indian from Great Britain, joined on bass. Stefani fell in love with him, and they were a couple for seven years. At first, they kept it a secret from the rest of the band.

Four days before Christmas 1987, Spence committed suicide just as the band was set to play the Roxy in Los Angeles, an important venue for new bands. Although the band announced it was their last gig, they decided to continue, believing that was what Spence would have wanted. From there the current lineup took shape over time. Tom Dumont auditioned and joined the band on guitar, successfully hiding his interest in heavy metal. Adrian Young was a No Doubt fan long before joining on drums in 1989.

A record deal with Interscope

After making a name for itself as a ska-pop band in Southern California, No Doubt signed with independent label Interscope in 1991. The band released a self-titled debut album on Interscope that wasn't even able to get airplay on Los Angeles rock station KROQ. As *Rolling Stone* noted, "No Doubt were trying to launch an album of quirky, bouncy girl-sung pop as **Nirvana** (see entry) and their compadres [friends] were exploding."

Tragic Kingdom was three years in the making

Older brother Eric remained the creative center of the group, so he wasn't happy when Interscope suggested the band work with different producers on the next album. He also continued to have artistic differences with other band members. When sister Gwen and guitarist Tom Dumont wrote "Just a Girl" in 1994, he couldn't see what everyone was so excited about. He stopped going to rehearsals and eventually quit, taking a job as an animator with *The Simpsons* television cartoon show. Rather than "lose" her brother, Gwen and Eric went through therapy together at the urging of their parents.

Also in 1994, Stefani and bassist Tony Kanal broke up after seven years together. As it turned out, they were able to remain friends and bandmates. The breakup provided Stefani with material for her songs, including "Happy Now?," where she teases her ex-boyfriend about being "happy now?" after dumping her, and "Sunday Morning," where she calls him a parasite.

No Doubt spent much of 1995 opening for **Bush** (see entry) on their American tour. Somewhere around this time Stefani began dating Bush's lead singer, Gavin Rossdale, a romance the media seized with relish.

"Just a Girl" became the first hit from *Tragic Kingdom* after it was released in the fall of 1995. Written by Stefani and Kanal, it makes fun of the way girls are looked down at. "I'm just a girl, all pretty and petite / So don't let me have any rights," Stefani sings. Delivered live, the song comes across as rousing and potent pop music. As *Rolling Stone* described one concert performance, "She breathlessly unspooled the song's opening lines, building to an eruptive [explosive], shout-along chorus that had a thousand kids on summer break pogo-ing as one."

Fame leads to tension

As No Doubt became more famous, media attention focused on lead singer Stefani at the expense of other band members. With her image of glamorous innocence, she drew fire and was branded by hostile critics as the "anti-Courtney Love" (see entry on **Hole**).

To many others, she was the media's darling. Arguments would flare up when she was featured on magazine covers and the others weren't. As guitarist Tom Dumont explained to *Rolling Stone*, "The reason I wanted to be a rock star when I was a kid, I thought that would be a way for people to like me. And now that I get

here, I'm not getting the payoff that I was always expecting."

Stefani was sympathetic to the problems associated with fame, and the band decided to make a video about it. Although "Don't Speak" was written when Tony and Gwen were breaking up, they decided to make the song's video be about the band breaking up. In the video, there are a series of situations in which Stefani gets all of the attention, and the other band members get angry about it.

Although the band remained together as they prepared for their 1997 tour, they continued to experience some tense moments. Just before shooting the video for "Don't Speak," Stefani got mad at guitarist Tom Dumont and told him he could quit the band if he wanted to, that she didn't care. One thing she did care about, though, was that her brother Eric would be involved with the next No Doubt project. "Because Eric is No Doubt," she said to *Rolling Stone*.

Selected Awards

Tragic Kingdom, certified platinum.

Grammy nomination, Best Rock Album, for *Tragic Kingdom*, 1997.

Grammy nomination, Best New Artist, 1997.

Selected Discography

Tragic Kingdom (Trauma/Interscope), 1995.

Further Reading

Browne, David, "Tragic Kingdom," *Entertainment Weekly*, August 2, 1996, p. 56.

Heath, Chris, "No Doubt," *Rolling Stone,* May 1, 1997, p. 36.

Holthouse, David, "No Doubt (Electric Ballroom)," *Rolling Stone,* September 5, 1996, p. 28.

Stovall, Natasha, "All the Music They Grew up With," *New York Times,* June 9, 1996, p. 36.

Contact Information

Interscope Music Publishing
10940 Wilshire Blvd., 20th Fl.
Los Angeles, CA 90024

Web Site

http://www.hallucinet.com/no_doubt

THE OFFSPRING

American alternative pop/rock band

Formed in Orange County, California, in 1984

ew bands better represent New School Punk than The Offspring. Their 1994 album, *Smash,* was exactly that, a smash hit that sold millions of copies around the world, and plastered the band's faces on magazine covers everywhere. Their overnight success was so out of the blue that many people thought they were a new band. They weren't; in reality they'd been around ten years and already had two albums under their belt.

Something to believe in

Before *Smash,* The Offspring were one of scores of punk bands that had grown up in the southern California area of Orange County. The groups all shared one thing in common, an enthusiasm for the music. Playing in a punk band was just a way to assert yourself and your opinions, and have fun. In fact, The Offspring formed at a party, when singer/guitarist Dexter Holland and bassist Greg Kreisel became so excited at hearing the influential Southern California hardcore group TSOL's album, *Change Today,* they decided they wanted to be in a band too.

"You might be gone before you know / So live like there's no tomorrow / Ain't gonna waste this life / There's no tomorrow." —from The Offspring's "Nitro"

Dexter Holland at the mike

When Lilja quit in 1987, he was replaced by sixteen-year-old Ron Welty.

The quartet started out playing "really, really bad hardcore," Holland remembers. But, slowly they grew better. At the time the members were all in school, and the band didn't change that (all eventually earned degrees, except guitarist Noodles). That didn't leave much time for the band, but The Offspring did find time to play shows every couple of months and put out their own single, "I'll Be Waiting"/ "Blackball."

A thousand days

By 1987, The Offspring started playing outside of California and the following year they recorded a demo tape. It wasn't until 1989 that the group finally signed a deal with Nemesis Records and released their first album, titled simply *The Offspring*.

The record didn't make much of an impact on the music scene, and even though the group went off on two national tours, they were still playing to small crowds in even smaller clubs. Still, The Offspring were starting to get attention in the punk scene, not just from their awesome live shows, but because of the many punk compilations they appeared on.

"It's funny, with the rise of our popularity, there's also been a steady rise in the number of people that hate us."

That wasn't enough. In 1992, The Offspring went label shopping again and came away with empty bags. Nobody

There were several line-up changes in the early days and a name change before The Offspring was officially born. By then, the group included Holland, Kreisel, guitarist "Noodles" (Kevin Wasserman), and drummer James Lilja.

wanted them. Their *Baghdad* EP (extended play) did nothing to change that, until finally Mr. Brett (Brett Gurewitz), hardcore band Bad Religion's guitarist and co-owner of the independent punk label Epitaph Records, heard it and offered the band a deal.

Crossroads

Their next album *Ignition* was a marked improvement from their first. "One of the finest SoCal [Southern California] melodic hardcore bands is alive and well," *Thrasher* raved. The Offspring had become much better musicians over time, and Holland was showing the makings of a great songwriter. However, nothing had really changed; they were still just opening for much bigger hardcore bands, like labelmates NOFX and Pennywise.

Certainly, *Ignition* sold many more copies than their first album, and The Offspring were becoming better known. Truthfully, they were now just a mid-sized punk band, and outside of that scene, few people had ever heard their name.

Smash came out in April 1994, and The Offspring celebrated by playing at an important snowboard competition in Alaska. The band was well-known to the skating and snowboard community, as their music had been featured on sports videos for the last two years. Holland credits them for the group's rising success.

Smash

Even so, nobody expected *Smash* to do as well as it did. Not the band, not Epitaph, not even the music press. The

---

Epitaph Records and The Offspring

Offspring created quite a stir among the punk rock community when they left Epitaph and signed with Columbia in 1996. Founded by hardcore band Bad Religion's guitarist, Brett Gurewitz, in the early 1980s, Epitaph Records was home to many Southern California punk rock bands. In addition to The Offspring, the label has recorded such bands as **Green Day** (see entry), **Rancid** (see entry), NOFX, and Pennywise.

Members of The Offspring justified the move by saying they would have more creative freedom at Columbia. They also thought that Epitaph was going to be sold to a major label. Even though label founder Brett Gurewitz denied that he was going to sell the label, the parting was not amicable. Epitaph's share of the revenues from Smash were estimated at more than $50 million.

Commenting on the band's growing fame following the success of Smash, guitarist Kevin "Noodles" Wasserman said, "It's funny, with the rise of our popularity, there's also been a steady rise in the number of people that hate us."

---

albums kept selling and selling and selling, and suddenly The Offspring were no longer playing clubs, but large theaters and auditoriums. They could scarcely take it all in.

In February 1995 Noodles discussed The Offspring's success. "Things are going really well ... if a bit sick and disgusting. We played Detroit the other night, it was really weird, there was twelve thousand people!" Commenting on the record becoming quadruple platinum, he added, "Quadruple platinum?!? Yeah, I guess it is. That's just sick!" After shows, The Offspring would stand outside and sign autographs. Often it would take a couple of hours to sign them all, but that didn't matter. The band was just so overwhelmed that people wanted to hear their music and meet them.

The meaning of life

What was equally surprising to them was how young their new audience was. Why not? The Offspring's songs spoke directly to kids, but never down to them. Anyone who's listened to their records knows that Holland has many important things to say, which he does without being patronizing. Best of all, he often says it in very witty ways. Whether he's mocking gang violence on "Come Out and Play" ("Like the latest fashion, like a spreading disease ... no one's getting smarter, no one's learning the score") or showing the result of having no "Self Esteem" ("I may be dumb, but I'm not a dweeb. I'm just a sucker with no self esteem"), Dexter writes lyrics that kids can understand, relate to, and want to sing along with.

That's something that's not changed on their latest album, *Ixnay on the Hombre,* their first on Columbia. What has changed is that The Offspring have become even more adventurous with their music. At its heart, their sound is still melodic pop-punk, based around Dexter's great surf guitar and Noodles' riffs and rock leads. But on *Ixnay,* the band stretched themselves even further, including great rockers and even a bubblegum song.

Although moving to a major label had alienated some of their hardcore punk fans, The Offspring refused to live by other people's rules. "It's my life and I'll do with it what I want," sings Dexter on "I Choose." What The Offspring have chosen to do is touch as many kids' lives as they can, whatever it takes.

Selected Discography

Offspring (Nemesis), 1989.

Ignition (Epitaph), 1992.

Smash (Epitaph), 1994.

Ixnay on the Hombre (Columbia), 1997.

Further Reading

Ali, Lorraine, "Offspring," *Rolling Stone,* September 22, 1994, p. 25.

Daley, Dave, "The Offspring: Shot by Both Sides," *Alternative Press,* April 1997, p. 52.

Eddie, Chuck, "Revenge of the Nerds," *Spin,* March, 1995, p. 44.

George, Alec, "Children of the Damned Never Mind the Sex Pistols: Here's Their Offspring," *Rolling Stone,* February 9, 1995, p. 42.

Greene, Jo-Ann, "Living Like There's No Tomorrow," *Goldmine,* September 15, 1995, p. 40.

Mettler, Mike, "Offspring Into Action," *Guitar Player,* January 1995, p. 19.

Schwart, Jennifer, "The Offspring's Gotta Keep 'Em Separated," *Bam,* January 10, 1997, p. 22.

Contact Information

Columbia Records
550 Madison Ave.
New York, NY 10022

Web Site

http://www.offspring.com
http://capsi.com/offspring/main.shtml

pavement

American alternative pop/rock band

Formed 1989 in Stockton, California

Prior to its 1997 release, *Brighten the Corners,* Pavement had a reputation as a band that didn't care. They didn't appear to ever rehearse, key members of the group lived in different parts of the country, and their live shows were mercifully described as "loose." That didn't keep them from developing a devoted following among fans and critics alike for their do-it-yourself, no-frills approach to rock music. Some characterized the group as the quintessential American independent band of the 1990s.

A "pathetic effort"

The band was formed in 1989 by singer/guitarist Stephen Malkmus (also known as SM) and his friend and former bandmate, Scott Kannberg (also known as Spiral Stairs) in their northern California hometown of Stockton. Malkmus told *Melody Maker,* "Pavement was originally a pathetic effort by us to do something to escape the terminal boredom we were experiencing in Stockton."

The two college-age friends recorded a single, picking up drummer Gary Young, a forty-something progressive rock fan who

Steve Malkmus, aka SM, singer and guitarist

Pavement: from "terminal boredom" a band is formed

also ran the recording studio where the single was made. Kannberg released the single on a label he called Treble Kicker, and Pavement was born.

"Slay Tracks (1933-1969)," as the single was called, generated a buzz in the world of independent recordings. Perhaps it was SM's free-association lyrics, sung with a flat-toned voice and cool passion over the band's low-fi, guitar-driven sound. Maybe it was the band's low-key way of self-promoting and packaging the single. In any event, reaction to the record caused SM and Spiral Stairs to rethink their commitment to Pavement, which until then had been more of project than a band.

Famous slacker band

During 1990 and 1991 they recorded a series of EPs on the independent Southern California label, Drag City. They added Mark Ibold on bass and a second drummer, Bob Nastanovich. During this period Pavement developed a reputation as a slacker band that didn't care about its live shows, often performing loose, unrehearsed renditions of its songs. The group's main drummer, Gary Young, became notorious for his drunken theatrics. *New Yorker* writer Alex Ross described one of Pavement's first East Coast performances from 1991. "They essentially murdered their songs. The effect was comic but also confrontational:

the band seemed to be trying to drive its new audience away."

Slanted and enchanted

Turning down big-bucks offers from major labels, Pavement signed with independent Matador Records in 1992 during the grunge explosion—when it was easy for guitar bands to get signed. The critics loved their first full-length album, *Slanted and Enchanted,* many of them ranking it among the year's best. Yet, as a group, Pavement did not appear serious about its future in the music business. In mid-1992 Malkmus told the fanzine *Option,* "We've actually spent less than 100 hours on Pavement—playing, recording, and practicing. We've had six practices. We don't even play together as a band when we record." Pavement was still more of a project than a band.

Original drummer Gary Young left the group in 1993 and was replaced by Steve West, a friend of Pavement's second drummer Nastanovich. At this time Malkmus, Ibold, and Young lived in New York, Kannberg remained in Stockton, and Nastanovich made his home in Louisville, Kentucky, to be near thoroughbred racing horses. *Rolling Stone* commented, "Geography has made it difficult for Pavement to be well rehearsed."

Crooked rain

Devoted fans of Pavement were rewarded with the 1993 compilation, *Westing (By Musket and Sextant),* which contained all of the group's early releases on the Drag City label. In 1994 Matador released the group's second original album, *Crooked Rain, Crooked Rain,* with a full-blown promotional effort. Pavement not only recorded a music video, they appeared on "The Tonight Show with Jay Leno."

Crooked Rain, Crooked Rain received even more critical acclaim than Pavement's first album. Again, critics were quick to point out Pavement's unique combination of loud noise and fragments of warm melodies. Malkmus told David Sprague of *New York Newsday,* "I guess there was more of a decision to just make songs instead of a noisy, indie-signifying record." In other words, Pavement was becoming a band that cared about its songs and how it sounded, and not just about being a poster band for independent labels. "Cut Your Hair," the first single from the album, explored the difference between relating to the music as a fan and as a professional musician; it became a moderate hit.

In 1995 Pavement recorded a double album for Matador called *Wowee Zowee.* It was not well received. One critic called it "scatterbrained," while Matador subsequently characterized it as "a stupidly misunderstood display of tensile strength," a comment on Pavement's roughly recorded, guitar-driven sound.

Brighten the Corners displayed a rehearsed Pavement

Perhaps taking some of the criticism of *Wowee Zowee* to heart, Pavement went into the recording studios in July 1996 to record another album. This time they did things differently. The album was recorded live under the direction of noted producer Mitch Easter (who produced **R.E.M.**'s [see entry] *Murmur* and *Reckoning)* in his studio in Kernersville, North Carolina. After extensive pre-production rehearsals at Steve Young's place in Virginia, all five band members recorded the songs together, quite a departure from past practices.

Released in February 1997, *Brighten the Corners* was widely and immediately reviewed. Nathan Brackett wrote in *Rolling Stone,* "*Corners* reaffirms what was likable about Pavement in the first place: their angular but graceful melodies, their languorous anti-anthems [songs that do not celebrate a belief or meaning] and, of course, Malkmus' labyrinthine [maze-like]—and often funny or poignant—lyrical turns." The critic was referring to Malkmus's ability to write catchy phrases, yet string them together in illogical and often nonsensical ways.

Writer Alex Ross described Malkmus's voice on this recording: "Malkmus's voice is closely recorded, and in several songs he half sings, half speaks in a style that falls somewhere between jazzy rap and talking blues." It's interesting that the first single from the album, "Stereo," is about the singing voice of Geddy Lee, the lead singer of classic rock band Rush. Lee sang in a high voice known as falsetto. Malkmus asks in the song, "What about the voice of Geddy Lee? How did it get so high? I wonder if he speaks like an ordinary guy?" A background voice chimes in, "I know him, and he does."

With a new album and solid reviews, Pavement was set to tour for much of 1997. It looked more and more like Pavement was a band, and not just a project.

Selected Awards

Slanted and Enchanted named Album of the Year by *Spin,* 1992.

Selected Discography

Slanted and Enchanted (Matador), 1992.

Westing (By Musket & Sextant) (Drag City), 1993.

Crooked Rain, Crooked Rain (Matador), 1994.

Wowee Zowee (Matador), 1995.

Brighten the Corners (Matador), 1997.

Further Reading

Brackett, Nathan, "Remain in Light," *Rolling Stone,* February 20, 1997.

Diehl, Matt, "Pavement Smooth out the Edges on 'Corners,'" *Rolling Stone,* November 28, 1996, p. 34.

Mulholland, Garry, "Odd Band Out," *Time Out,* January 22-29, 1997.

New York Newsday, February 15, 1994.

Ross, Alex, "The Pavement Tapes," *The New Yorker,* May 26, 1997, p. 85.

Contact Information

Matador Records
676 Broadway, 4th Fl.
New York, NY 10012

Web Sites

http://www.matador.recs.com

http://www.slip.net/~pavement/

Pearl Jam

American alternative pop/rock band

Formed in Seattle, Washington, in 1990

Pearl Jam was a frontrunner, along with **Nirvana** (see entry), in helping to spread the style of alternative rock that became known as grunge. Both bands achieved tremendous success and their albums sold millions of copies. Yet both groups had trouble coping with the burdens that success brought. Neither sought to become rock stars, and when they found fame thrust upon them, they weren't very happy about it. After they became famous, many of their songs complained about a loss of privacy and other woes that came with success. In the case of Nirvana, lead singer, guitarist, and songwriter Kurt Cobain committed suicide.

On the other hand, Pearl Jam's lead singer and lyricist Eddie Vedder continued to fight against the rock establishment, both in his songs and in his deeds. Vedder seemed able to remain focused on his music, which for him remained the most important thing. He once told the British music weekly, *Melody Maker,* "My upbringing was like a hurricane, and music was the tree I held onto."

Pearl Jam's grunge sound featured a hard-hitting sound complete with roaring guitars and raw, emotional power. They took a

"I know who I really am. It's a long story, and it won't fit in a *Rolling Stone.*" —Eddie Vedder, lead singer and lyricist

Eddie Vedder, lead singer

"no frills" approach to rock and successfully created an alternative to mainstream rock. Along with Nirvana, Pearl Jam helped define the end of 1980s mainstream rock and the beginning of 1990s alternative rock.

Pearl Jam featured the voice and lyrics of Eddie Vedder

Eddie Vedder's "raw-throated, rageful singing" combined perfectly with the guitar-driven sound produced by Pearl Jam's musicians Mike McCready (lead guitar) and Jeff Ament (bass). Another important element of Pearl Jam's sound were the driving rhythms produced by rhythm guitarist Stone Gossard and original drummer Dave Abruzzese (later replaced by Red Hot Chili Peppers' drummer Jack Irons).

"My upbringing was like a hurricane, and music was the tree I held onto."

Vedder's lyrics reflect a difficult childhood. His family situation made it difficult to feel secure. He was born Edward Louis Severson III in 1964 in Evanston, Illinois. His father, a musician, divorced his mother two years after his birth. His mother remarried, and Vedder was raised believing his stepfather was his biological father, and that his mother's three other sons by her new husband were his full brothers. He was raised as Eddie Mueller, after his stepfather. He didn't change his name to Eddie Vedder, after his mother's maiden name, until after leaving high school and earning a high school equivalency degree.

Pearl Jam's first big hit, "Alive," contains a retelling of Vedder's discovery of who his real father was. "Son, she said/Have I got a little story for you/What you thought was your daddy/Was nothin' but a .../While you were sittin'/Home alone at age 13/Your real daddy was dyin'.../Sorry you didn't see him/ But I'm glad we talked." Like many other Vedder-written songs, this one contains a "slice of life." Vedder paints a situation that many in Pearl Jam's audience who came from broken homes could relate to.

Vedder's family moved to southern California in the mid-1970s, and he attended San Dieguito High School in San Diego. The family lived in a solid middle-class neighborhood in the San Diego suburb of Encinitas. Vedder showed musical aptitude in school, but he was better known as an actor and played leading roles in several high school productions. After he broke up with his girlfriend in his senior year, though, things seemed to fall apart. He dropped out of the theater program and left school just before graduating.

Vedder was part of the San Diego musical scene

Vedder spent a couple of years in the Midwest, then returned to the San Diego area and settled in the beach community of La Mesa, California, in 1984. In 1986 he responded to an ad for a lead singer with a band called Bad Radio. By this time, Vedder wanted to make it as a singer and songwriter. He auditioned by singing several cover songs. Then, when

Pearl Jam accepts their Grammy for "Spin the Black Circle," 1996 Grammy Awards

the band accepted him, he revealed that he had several finished songs of his own that they could play and record.

Vedder stayed with Bad Radio for three years, taking control of the band, hustling for gigs, and designing the artwork for their posters and cassettes. His main base of operations was a club called the Bacchanal, where new alternative acts played. He helped out when other bands played there, loading equipment for free so he could meet other rock musicians. It was there that he met the **Red Hot Chili Peppers** (see entry) and their drummer, Jack Irons, who would later introduce Vedder to Gossard and Ament. In fact, Vedder took the

Chili Peppers on a backpacking trip to Yosemite National Park.

Around this time Vedder met his future wife, Beth Liebling, who was attending San Diego State University and interning at Virgin Records. Like Vedder, she was actively involved with promoting bands around the San Diego music scene. Together, they knew just about everyone of importance in the local music business.

Pearl Jam formed in Seattle in 1990

Vedder was free from Bad Radio when, up in Seattle, Washington, Gossard and Ament were forming a new band. They had been in Green River, a Seattle-based band that featured lead singer Mark Arm, who would later join **Mudhoney** (see entry). When Green River broke up, Gossard and Ament formed Mother Love Bone, which was more of a mainstream band. It was signed to PolyGram, but in March 1990, a few months before its debut album was to be released, lead singer Andrew Wood died of an accidental heroin overdose.

Gossard and Ament quickly recruited guitarist Mike McCready to form a new band. McCready had played in a commercial band called Shadow for a while, even moving to Los Angeles in pursuit of success. He'd returned to Seattle, though, disillusioned with the music business. He even stopped playing guitar for a while, but was spotted by Gossard while playing in a new band.

Gossard, Ament, and McCready recorded some instrumentals using **Soundgarden**'s (see entry) drummer, Matt Cameron. The songs were built around Gossard's heavy guitar riffs. The group needed a vocalist, though, and former Red Hot Chili Peppers' drummer Jack Irons suggested Eddie Vedder from San Diego.

Vedder was inspired by Gossard's music

Vedder told *Rolling Stone* in 1991 that writing the lyrics and melody line to Gossard's demos marked a turning point in his creative and personal lives. "I started dealing with a few things that I hadn't dealt with. It was great music—it was bringing things out of me that

hadn't been brought out." With long-buried emotions swelling up inside of him, Vedder wrote the words to "Alive" to a Gossard track titled "Dollar Short."

Upon forming late in 1990, Pearl Jam was an overnight sensation in Seattle. Vedder flew up to Seattle to meet his bandmates. Together, they wrote eleven songs in five days. At the end of the week they played their first live gig at a Seattle club, calling themselves Mookie Blaylock, after a New Jersey Nets basketball player. After Blaylock complained, though, they changed their name to Pearl Jam. But their first album, *Ten*, was named in honor of Blaylock's jersey number.

Ten released in August 1991

The initial single from *Ten*, the furious rocker "Alive," became a major hit, thanks in part to a video that showed a raucous live performance. It was the mainstream music audience's first exposure to Vedder, whose anguished yet resilient presence became an overnight sensation. The singer later revealed to *Rolling Stone* that "Alive"—despite having been adopted as a survival anthem by critics and fans alike—was a far darker and more despairing tale than anyone seemed to realize. The song "Evenflow" also fared well, and the band's appearance on *MTV Unplugged* broadened its audience considerably.

It was the first "concept video" for a Pearl Jam song—something the group had initially vowed not to do—that took them over the top. "Jeremy," a tragic story of a misunderstood boy who kills himself before his classmates, became the group's biggest hit, thanks in large part to a dramatic video by Mark Pellington that won three trophies at the MTV Video Awards. The group resisted Epic's efforts to make a video for the emotional "Black," believing it would compromise the song's personal meaning. Even so, *Ten* became a multi-platinum sensation, selling several million copies. Pearl Jam was suddenly one of the biggest bands in the music world. Among other honors, they took home trophies at the 1993 American Music Awards for favorite new artist in both the pop/rock and heavy metal/hard rock categories.

Bona fide rock stars

Pearl Jam's second album, originally titled Five Against One but changed to *Vs.* after its initial pressing, hit retail outlets in the fall of 1993. It set a record by selling 950,000 copies in its first week. It went on to sell more than five million copies. Another sign of the band's popularity was the fact that their first album, *Ten,* remained in *Billboard*'s Top Thirty some ninety weeks after its release.

By the time of *Vs.'s* release, Vedder had emerged as a bona fide rock star. He sang in front of the reunited 1960s band The Doors—in place of the band's late and legendary vocalist Jim Morrison—on the occasion of their induction into the Rock and Roll Hall of Fame. He participated in the 1992 anniversary tribute to visionary singer/songwriter Bob Dylan.

The band chose its booking to keep in touch with its fans, though, and maintain continuinty with its roots. Pearl Jam played the 1992 Lollapalooza tour, but the band also rubbed shoulders with other rock idols: they opened for Rolling Stones guitarist Keith Richards at a New Year's Eve concert and joined rock survivor Neil Young onstage at the MTV Video Music Awards for a raucous version of Young's "Rockin' in the Free World." They joined Young for a tour and shared a European bill with Irish superstars U2. The group also participated in a number of benefit albums.

It was natural, then, that some of the songs on *Vs.* dealt with the subject of fame. In Pearl Jam's view—and all of the songs on *Vs.* are credited to the band rather than just to Vedder—being famous is like taking abuse. Throughout the album's lyrics, the theme of abuse recurs in different settings. "Go," the album's opening song, contains the lines, "Don't go on me," and "Suppose I abused you." In "Animal," Vedder asks his audience, "Why would you want to hurt me?" Finally, abuse is linked to government oppression through the images of police brutality found in the song, "Rearviewmirror," in which Vedder testifies, "I tried to endure what I could not forgive."

Fame and pain

Released in December 1994, *Vitalogy* sold 877,000 copies in its first week and went on to sell more than five million copies. Although Dave Abruzzese played drums on the album, he had left the band earlier in 1994 and was replaced by former Red Hot Chili Peppers' drum-

Neil Young and Pearl Jam

Pearl Jam has enjoyed a special relationship with Neil Young. Both Young and the band share a passion for "no frills" rock, especially the guitar-driven sound that is Pearl Jam's trademark. Young jammed with the group at the MTV Video Music Awards for a grunge-rock version of Young's "Rockin' in the Free World." Pearl Jam also toured with Young as his opening act. In 1995, when Eddie Vedder was too sick to continue performing in a San Francisco concert, Young took his place in the lead of Pearl Jam.

In mid-1995 Neil Young's Mirror Ball was released. The album featured Pearl Jam as Young's backup band, with Vedder and Young providing some vocal duets. Comparing Pearl Jam's version of "Act of Love" with Young's old band Crazy Horse's version, Rolling Stone credited Pearl Jam with bringing a "rhythmic vitality" to the song and noted that the song was much shorter and lacked the usual extended guitar solos characteristic of Crazy Horse. It also credits the two musicians with breaking through the gap between rock of the 1960s and rock of the 1990s.

mer Jack Irons for live performances. Two popular songs from the album, "Corduroy" and "Better Man," became staples on alternative radio stations. In "Corduroy" Vedder sings of the feeling of not being in control of his destiny because of his fame. "I'm already cut off like I feared/I'll end up alone like I began," he sings, continuing with "All the things that others want for me/Can't buy what I want because it's free." Another song on *Vitalogy* that criticizes fame is "Immortality," which contains the line that describes Pearl Jam as "Victims in demand for public show."

An older Vedder reveals some nostalgia for lost youth in the tormented song, "Not for You," when he sings, "All that's sacred comes from youth/Naive and true with no power... " Death and suicide also seem to occupy Vedder's thoughts in *Vitalogy*. In the album's opening track, "Last Exit," Vedder imagines his decaying corpse, "Let the sun climb, burn away my soul." The album's closing song, "Stupidmop," contains a meditation on suicide. The album's title contains a double meaning on the themes of life and death. While "vitalogy" means the study of life, "Vitalogy" was the name of an early twentieth-century pamphlet promoting bogus health cures.

In *Vitalogy* Pearl Jam expanded on its muscular hard rock to include some "fast but brutal punk, fuzz-toned psychedelia, and judicious folk-rock," wrote Jon Pareles in the *New York Times*. *Rolling Stone* found the album "wildly uneven and difficult .. .sometimes maddening, sometimes ridiculous, often powerful." *Time* magazine's Christopher John Farley noted, "The album has its share of stinkers." Still, the combination of Pearl Jam's guitar-driven sound and Vedder's impassioned baritone voice proved the perfect vehicle for delivering songs expressing a wide range of emotions.

1994 and 1995 tours were disrupted, then cancelled

Pearl Jam had already demonstrated its willingness to defy the rock establishment when it refused to produce any videos from *Vs.* Then in May 1994, the band took on Ticketmaster, the national ticket-selling agency, filing a brief with the Justice Department accusing Ticketmaster of being a monopoly. Band members Ament and Gossard testified before Congress about Ticketmaster's alleged monopoly. Pearl Jam's objection to Ticketmaster was that the ticketing giant forced stadiums, arenas, concert halls, and other venues to sign exclusive agreements. That meant that any acts that played those places had to have their ticketing done through Ticketmaster, which was accustomed to adding a $3 to $8 service charge to each ticket sold. Objecting to the amount of the service charge, Pearl Jam tried to book a 1994 tour without using Ticketmaster's services. It proved impossible, and the tour was scrapped.

In 1995 Pearl Jam again attempted to line up a summer tour for June and July, this time using the ticketing services of ETM Entertainment Network. The tour was to open June 16 at a basketball arena in Boise, Idaho, and end July 9 at a fairgrounds in Milwaukee, Wisconsin. Circumstances plagued the tour right from the start. The opening date had to be cancelled and moved to Wyoming. The second date, in Salt Lake City, Utah, was rained out, sending 12,000 fans home. Hassles with the local authorities disrupted a planned San Diego date. Then Vedder checked into a local hospital on June 23, suffering from digestive problems. A week later the tour was abruptly cancelled. On July 5, 1995, the Justice Department quietly dropped its investigation of Ticketmaster. And even though the band made up most of its tour dates by the end of 1995, its reputation suffered as the press accused it of leaving its fans out in the cold.

No Code

Pearl Jam won its first Grammy in February 1996 when the song, "Spin the Black Circle," won for Best Hard Rock Performance. Upon accepting the award, Vedder displayed his indifference to the musical establishment once again, saying that the honor "doesn't mean anything."

Pearl Jam's fourth album, *No Code,* was released at the end of August. It showed a band willing to absorb new influences and play in a variety of styles. *New York Times* music critic Jon Pareles noted that the songs "I'm Open," "Who You Are," and "In My Tree," "may reflect Vedder's collaboration with Nusrat Fateh Ali Khan, the Pakistani master of qawwali devotional singing, on the *Dead Man Walking* soundtrack. He has learned the meditative and dramatic potential of the drone."

Other songs on the album display Pearl Jams' hard-rock muscle. "Hail, Hail" is a rocker that's about troubled relationships. Vedder sings, "All hail the lucky ones/I refer to those in love." "Habit" is another rocker that bemoans friends turning into drug addicts. "Smile" pays tribute to Neil Young, complete with an introductory harmonica riff, before shifting into a Pearl Jam-style chorus.

Even though Pearl Jam fought unsuccessfully against Ticketmaster, tickets for the band's fall 1996 tour in support of *No Code* were sold through Fans Tours and Tickets. The tour's opening date in Seattle was Pearl Jam's first concert in a year, not counting a warm-up club performance two days before. According to a review of the concert in *Rolling Stone,* Vedder "had a platform of issues to discuss onstage." The concert was a mix of songs from the new album and old favorites. At the start of its thirty-one-date, fifteen-nation tour, Pearl Jam appeared to be a band that knew who it was, but was also willing to move in new directions.

Selected Awards

Multi-platinum records for *Ten, Vs., Vitalogy,* and *No Code.*

Favorite new artist, pop/rock and favorite new artist, heavy metal/hard rock, 1993 American Music Awards.

Best video of the year, best group video, and best metal/hard rock video for "Jeremy" (director: Mark Pellington), MTV Video Music Awards, 1993.

Rolling Stone artists of the year, 1994.

Best Hard Rock Performance for "Spin the Black Circle," 1996 Grammy Awards.

Selected Discography

Ten, (Epic), 1991

Vs., (Epic), 1993

Vitalogy, (Epic), 1994

No Code, (Epic), 1996

Further Reading

Colapinto, John, "Who Are You? Pearl Jam's Eddie Vedder," *Rolling Stone,* November 28, 1996, p. 50.

Cross, Charles R., "Pearl Jam: Key Arena, Sept. 16, 1996," *Rolling Stone,* October 31, 1996, p. 34.

Pareles, Jon, "Pearl Jam Is Tired of the Pearl Jam Sound," *New York Times,* August 25, 1996, p. 28, section 2.

Wall, Mick, *Pearl Jam,* Music Book Service, 1994.

Weiderhorn, Jon, "Tickets to Ride," *Rolling Stone,* May 18, 1995, p. 28.

Weisel, Al, "Lifestudy," *Rolling Stone,* December 15, 1994, p. 91.

Contact Information

c/o Epic Records
2100 Colorado Ave.
Santa Monica, CA 90404

Web Site

There are more than 100 web sites with information on Pearl Jam.

Porno For Pyros

Alternative pop/rock band

Formed in Los Angeles, California, in 1991-92

Most bands have to work very hard to get even a little recognition, not to mention a recording contract, but Porno for Pyros only had to come up with their name before they signed a major record deal. Most bands don't have Perry Farrell (former leader of the art-rock band **Jane's Addiction** [see entry], and co-creator of the very successful summer music festival Lollapalooza) as their lead singer either. In fact, it's difficult to think of Porno for Pyros without thinking of the flamboyant and outrageous Farrell, who has been called the "all-around alternative-rock shaman [high priest] and showman."

Jane's not home

When Farrell disbanded his group Jane's Addiction toward the end of 1991, they had built a near cult following and were at the peak of their popularity. With their blend of exotic yet catchy hybrid of rock, metal, jazz, funk, and folk, with outrageous stage antics and costumes, they helped open the door to the mainstream music market for other "art-rock" performers. Fans and

"The biggest thing I've learned is that you've got to delegate responsibility and trust people. That's the most important thing. I have a lot of people who work with me on things. It's a little scary but it's okay. You know, checks and balances." —Perry Farrell, vocals/frontman/songwriter

Perry Farrell

Porno for Pyros

critics alike were shocked and disappointed at the news of the band's split, but the band's founder, Perry Farrell, was interested in moving on. Some personal conflicts among the band members had gone unresolved, and Farrell had grown tired of the whole situation. He decided it was time to put Jane to bed.

Farrell wasted no time putting his energy into other projects, immediately beginning work on a video documentary of the first Lollapalooza tour of 1991. His interests soon turned back to music, and he decided to form a new music project. With former Jane's Addiction drummer Stephen Perkins, Peter DiStefano on guitar, and Martyn LeNoble on bass, Farrell assembled Porno for Pyros. He spent the next few months writing new material and working the band into shape. Farrell knew that expectations for Porno for Pyros would be big because of the huge success of his last band, so he was in no hurry to bring the band out before they were ready.

First album is no let down

Warner Bros. released Porno for Pyros' self-titled debut album in May 1993 to mostly good reviews. Although *Porno for Pyros* tried to capture the band's own unique sound, some critics argued it sounded like "Jane's Withdrawal." Yet, if the worst things the critics could say about Farrell's new album was, "It sounds too much like your last million-selling record," then things couldn't be all that bad.

Indeed, *Porno for Pyros* had silenced most of the critics who said that Farrell would be unable to recapture the magic that helped his former group make such a big impact in the music business. Farrell leads off the CD with his trademark high pitched whine saying, "I got the devil in me" (some critics claim Farrell's singing grates on the listener).

Airy guitar chords and a spacy murky mix give the debut album a certain charm. The band performed several times on the second stage at Lolla-

palooza that year to help promote record sales. Sales had started off strong, but soon after its release the album slipped down the charts.

Getting back to business

Farrell's involvement with Lollapalooza and his excessive drug use left him little time to devote to his new band over the next couple years after the release of their first album. By 1996 however, Farrell was ready to release his second Porno for Pyros album, entitled *Good God's Urge*. The album was given high marks by music critics. *Guitar Player* claimed the second album "paints a more expansive soundscape than the band's crudely produced 1993 debut." It seemed Farrell had finally succeeded in his vision of mixing jagged rock tunes with unusual textures.

The second release also covered a broad spectrum of music styles and sounds that Farrell is known for creating. Each track on the album was recorded, produced, and mixed by the band from start to finish, before they moved on to the next song. With a stronger guitar presence than the band's first album, songs like "Freeway" (featuring former Jane's Addiction guitarist Dave Navarro), "Dogs Rule the Night," "Wishing Well," and "Porpoise Head" help make *Good God's Urge* a strong sounding but very smooth and diverse collection of music.

Selected Discography

Porno For Pyros (Warner Bros.), 1993.

Good God's Urge (Warner Bros.), 1996.

Further Reading

Browne, David, "Porno for Pyros," *Entertainment Weekly*, May 7, 1993, p. 54

Farley, Christopher John, "Porno for Pyros," *Time*, May 31, 1993, p. 68

Ransom, Kevin, "Porno for Pyros: Peter DiStefano's Nylon Alternative," *Guitar Player*, September, 1996, p. 27.

Sinclair, Tom, "Farrell Faucet," *Entertainment Weekly*, August 16, 1996, p. 60.

Contact Information

Warner Bros.
3300 Warner Blvd.
Burbank, CA 91510

Web Site

http://www.wbr.com/pornoforpyros/

THE PRESI-DENTS OF THE UNITED STATES OF AMERICA

American alternative pop/rock band

Formed in Seattle, Washington, in 1991

've been watching MTV's 'It Came From The '80s,' and I started thinking that we are the Men At Work of the '90s. We are Kajagoogoo," said Chris Ballew, lead singer of the Presidents of the United States of America, in *Billboard* magazine. It could happen. With 1995's double-platinum *Presidents of the United States of America* and 1996's *II,* the band has perfected the art of making fun, lightweight songs like "Lump" and "Peaches." *Rolling Stone* calls their music "something like a processed-sugar-fueled pajama party gaining air on a trampoline," and *Billboard* calls it "happy pogo/pop-core." To Ballew, writing disposable pop songs is not a bad thing; in fact, it's the whole point. And in the view of many critics and fans, the rock world in the mid-1990s needed a jolt of the Presidents' anxiety-free humor. "Like the Ramones did for 1970s dinosaur rock, the Presidents pop the balloon of 1990s self-absorption without mocking it," said the *Los Angeles Times.*

"I'd get bored singing sad songs." —Chris Ballew, lead singer of the Presidents of the United States of America

From left to right: Jason Finn, Dave Dederer, Chris Ballew

In the beginning

The Presidents are one rock band that admits to having happy childhoods. "If you're really hurting, that's fine. But if you had a well-adjusted childhood and you're trying to give yourself an ulcer, it's obvious who's for real and who's not," said Ballew to *Rolling Stone*. Ballew came up with many of his crazy characters, like "Lump," as a boy, happily playing with Legos with his little brother. Ballew and Dave Dederer came from well-off families, grew up in Seattle, and went to junior and senior high together.

The two went to separate colleges—Ballew to the State University of New York and Dederer to Brown University. After graduation, Ballew moved to Boston and started playing with Morphine's Mark Sandman in a band called Supergroup. He also toured with Beck. Ballew and Dederer got back together in Seattle and started cowriting songs. Jason Finn, who was working as a bartender and band booker, saw them playing and begged them (for one or two years, depending on who you ask) to let him join the band. They relented. Finn took drums, Ballew played two strings on his "basitar," and Dederer was on three-string "guitbass." They set out to conquer the world with what they called "five strings and one tub-banger united under a single groove."

That name

From the start, the Presidents never took themselves too seriously. In the early days of the band, they would make up a new name each time they played. They finally picked a name one night while playing at a house party. "Between every song I'd say we were a different band," said Ballew to *Rolling Stone*. "'We're the Electric Blueberries!' One was 'We're the Presidents of the United States of America!' The whole party fell apart."

"To feel really secure on stage, I gravitate toward those songs that make people smile and laugh and jump up and down."

The Presidents' first record, *The Presidents of the United States of America,* became popular almost immediately. It helped that "Lump," a song about a fat lady sitting in a swamp, made MTV's "Buzz Clip" rotation. Two more absurd songs, "Peaches" and "Kitty," made the top forty. The Presidents were just as silly live. They made a point of playing weird venues like Pink's Hot Dog Stand in Los Angeles and a bowling alley in Chicago. For Presidents Day, they played a live MTV concert in front of Mount Rushmore. The goal with it all is just to have fun. "I personally base a good performance and a good song on a physical reaction from the audience. To feel really secure on stage, I gravitate toward those songs that make people smile and laugh and jump up and down," said Ballew to *Billboard. Spin* described a typical performance like this: "Ballew spreads his legs wide and 'sprays' the crowd with his red Flying V guitar, indulging in an array of 'Look at me, I'm rockin'' poses. Dederer jumps up and down as if elastic, leaps off the drum riser in tandem with Ballew, and repeatedly sails guitar picks into the crowd."

Parents Aren't Supposed to Like It

Stick with what works

For *II,* the band kept up the formula—short, tight, upbeat songs about strange subjects. Humor is still key to the band. "Tiki God," for example, is about the Hawaii episode of "The Brady Bunch." The video for "Volcano" looks like an out-of-date school science film with the band acting like nerdy professors explaining geological concepts. *Rolling Stone* called the Presidents' music "insidiously catchy," but seemed to be getting sick of the joke, calling the band "a joke band that isn't always funny." Others weren't so harsh. *Billboard* said the record would "certainly make fans want to smile, laugh, and jump up and down as much as did the gems on the last album." Whatever the reaction of the critics, the band is going to stick with what they like doing. "We're entertainers, not artists. We want to be mainstream; we're not in this to be cool," said Dederer to *Rolling Stone.*

Selected Awards

Presidents of the United States of America, certified double platinum, 1996.

Grammy nomination, Best Alternative Music performance, for *Presidents of the United States of America.*

Selected Discography

Presidents of the United States of America (Columbia), 1995.

II (Columbia), 1996.

Further Reading

Borzillo, Carrie, "Columbia's Presidents Take The Lighthearted Approach," *Billboard,* October 5, 1996, p. 16.

Clay, Jennifer, "Talking to ... The Presidents of the United States of America," *'Teen,* April 1996, p. 82.

Cross, Charles, R., "Can The Presidents of the United States of America Live Up To the Majesty and Stupidity of Their Name?" *Rolling Stone,* March 7, 1996, p. 30.

Scribner, Sara, "Presidents of the United States of America," *Rolling Stone,* October 5, 1995, p. 35.

Stovall, Natasha, "At Home in Seattle, Cheerfully Singing Against the Current," *New York Times,* April 26, 1996, p. 30 (section 2).

Tomashoff, Craig, "Hail to the Chiefs," *People,* October 30, 1995, p. 26.

Contact Information

P.U.S.A. Fan Club
PO Box 12265
Seattle, WA 98102

e-mail:
PUSAFAN2@aol.com

Web Site

http://www.music.sony.com/Music/ArtistInfo/Presidents/index.html

Primus

American alternative pop/rock band

Formed in San Francisco, California, in 1984

"Anybody who hears it is probably going to love us or hate us." —Primus bassist and singer Les Claypool on his music

Les Claypool

The early 1990s was a great time for Primus to break out. Alternative music was becoming a huge force in the music world, and Primus's music is about as alternative as it gets. "Imagine a punkier, thrashier Rush fronted by Mel Blanc," said *Rolling Stone,* referring to the man who did the voices for Warner Bros. cartoon characters Bugs Bunny, Yosemite Sam, and Daffy Duck. A press release for 1995's *Tales From the Punch Bowl* explained the music as: "Songs about working blokes, redneck goons, race car drivers and visits to the Department of Motor Vehicles, all done up in skewered time changes that could only be danced to if you have a master's degree in calculus."

It's strange music and Primus found throngs of fans who were waiting for just that. Their music scored the band two big selling records, 1991's *Sailing the Seas of Cheese* and 1993's *Pork Soda,* as well as a spot on the 1993 Lollapalooza tour, and multitudes of fans who affectionately yell "Primus sucks!" at Primus concerts. "I think young musicians appreciate us a lot, people who are into trippy, not-normal stuff. We're not a party band," said Primus bassist and singer Les Claypool in *Rolling Stone*.

Young Les

Claypool grew up in El Sobrante, in northern California, and describes his environment as "blue collar, almost redneck." He came from a family where most of the men were mechanics. Claypool learned about country music from his stepfather. "When I was a kid that's where I got my exposure to what he (his stepfather) calls Okie music," he said in *Guitar Player*. "He had an Okie station going. That's all he would listen to. I'd be out in the garage raising the banana seat on my bike, and I'd hear Waylon [Jennings] and Willie [Nelson]."

Claypool chose to play bass because it only has four strings and he thought it would be easier to play than a guitar. He was fifteen. "I heard Ted Nugent when he was nine so I figured I had to catch up fast," said Claypool in *Rolling Stone*. "I sat in front of the television and noodled. I didn't have an amp, but I developed a lot of dexterity [skill]."

When Claypool was eighteen, he joined a band that played R & B covers at biker bars. "It was four sets a night, up to five nights a week—that's how I learned discipline and how to actually groove," he said in *Guitar Player*.

Early Primate

Claypool started auditioning for other bands because he wanted to find a band "that would make it big." When he wasn't impressed by any of the other local bands, he decided he would have to start his own. His first recruit was guitarist Todd Huth, and in 1984, with Huth and a drum machine, a new band called Primate was born. They were almost ready to go, except that when Claypool got new drummer Tim "Herb" Alexander, Huth quit. With his own band in shambles, Claypool decided to audition for a spot in the rising band Metallica. When he didn't get the job, he decided to revive his old band. He named it Primus and brought in a friend, guitarist Larry "Ler" Lalonde, who had played in a metal band.

Finally, a record

Five years after first forming as a band, Primus put out its first record *Suck on This,* a live recording of a club show. Claypool borrowed $3,000 and put it out on his own label, Prawn Song (a reference to Led Zeppelin's label Swan Song). On the record the band already had their signature sound—weird lyrics, thumping bass, and Claypool's odd, cartoony singing voice.

> **"We'd go down the street, and someone will yell, 'You suck,' and I'll say, 'Oh, thank you very much,' which freaks out whoever's with you."**

Caroline Records heard the record and signed them to make their studio debut, *Frizzle Fry.* Meanwhile, Primus was selling out 500-seat theaters and getting a devoted cult of fans who formed the tradition of yelling out "Primus sucks!" at shows. "People would follow us around telling us how cool we were, and we'd be

with *Sailing the Seas of Cheese.* Bolstered by an appearance in the film *Bill & Ted's Bogus Journey,* the record was a hit and scored with typically oddball songs like "Jerry Was a Racecar Driver" and "Tommy the Cat," featuring an appearance by Tom Waits. Tours with heavy metal band Anthrax and rap group Public Enemy helped *Sailing the Seas of Cheese* become Primus's first gold record.

In 1992 Les Claypool took Primus on tour with his high school heroes Rush. Both bands, said Claypool in *Rolling Stone,* are favorites of young high school musicians but bad for "getting any girls." Primus also toured on U2's Zoo TV tour, then took a spot at 1993's Lollapalooza. Often Primus would start its shows with odd circus music to set the stage. The *New York Times* complained that Primus was "aiming for the Beavis and Butt-head market," but instead "simply sounded contrived, coldly displaying its cleverness."

By the time *Pork Soda* came out, Primus was so popular that the record debuted at number seven. They made a strange video for "My Name Is Mud," which got a lot of airplay on MTV. *Rolling Stone* called the record "a weird, whimsical grab bag." Later, Claypool described the record as "a fairly dark record" and "eerie." "It was a sign of the times. We were getting a lot of flak for being goofy guys. That was our less goofy album," he said in *Guitar Player.*

A break, then *Punchbowl*

After the whirlwind of the preceding few years, Primus took a break from

like 'Nah, we suck.' It evolved, and then it became good marketing. We'd go down the street, and someone will yell, 'You suck,' and I'll say, 'Oh, thank you very much,' which freaks out whoever's with you," said Claypool in *Rolling Stone.*

More than cult fame

A representative from Interscope Records signed the band after seeing a wild audience going crazy for the band at a San Francisco show. Primus came up

being Primus. Claypool toured with his side project Sausage and spent a lot of time working on computer artwork. "We needed to do other things and be apart," said Claypool in a press release for *Tales From the Punchbowl.* "Green beans may be your favorite food but every now and then you're gonna have to eat something else."

They came back with *Tales From the Punchbowl,* which *Guitar Player* called "worth the extra wait." "It's the band's most consistent and accessible album, with all of Claypool's wacky humor and twisted imagination intact." The record didn't do as well as *Pork Soda,* but it still went gold. The band put out a CD-ROM for *Tales.*

Another break, then *The Brown Album*

After *Tales,* Claypool took a break from Primus and worked on a solo project called Les Claypool and Holy Mackerel. Primus then reunited with big plans for 1997. There was a new drummer, Brian "Brain" Mantia, a spot on the H.O.R.D.E. tour, and a record *The Brown Album* out in July. The time-out, the side projects, and the CD-ROM should help Primus's music stay just as weird as ever. "Our stuff has always been a combination of everything— not deliberately, but because we've all been involved in so many different projects," said Claypool in *Guitar Player.* "We've been around the block."

Selected Awards

Pork Soda, certified platinum.

Tales from the Punch Bowl, certified gold.

Sailing the Seas of Cheese, certified gold.

Selected Discography

Suck on This (Prawn Song), 1989.

Fizzle Fry (Caroline), 1990.

Sailing the Seas of Cheese (Interscope), 1991.

Pork Soda (Interscope), 1993.

Tales from the Punch Bowl (Interscope), 1995.

Further Reading

Borzillo, Carrie, "Primus Spikes Its 'Punchbowl,'" *Billboard,* April 29, 1995, p. 12.

Gill, Chris, "21st Century Schizoid Band," *Guitar Player,* July 1995, p. 82.

Kot, Greg, "Les Claypool of Primus," *Rolling Stone,* September 2, 1993, p. 16.

Pareles, Jon, "With a Clank, a Thunk and a Boom-Chunk," *New York Times,* August 7, 1995, p. C11.

Richardson, Ken, "Tales from the Punchbowl," *Stereo Review,* August, 1996, p. 80.

Contact information

Interscope Records
10900 Wilshire Blvd., Suite 1230
Los Angeles, CA 90024

Web Site

http://www.ram.org/music/primus/
primus.html

Rage Against the Machine

American alternative pop/rock band

Formed in Los Angeles, California, in 1992

After the conservative Reagan era in American politics in the 1980s, along came the 1990s and Rage Against the Machine, an inspired and powerful band who surfaced to stand in musical defiance of the "powers that be." RATM began feeding a new truth-starved generation of youth their own blend of high-energy heavy metal and hip-hop. Their songs contained radical lyrics with messages that held no social or political topic sacred. They blasted out at racism, police brutality, oppressive governments, big business, and many other social and political issues. With their unique hardcore music and heavy issue-oriented lyrics, RATM spearheaded a mission to cut through cynicism and reaffirm the potential "power of the people."

Building the machine

Emerging from relative obscurity in Los Angeles in 1992, Rage Against the Machine is made up of fiery vocalist/frontman Zack de la Rocha, Harvard graduate Tom Morello on guitar, Tim Bob Commerford on bass, and Brad Wilk on drums. Wasting no

Zack de la Rocha (left) and Tom Morello

time making their mark in the music world, they released a self-produced twelve-song cassette that sold more than 5,000 copies that year. It included the band's first collaborative songwriting effort, "Bullet in The Head," which would also appear in its original version on the group's major label debut album.

With unyielding and blistering performances, the band started developing a strong following in West Coast music circles. As a result, several record labels began showing interest in the group. RATM's compelling live show also earned them a spot as a support act on several significant shows in 1992, including opening for the debut performance of **Porno For Pyros** (see entry), two second-stage performances at Lollapalooza II, and a European tour opening for Suicidal Tendencies.

Releasing the rage

After talking with several record labels who did not share their vision, RATM decided to sign with Epic Records. Epic agreed to allow the band the musical freedom they sought, and to follow through with the support the group needed. On November 6, 1992, Epic released the band's self-titled debut album. Almost immediately, *Rage Against the Machine,* with the songs like "Killing in the Name," "Bullet in the Head," and "Bombtrack," began earning the band critical acclaim and heavy radio and TV airplay. In the December 26, 1992, issue of *Billboard,* music critic Timothy White noted, "On the strength of the [debut] album, they [RATM] must be viewed as

RATM relish controversy

RATM has used its success to stretch the limits of musical expression and political understanding at every opportunity. Known as an uncompromising, hard-hitting band whose expletive-riddled music is commonly censored by mainstream radio and television, Rage Against the Machine once protested music censorship at Lollapalooza III (1993) in Philadelphia by standing motionless on stage, naked except for duct tape across their mouths, for twenty-five minutes without singing or playing.

Another controversial moment in the band's history came when a two-song performance on "Saturday Night Live" in 1996 was cut to just one song after the band attempted to hang inverted American flags from their amplifiers to protest the unfair influence of the wealthy on American politics. Not coincidentally, Steve Forbes, the multimillionaire ex-presidential candidate was the host that night. Morello claimed the SNL staff cut the band's second song from the show as revenge, while SNL claimed the show was running long and that's why the second song was dropped.

one of the most original and virtuosic [skilled] new rock bands in the nation." The album went on to sell more than one million copies in the United States and two million throughout the rest of the world.

Getting the message out

Rage Against the Machine continued to tour throughout the world for most of

American activist who many think was unjustly prosecuted for the 1975 murder of two FBI agents at the Pine Ridge Indian Reservation in South Dakota. Public reaction to the video was overwhelmingly positive, and by February 1994, it was the #1 video in the United States.

Was the machine breaking down?

With more than three years passing since the band's first album, fans and critics alike wondered if there would ever be another. When the band finally went to Atlanta to record their second album in 1995, word spread that there was disagreement among the band members. It was feared that the "Machine" would be no more. The band had spent so much time with each other over the course of the past few years that some personal differences had developed that needed to be sorted out. Fortunately, after a few weeks away from each other, the band was able to regroup to finally record their next album.

On April 16, 1996, Epic released the long-awaited second album, *Evil Empire*. Viewed as a strong effort by industry insiders, the CD dispelled the myths surrounding the bands longevity. In fact, *Evil Empire* debuted on the music charts at #1, knocking **Alanis Morissette's** (see entry) multiplatinum album, *Jagged Little Pill,* from that spot, and securing the respect that RATM had fought so hard to earn.

The second effort picked up where the first CD left off, except the band had fine-tuned their song-crafting skills and

the three years following the release of their first album. They had now become a headlining act, receiving top billing on a series of Rock for Choice benefit concerts in 1993 as well as a sold-out Anti-Nazi League benefit in London, England, among many other notable shows.

In late 1993, MTV's *120 Minutes* premiered the band's "Freedom" video, which RATM used to bring attention to the plight of Leonard Peltier, a Native

sharpened their focus, helping them go to a new musical level. *Rolling Stone* writer Jon Wiederhorn proclaimed, "If the band's first album was a call to arms, *Evil Empire* is a declaration of war." Not only did RATM live up to the critics' expectations, it hit them right between the eyes. Ripe with catchy yet quirky guitar riffs and the band's trademark heavy-grooving rhythm section, *Evil Empire* has De La Rocha smearing his critical lyrics across the music with a powerful sense of urgency over a smooth, calculating undertone. Called the "world's most dangerous band" by *Spin,* RATM would not let their message be suppressed.

Selected Discography

Rage Against The Machine (Epic), 1992.

Evil Empire (Epic), 1996.

Further Information

Arenas, Norm, "Rage Against The Machine: You Say You Want a Revolution?" *Alternative Press,* July 1996, p. 56.

Farley, Christopher John, "The Guitar God is Back," *Time,* September 23, 1996.

Morales, Ed, "No Apologies," *The Village Voice,* May 28, 1996.

Smith, R. J., "Red, Hot, and Bothered," *Spin,* October 1996, p. 56.

Wiederhorn, Jon, "Blows Against The Empire," *Rolling Stone,* April 18, 1996, p. 67.

Contact Information

Rage Against The Machine
P.O. Box 2052
Los Angeles, CA 90069

email:

RAGEemail@aol.com

Web Site

http://home.aol.com/RAGEemail

THE RAMONES

Influential American punk rock band

Formed in 1974 in
Forest Hills, New York

"We just played a twisted bubble gum music...and it caught on." —Johnny Ramone, guitarist

In the early 1970s, rock music was moving away from the short, three-minute-or-less, pop-song structure of its roots towards longer forms that became known as progressive rock. Progressive rock of the 1970s featured exceptionally flashy musicianship and song structures that sometimes borrowed heavily from classical music. Songs by groups such as Emerson, Lake and Palmer, ELO, and Yes could have many movements and last up to twenty minutes. For four New Yorkers with a do-it-yourself, "no frills" approach to rock and roll, it was easy to lead a rebellion against such a bloated state of music. It was simply a matter of buying some guitars and drums and learning the three or four chords necessary to write a song. Rock and roll would never be the same.

"Hey, Ho! Let's Go!"

The Ramones were formed in 1974 by singer Joey Ramone (real name: Jeffrey Hyman), guitarist Johnny Ramone (John Cummings), drummer Tommy Ramone (Tommy Erdelyi) and bassist Dee Dee Ramone (Douglas Colvin). They changed their last

From left: Johnny, Marky, Joey, and C.J. Ramone

names to Ramone as a tribute to Paul McCartney, who played under the name Paul Ramon in the Beatles' early years. When they set out to make music, the fact that they could barely play didn't keep them from having a solid idea of what they wanted to do. "It had to sound loud and fast and heavy rock with no guitar solos or anything like that. Just heavy power chords and exciting songs," Dee Dee told *Guitar Player* magazine.

They played their first public show at CBGB's, a bar in New York City's run-down Bowery district. Originally a country bar (CBGB means "Country, Bluegrass and Blues), CBGB's eventually became the center of New York's growing punk music scene. Future punk superstars like Blondie, the Talking Heads, the Patti Smith Group, and Television were among the bands that regularly played there in the late 1970s. That would have been hard to tell from the first Ramones show; they played to a tiny crowd ("The bartender and his dog," they would later joke). Legend has it that they played seventeen short, fast, and loud songs in twenty minutes. Bar owner Hilly Cristal told them, "No one's gonna like you, but you can come back again."

Blitzkrieg bop

Led by Dee Dee's classic, shouted "1-2-3-4!" song countdowns, the Ramones built a sizable following that was attracted to the band's defiant, raucous music and their anti-rockstar "fashion" of matching black leather jackets, ripped-up blue jeans, and sneakers. They were signed to Sire Records after about a year-and-a-half of live performances and recorded their debut album, *Ramones,* for $6400. It was released in May 1976 and demonstrated the band's trademark short, fast song style. It contained such favorites as "Blitzkrieg Bop," "Beat On the Brat" and "Now I Want To Sniff Some Glue." The record sold poorly in America (peaking at #111 on the *Billboard* album chart) but did better in Europe, particularly England.

> **"It had to sound loud and fast and heavy rock with no guitar solos or anything like that. Just heavy power chords and exciting songs."**

When the Ramones played the Roundhouse in London on the same day as America's Bicentennial, July 4, 1976, it sparked a second revolution. Punk records had been coming into economically depressed England for a while, but it was the foursome's show that was credited with providing the spark for the explosion that came in the wake of their appearance. The Ramones' powerful music and do-it-yourself approach inspired British punk bands like the Clash and the Buzzcocks, as well as the newly formed Sex Pistols, to pick up guitars and write songs about their lives, even if they hadn't played before.

"Gabba-Gabba-Hey!"

The Ramones' second album, *The Ramones Leave Home,* was more of the same: "1-2-3-4!" count-offs, two-minute song lengths, and songs that would become punk-rock classics, like "Pinhead" and

Phil Spector produces the Ramones' *End of the Century*

When their tracks were given to Phil Spector to be remixed for a soundtrack album, the Ramones embarked on an interesting adventure. The legendary producer, known for his work in the 1960s with groups like the Righteous Brothers and the Ronettes, developed a recording style he dubbed the "Wall of Sound," which sometimes had two drummers, two pianists, four guitarists, horn sections and others all playing at the same time. He also produced the Beatles' Let It Be in the early 1970s, then became known for his eccentric behavior later in the decade.

Spector's eccentricities showed themselves in the making of the Ramones album End of the Century. Obsessive about the smallest detail (he once listened to the opening chord of "Rock 'n' Roll High School" over and over for ten hours), he clashed with the band. At one point he pulled a gun on them and made them listen to their remake of the Ronettes' "Baby I Love You" many times over before recording their version for the album. Needless to say, the band was pretty frightened by the experience, but the song hit #8 in Great Britain. Later, the band dismissed the album as their worst. It wasn't a total disaster, though, for the track "Do You Remember Rock and Roll Radio?" is a showcase for what the album could have been.

The decision for the Ramones to work with the big-name producer had been motivated by the record company's desire to squeeze some hits out of punk music. In the late 1970s there was a "new wave" of bands that shared the punk band's do-it-yourself ethic but not their sound. While groups like the Cars and Blondie were crossing over to the mainstream with softer and more highly produced sounds, the Ramones' popularity derived from the live shows and their spontaneous, accessible punk sounds. Spector's proven skills, precision, and sense of style were clearly brought in to channel the band's rock charisma for a wider audience. Other music produced by Spector:

All Things Must Pass, George Harrison

Death of a Ladies' Man, Leonard Cohen

Imagine, John Lennon

River Deep, Mountain High, Ike and Tina Turner

"Gimme Gimme Shock Treatment." (Live performances of "Pinhead" sometimes featured a roadie dressed in a Zippy the Pinhead costume, waving a sign saying "Gabba-Gabba-Hey!," and leading the audience in the chant.) The album also contained a speeded-up, punk rock version of the rock and roll classic, "California Sun."

However, the United States was still ignoring the Ramones. The songs didn't fit into the formats of radio stations that were playing disco music and bands such as the Eagles and Fleetwood Mac. Their singles and albums routinely charted much higher in England than in America. For example, "Sheena Is a

Punk Rocker" off their definitive third album, *Rocket to Russia* (1977), reached #22 in the United Kingdom while peaking at #81 in the United States.

In addition to "Sheena Is a Punk Rocker," *Rocket to Russia* contained other songs that would become well-known to punk rockers. "We're a Happy Family" demonstrated the Ramones' ability to write humorous, satirical songs, as they lampooned the notion of traditional family values ("We ain't got no friends/Our troubles never end/No Christmas cards to send/Daddy likes men"). The band also covered rock classics, including "Surfin' Bird" and "Do You Wanna Dance?," turning them into speeded-up punk rock songs.

Tiring of the constant nine-months-a-year touring and desiring a career change into record production, Tommy left the band and was replaced by Marky (Marc Bell) of the New York band the Voidoids. Tommy remained involved in producing the band. After co-producing *Rocket to Russia,* he co-produced and co-engineered their next album, *Road to Ruin,* among others. He also produced the Ramones' thunderous 1984 album *Too Tough To Die.*

"I Wanna Be Sedated"

The sound of the band was beginning to undergo subtle changes with the release of album number four, *Road To Ruin,* in 1978, which was the first with Marky on drums. Some songs went beyond the two-minute mark, others featured acoustic guitars, and there were even some short guitar solos. The anthem "I Wanna Be Sedated" was included on this album along with some power ballads and even a country song. The band also chose to cover the rock classic, "Needles and Pins," on this album.

Their New Year's Eve 1977 show at the Rainbow Theatre in London was recorded and released as the double-album *It's Alive* in 1979. It captured the band at the peak of its powers for an entire Ramones set of blistering speed and fury.

The Ramones also appeared in low-budget movie mogul Roger Corman's film *Rock 'n' Roll High School* as star P. J. Soles' favorite band. The forgettable plot about parents opposed to the Ramones playing in their town (because lab rats explode when exposed to their music) is redeemed for punk rock fans by the band's entrance in a slow cruising convertible, singing "I Just Wanna Have Something To Do" and a live performance at the film's end playing "Pinhead." They also performed the film's title song.

Howling at the moon

In the early 1980s, a variation of punk called "hard-core" started to appear in America. Rawer, faster, and typically more political than the music of the Ramones, it threatened to make the band look slow in comparison. Although hard-core bands such as Minor Threat, Black Flag, and the Dead Kennedys never attained much beyond cult status, they were a natural evolution from the 1970s punk of the Ramones and the Clash. Not to be shown up, the Ramones released *Too Tough To Die* in 1984. A powerful record, it com-

A Comment on the Influence of the Ramones

The first edition of the Trouser Press Guide to New Wave Records, published in 1983, had this to say about the Ramones: "With no more than four chords, the Ramones blasted open the closed arteries of mid-70s rock, reanimating the music. Their genius was to recapture the short/simple esthetic from which pop had strayed, adding their own caustic sense of humor and minimalist rhythm guitar sound. The result not only spearheaded the original new wave/punk movement, but also drew the blueprint for more recent hardcore bands."

bined the usual great power-pop/punk songs with crisp production that really delivered the band's live wallop. It marked the debut of new drummer Richie, and Dee Dee contributed his strangled vocal stylings to the hard-core punk tunes "Wart Hog" and "Endless Vacation." The song "Howling at the Moon (Sha-La-La)" was produced by Dave Stewart of the band Eurythmics and was a minor hit.

Another political shot was the controversial single "Bonzo Goes to Bitburg" in 1985. The song dealt with President Reagan's visit to a cemetery in Bitburg, Germany, which had some Nazi SS troops buried in it. The political fallout was chronicled in this angry, yet still poppy, song. In 1986 they continued their move to back-to-basics punk with *Animal Boy,* which contained "Somebody Put Something in My Drink."

We're a happy family

Marky rejoined on drums in 1987, but in 1989 founding bassist (and count-off master) Dee Dee left the band, citing that he was tired of the constant touring and the stagnation in the band's musical direction. After all, the band had been together for fifteen years. Dee Dee renamed himself Dee Dee King and released a rap-rock album entitled *Standing in the Spotlight.* Dee Dee later moved to Michigan where he started a band called Dee Dee Ramone and the Chinese Dragons. He was replaced by C. J. Ramone (born Christopher Joseph Ward), who re-energized the band by contributing to the songwriting and taking lead vocals on songs like "Strength To Endure." That year they also contributed the title song to Stephen King's horror film, *Pet Semetary.*

Adios amigos

After several compilation and live releases, the band switched labels to Radioactive Records in 1992. Their label debut release, *Mondo Bizarro,* made the *Billboard* album chart for one week, peaking at #190 in the US. Their 1994 effort *Acid Eaters* (the title is taken from an old schlock-horror film) consisted of covers that influenced them in their earlier years, including The Who's "Substitute" and the Jefferson Airplane's "Someone To Love." *Ramones Mania,* a greatest hits compilation, was certified gold (500,000 units sold) in 1994, a mere five years after it's release.

The Ramones announced that they were retiring in the press preceding the release of the aptly titled *Adios Amigos* in 1995. Although Johnny and Joey weren't getting along that well, they coyly said that they might reconsider if the sales were exceptional. Sales weren't, and the Ramones played their last show on August 6, 1996, at the Palace in Los Angeles after a sold-out tour that included a spot on the Lollapalooza festival.

In an interview promoting *Adios Amigos,* Johnny said "My ambition in life was to do nothing and the Ramones got in the way of that. Now I wanna realize my ambition." Immediately after the tour, Johnny sold all of his gear. His trademark Mosrite Venture's Model guitar was reportedly purchased by Pearl Jam's Eddie Vedder. The other Ramones were busier: Joey wrote for the Internet magazine *Addicted to Noise,* Dee Dee published a fanzine called *Taking Dope,* and Marky released an album with his band The Intruders.

The next generation

Even though the Ramones never sold massive quantities of records, their influence can be felt today. They were named one of *Spin* magazine's "Seven Great Rock Bands of All Time," and *Rolling Stone* named their first album to the #69 spot on their list of the top 100 albums of 1967-1987.

The impact of the Ramones is apparent today in bands like **Green Day** (see entry), **Offspring** (see entry), and **Rancid** (see entry). Every band probably knows a couple of Ramones' songs, if only to play for fun at practice. A case can also be made for their influence on

the development of speed-metal, with it's warp-speed tempos. It's hard to imagine groups like **Metallica** (see entry) and **Slayer** (see entry) without acknowledging the four 'brothers' from New York who, in their words, "Just want(ed) to have something to do."

Select Discography

Ramones (Sire), 1976.
The Ramones Leave Home (Sire), 1977.
Rocket To Russia (Sire), 1977.
Road To Ruin (Sire), 1978.
It's Alive (Sire), 1979.
End of the Century (Sire), 1980.
Too Tough To Die (Sire), 1984.
Ramones Mania (Sire), 1989.
All The Stuff & More, Vol. 1 (Sire), 1990.
All The Stuff & More, Vol. 2 (Sire), 1990.
Mondo Bizarro (Radioactive), 1992.
Acid Eaters (Radioactive), 1994.
Adios Amigos (Radioactive), 1995.
Greatest Hits Live (Radioactive), 1996.

Further Reading

Ferguson, Jason, "Greatest Hits Live," *Entertainment Weekly,* July 19, 1996, p. 75.

Gill, Chris, "Faster and Louder: A Punk Guitar Primer," *Guitar Player,* January 1994, p. 108.

Guitar Player, April 1985.

Kenny, Glenn, "Joey Ramone" (interview), *Rolling Stone,* March 24, 1994, p. 16.

"Rock & Roll," PBS Documentary Series.

Rolling Stone, August 27, 1987.

Contact Information

The Ramones
c/o Radioactive/MCA Records

70 Universal City Plaza
Universal City, CA 91608

Web Site

http://radioactive.net/radioactive/BANDS/
   RAMONES/ramone.html

Parents Aren't Supposed to Like It

RANCID

American alternative pop/rock band

Formed in Berkely, California, in 1991

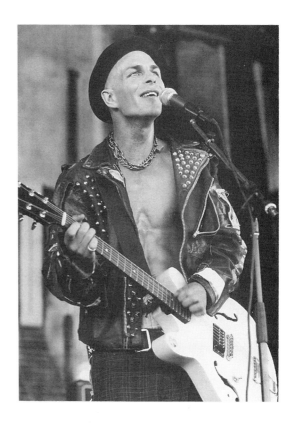

R ancid was formed for one reason alone; to save guitarist/ vocalist Tim Armstrong. His best friend, bassist Matt Freeman was afraid for him. He'd watched Armstrong go from one "McJob" to another. He'd seen him lose his apartment, then slide from friends' couches onto the streets. Armstrong couldn't stop drinking, and he was throwing his life away. Freeman had known the guitarist since the two were five years old. He knew what would help his friend ... a band. And so in late 1991, the pair, along with drummer Brett Reed, formed Rancid. Armstrong had found a reason to live.

Journey to the end of the East Bay

The guitarist had never really recovered from the break-up of his and Freeman's last band, Operation Ivy. "All these friends and all these people, we were equals. But what you gonna do when everybody goes on without you?" That's how the guitarist explained it on "Journey to the End of the East Bay." "Started in '87, ended in '89. You got a garage, hall, and we'll play anytime. It's

"Through all this evil and wreckage he maintained a sense of himself." —from "The Wars End"

Tim Armstrong

145

just the four of us, getting in the tour bus, too much attention unavoidably destroyed us. Four kids on tour, 3000 miles, in a four door car, not knowing what was going on. Not in a million years, thought it would turn out like this, hell no, no premonition could have seen this!"

Although Op Ivy only lasted two years, it became the most influential ska-core band of all time (a mix of ska and hardcore rhythms). They group grew so big, so fast, that the members couldn't cope. "I think the bigger you get the more pressures are put on you," Freeman explained. "We were all young and just didn't want to do it like that any more. I'm sort of glad it stopped when it did, because it didn't have time to really degenerate into.... Who knows what would have happened."

Salvation

But without the band, Armstrong had nothing. Rancid offered salvation, and the independent Lookout label offered a home. In 1992, Rancid released a five-song single. It was very different from the ska-based Op Ivy, straight hardcore with hints of the melodic punk that was to come. As soon as Epitaph, a Southern California label specializing in hardcore bands, heard it, they offered the trio a contract. And early in 1993, Rancid began recording their first album for their new label.

By then, the trio had already played shows around Berkeley, California, and decided they needed a second guitarist. Originally, **Green Day**'s (see entry) Billie

Joe Armstrong (no relation to Tim) was brought in. He even played a show with them and co-wrote a song, "Radio Radio Radio." But the Green Day guitarist was too busy with his own band. So, another Berkeley guitarist, Lars Frederickson, was asked to join.

Hopin' for better days

The album *Rancid* was a surprise for many in the punk and ska scenes. They assumed the new band would continue where Op Ivy left off. But *Rancid* didn't have ANY ska on it at all. Where Op Ivy was a pretty sloppy band, Rancid was not. They wrote fast, sharp, high-energy songs and played them very well. Then there were the lyrics. Most of them were taken from Armstrong's own experiences. "Hyena" was all about being broke and having nowhere to go. "The Bottle" is a song about spending all one's life getting drunk. And so on. The members of Rancid weren't afraid to talk about the bad things that had happened in their lives.

Let's go

After a national tour, Rancid went to work on their next album. *Let's Go* was even more polished than their debut. Within it, the quartet showcased virtually the entire punk genre. From the pure pop punk of "Radio" (cowritten by Billie Joe) to the reggae touches of "Burn," on to the anthemic shout-along of "Salvation" through the hardcore of "Black & Blue," *Let's Go* had it all.

The band's Old School punk influences shone clearly through. They included punk and hard rock bands like The Clash, Sham 69, Stiff Little Fingers, Johnny Thunders, and all the other great punk bands of yesteryear. Only Rancid were better musicians than many of these groups. They also had three singers. Tag team vocals that switched between Armstrong, Freeman, and Fredrickson gave Rancid a sound very different from Old School punk.

Solidarity

Punk was taking off. Suddenly, every major label wanted a punk group. "You had all these bands going crazy (sales-wise)," Freeman explained. "We're only human, and we talked to Epic; if anything, it was a quest for knowledge. If anyone's throwing that much money in your face, and you see all these other bands selling like crazy, you're going to consider it. You'd be a fool not to."

The punk scene was horrified that Rancid would even consider moving to a major label. Interestingly, one of the reasons Epic was considered was because it had been the Clash's label. "In the end," Freeman continued, "when all was said and done, we made a band decision that we wanted to stay with Epitaph. No matter what happened that's where we should be, just because all our friends were there."

Great punk

After the dust settled, Rancid went into the studio and recorded an even better album than their last. Most reviewers compared *...And Out Come the Wolves* to the Clash. While there are many Clash influences on the record, the reviewers all seemed to miss the Sex Pistols riff, the nod to Ian Dury, and the Johnny Thunders-esque lead guitar lines. More importantly, they missed what makes Rancid special. Freeman is such a talented bassist that often he plays the melody line, something that no Old School punk band had even considered. The songs are all very catchy, while the lyrics talk about problems through the band's and their friends' experiences. Of the many punk bands around today, few have stayed as true to punk's vision and ethics as Rancid.

Selected Discography

Rancid (Epitaph), 1993.

Let's Go (Epitaph), 1994.

...And Out Come The Wolves (Epitaph), 1995.

Further Reading

Christie, Ian, "The Unheard Music?," *Alternative Press*, February, 1995, p. 44.

Goldman, Jonathan, "Meet Lars Frederiksen," *Spin* October, 1995.

Greene Jo-Ann, "Salvation Through Punk," *Goldmine*, September 15, 1995, p. 58.

Jenison, David, "Wolves In Cheap Clothing," *Huh* October, 1995 p. 54.

Contact Information

Epitaph Records
2798 Sunset Blvd,
Los Angeles, CA 90026

Website

http://www.arrowweb.com/Rancid

THE RED HOT CHILI PEPPERS

American alternative pop/rock band
Formed in 1978 in Los Angeles, California

"Should have been/Could have been/Would have been dead/If I didn't get the message going to my head"—from "Suck My Kiss"

In the mid-1980s, The Red Hot Chili Peppers combined hard rock, funk, rap, and punk into a distinctive brew that made them trailblazers in the world of alternative rock. Formed in 1978 by four sixteen-year-old Fairfax High School students in Los Angeles, the band was originally known as Los Faces, then as Anthem. Lead vocalist Anthony Kiedis was the son of cult-film actor Blackie Dammett and had moved to Los Angeles from Grand Rapids, Michigan. Bassist Flea (real name: Michael Balzry) was born in Melbourne, Australia. Guitarist Hillel Slovik was born in Haifa, Israel. The only Los Angeles native was drummer Jack Irons.

After high school, Flea quit the band to join the hardcore-punk band Fear. Slovik and Irons formed a band called What Is This? that managed to get signed to a record deal. After some time, Kiedis and Flea invited the other two to get back together as the Red Hot Chili Peppers. During an early show that they played under the name Tony Flow and the Miraculous Majestic Masters of Mayhem, they inaugurated their trademark stage act of performing nude, with tube socks placed over their groin areas.

Anthony Kiedis

Rolling tape

They were signed to EMI America in 1983 and recorded their debut album with British new wave band Gang of Four's Andy Gill producing. Due to Irons's and Slovik's record contract, session musicians filled in for them for the recording. The self-titled album was released in April 1984.

Their second album *Freaky Styley,* was produced by P-Funk wizard George Clinton and featured the full line-up of the band for the first time on record. Musicians Maceo Parker and Fred Wesley (both from soul singer James Brown's backup band) also contributed to the Peppers' evolving punk/funk/trash melange.

Their first charting album was 1987's *The Uplift Mofo Party Plan.* As their sound coalesced around songs like "Fight Like a Brave," "Me and My Friends," and "Behind the Sun" (which became a hit for them in 1992 as a remixed version on the *What Hits?* album), the album showcased subjects ranging from friendship to social commentary to sex.

In May 1988, they released *The Abbey Road E.P.* The cover, a spoof of the cover of the Beatles album of the same name, recreated the poses of the Fab Four with one important difference: the Red Hot Chili Peppers were naked except for their strategically placed socks.

Drugs take their toll

The Red Hot Chili Pepper's "good times" lifestyle extended to the use of various drugs. The lifestyle caught up to Slovik, who died of a heroin overdose on June 25, 1988. He was only twenty-six years old, and his death devastated his close friends in the band. Slovik's death so disturbed Irons that he quit the band the following month. After forming the band Eleven and recording with the band Sun 60 (among others), he took over the drum throne in **Pearl Jam** (see entry) in 1994. Kiedis ended up in a fishing village in Mexico's Baja peninsula, where he struggled with his own addictions. While Flea had used heroin, he said he never got too strung out and eventually quit using it.

After auditioning many drummers, the Peppers hired Chad Smith, who hailed from Detroit, where he had been in local band Toby Redd. Various guitarists jammed with the Peppers before Flea met John Frusciante, a member of the band Thelonius Monster. The regrouped Chili Peppers returned to the studio to record what would be their biggest album yet, *Mother's Milk.*

Mother's milk

The new edition Peppers hit hard on *Mother's Milk* with their first single, "Knock Me Down," which dealt with drug addiction with lyrics like, "If you see me getting mighty/If you see me getting high/Knock me down/I'm not bigger than life." The album also featured a muscular cover of Stevie Wonder's 1973 hit, "Higher Ground." Flea's background in classical trumpet was showcased on the instrumental "Pretty Little Ditty." (He had played first trumpet in the Los Angeles Junior Philharmonic.) Other songs covered their beloved Los Angeles Lakers

Red Hot Chili Peppers, in and out of stage costume

("Magic Johnson") and, of course, sex. *Mother's Milk* was certified gold (500,000 units sold) after just six months.

With their growing "Good Time Boys" attitude came some trouble. While playing for MTV's Spring Break in Daytona Beach, Florida, Flea and Smith jumped off stage and grabbed a bikini-clad fan and spanked her. They were arrested and charged with battery and sexual assault. They pled guilty and were ordered to apologize, pay $1,000 fines, and donate $5,000 each to a rape crisis center.

Musical growth

With their contract with EMI up, the Chili Peppers signed with Warner Bros. Records and settled into a reputedly haunted mansion in Los Angeles to work on the follow-up to *Mother's Milk.* Under the direction of producer Rick Rubin (Beastie Boys, Tom Petty) and engineer Brendan O'Brien (who would go on to produce **Pearl Jam** and **Stone Temple Pilots** [see entries]), they crafted their most ambitious album, *Blood Sugar Sex Magik.* Combining their trademark hard metal/funk with mellow ballads and some surprisingly jazzy textures on songs like "Breaking the Girl," the Peppers showed growth and new maturity without losing their "bad boy" touch.

Following the lead single "Give it Away," with its visually striking video featuring the band painted silver out in the desert, came "Under The Bridge." The song about Los Angeles and heroin abuse reached number two on the singles chart. Lyrics like "Sometimes I feel like I don't have a partner/Sometimes I feel that my only friend/Is the city I live in/The city of angels," and "Under the bridge downtown/Is where I drew some blood ... I could not get enough ... Forgot about my love...I gave my life away," convey the loneliness of a big city and drug addiction.

While on tour in Japan in May 1992, Frusciante abruptly announced that he was quitting. Speculation that the pressures of touring were to blame were hard to confirm because the guitarist became a virtual recluse and would not return the band's efforts to contact him. He released a solo album in 1994 to no success.

New kids in the sock

Arik Marshall joined up to complete the tour, which included a thirty-four-date stint as headliners for the Lollapalooza '92 festival. After a year, when attempts to write new material were frustrated by the lack of chemistry with his band mates, Marshall left the band. In a move widely perceived as a publicity stunt, the band placed an ad in the *Los Angeles Weekly* seeking a new guitarist. As news spread, the telephone number received over 3,000 calls in three days before it was disconnected. Any guitarist who could make it out to Los Angeles was given a preliminary audition by representatives of the band. Those who made the cut were advanced to jamming with Flea and Smith.

The cattle-call was for naught, because Kiedis spotted Mother Tongue guitarist Jessie Tobias in a Los Angeles club and invited him to join. He lasted a month before he was replaced by Dave Navarro (formerly of **Jane's Addiction** [see entry]). Tobias went on to join **Alanis Morissette's** (see entry) touring band in 1995. In an ironic twist, Flea and Navarro appeared on Morissette's debut single "You Outta Know."

Tragedy continued to stalk the band as Flea was present when the actor River Phoenix succumbed to a drug overdose in front of the notorious Viper Room in Los Angeles. Flea rode the ambulance to the hospital with Phoenix.

A new style?

One Hot Minute (1995) was the first release of this new lineup. The sound was different from the previous incarnations of the Peppers, due in large part to new guitarist Dave Navarro's playing style. Critic Jas Obrecht described it in *Guitar Player*, "Navarro experiments with long, spacey reverbs, clean arpeggiated lines, retro bad-for-good tones, and cool wah clucks, but his focused power riffing really brings out the band's hard-edged side ... and tightens their funk...." There was much debate as to whether it was a change for the better, though, with *People Weekly's* rock critic Jeremy Helligar feeling the album sounded "as if they left the studio too soon" with its "frayed edges and mazy meandering." Despite critical concerns, the album was certified platinum after only six weeks. It went on to sell over four million copies in less than a year.

Controversy also followed the band's videos. "Warped" included quick shots of Flea and Navarro kissing, and the clip for "My Friends" showed the band in full ball gowns in a row boat on a surrealistic ocean. The video for "Aeroplane," however, was a gorgeous tribute to the style of Esther Williams's water ballet films. It even had small children (including Flea's daughter) dressed as airplanes.

Selected Awards

Grammy Award: Best Hard Rock Song for "Give It Away," 1993

MTV Video Music Awards: Best Art Direction, Breakthrough Video for "Give It Away"; Viewers Choice for "Under The Bridge," 1992.

Flea named Best Bassist in *Rolling Stone* Readers Poll, 1993.

Blood Sugar Sex Magik certified platinum, 1992; triple platinum, 1993; quadruple platinum, 1996.

What Hits? certified platinum, 1993.

One Hot Minute certified platinum, 1995.

Selected Discography

The Red Hot Chili Peppers (EMI), 1984.

Freaky Styley (EMI), 1985.

The Uplift Mofo Party Plan (EMI), 1987.

The Abbey Road E.P. (EMI), 1988.

Mother's Milk (EMI), 1989.

Blood Sugar Sex Magik (Warner Bros.), 1991.

What Hits? (EMI), 1992.

Out In L.A. (EMI), 1994.

One Hot Minute (Warner Bros.), 1995.

Further Reading

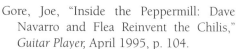

Foege, Alec, "Once Death-Defying Clowns, the Red Hot Chili Peppers Grow Up To Become Sensitive White Males," *Rolling Stone*, October 19, 1995, p. 52.

Gore, Joe, "Inside the Peppermill: Dave Navarro and Flea Reinvent the Chilis," *Guitar Player*, April 1995, p. 104.

Helligar, Jeremy, "One Hot Minute," *People Weekly*, October 16, 1995, p. 27.

Marvel, Mark, "Anthony Kiedis of the Red Hot Chili Peppers," *Interview*, October 1994, p. 158.

Neely, Kim, "Flea of the Red Hot Chili Peppers," *Rolling Stone*, November 17, 1994, p. 66.

Obrecht, Jas, "One Hot Minute," *Guitar Player*, December 1995, p. 129.

Rotondi, James, "Pleasure Spiked with Pain: Dave Navarro Braves the Darkness and Finds the Light," *Guitar Player*, August 1996, p. 42.

Books:

Harvey, Spike, *Red Hot Chili Peppers*, Omnibus Press, 1995.

Thompson, Dave, *Red Hot Chili Peppers*, St. Martin's Press, 1993.

Watts, Chris, *Red Hot Chili Peppers: Sugar and Spice*, Castle Communications, 1994.

Contact Information

Warner Bros. Records, Inc.
300 Warner Blvd.
Burbank, CA 91505-9090

Web Sites

http://www.wbr.com/chilipeppers/
http://www.coast.net/~rhcpfans/
http://www.treknet.is/saemund/redhot.htm

R.E.M.

American alternative pop/rock band

Formed in Athens, Georgia, in 1980

According to *Maclean's* magazine, R.E.M. is "one of the biggest bands in the rock 'n' roll universe." The group's thoughtful, well-constructed material and professional precision earned it a reputation as one of the best and most consistent rock bands ever. Known for arty touches and recurring themes, R.E.M. offers listeners artful melodies with lyrics that appeal to listeners' emotions. Featuring dense layers of guitar playing and sometimes inaudible, obscured lyrics from murmured singing, the group's songs seem like blurs from the unconscious, thus reflecting the band's name. (R.E.M. stands for Rapid Eye Movement, which occurs while sleeping and especially while dreaming.)

Attracted by the mystery of the sound and lyrics, loyal fans have been drawn to R.E.M. since 1980, giving the group a rare longevity in the music industry. Though frequently imitated, R.E.M.'s signature style was unprecedented and secured it a place in the history of popular music. As Christopher John Farley explained in *Time*, "Good bands hit and fade. Great bands, like R.E.M., endure."

"We made a contract with the world that says, 'We're going to be the best band in the world; you're going to be proud of us.' But we have to do it our way."—Peter Buck, lead guitarist

Michael Stipe

It started in the South

R.E.M. began as a party band at the University of Georgia in Athens, Georgia. Vocalist Michael Stipe and guitarist Peter Buck met in a record store and learned that they both liked British new wave music. They then met drummer Bill Berry and bassist Mike Mills at a party, and R.E.M. was born. Their world debut occurred at a college party held in a converted Episcopalian church.

R.E.M. released their first single, "Radio Free Europe," in 1981, when British new wave music was going strong (compare British band The Clash's "This Is Radio Clash," also from 1981). However, immediate success was not to be. The band received little support from radio stations and MTV, so they toured college towns and played small clubs to gain exposure. "We were playing five nights a week," Peter Buck explained in *Guitar Player,* "usually three weeks out of the month, doing two or three sets a night. If anything, that's why we got to be an okay band."

Developing its own style

It took two years for R.E.M. to establish its unique style of melody and mumble. Much of the distinctive sound of the whole came from the individual talents of the parts. Each member of R.E.M. gave the group's sound a valuable edge. Bill Berry, for example, provided strong drumming. Mike Mills played melody instead of using the bass for rhythm only. Peter Buck established himself as an accomplished guitarist. He offered tightly focused riffs and bursts. Often Buck would pick instead of strum

chords, utilizing arpeggios (playing the tones of a chord one at a time) effectively. He achieved the status of a rock guitar hero equal to Jimi Hendrix or Eric Clapton, though Buck was not given to showy solos during performances.

Overall, though, Michael Stipe's singing defined R.E.M.'s sound. His garbled vocals—the indecipherable words with changing interpretations—became the group's trademark. Stipe delivered lyrics that, according to Deborah Feingold in *Rolling Stone,* "combined vivid imagery with pithy telegraphic phrasing, sacrificing grammar for impact."

Murmurs of success

In 1983, with the release of the album *Murmur,* R.E.M.'s unique style solidified. With some trepidation, the band sought to combine an art concept with mass-market media, using overdubs and studio devices to create a distinctive sound. Listening to the album was compared to eavesdropping, because its songs were alluring yet indecipherable. "We were conscious that we were making a record that really wasn't in step with the times," Peter Buck told *Rolling Stone.* "It was an old-fashioned record that didn't sound too much like what you heard on the radio. We were expecting the record company to say, 'Sorry, this isn't even a record, it's a demo tape. Go back and do it again.'" In the end, though, *Rolling Stone* magazine named *Murmur*—a certified gold record for selling 500,000 copies—one of the best albums of the 1980s.

A string of well received albums followed *Murmur.* According to *Time's* Far-

Parents Aren't Supposed to Like It

R.E.M., rock professionals

ley, "The rock group R.E.M. is not only one of the best bands in America, it is also one of the most consistent. Since its debut in 1983, the band has released nine major albums, and every one has set a high standard; several ... have become classics." Indeed, each album issued in the 1980s was well received by the public. In 1984—a year after *Murmur*'s success—the band released *Reckoning*. Recorded in just twelve days, this certified gold album stayed on the charts for more than a year despite being very different from the rest of the contemporary music field.

The next year R.E.M. issued another gold album, *Fables of the Reconstruction*, which sold more than 300,000 copies in just three months. Still resisting any commercial orientation, R.E.M. hired producer Don Gehman to add a new dimension to their sound. *Fables of the Reconstruction* featured more instruments—big drums, organs, pianos, banjos, and accordions that helped the band's sound evolve futher. Similarly, 1986's *Life's Rich Pageant* was heralded as "brillant and groundbreaking" by critics. Less than one year after its release in 1986, this album also earned gold record certification.

R.E.M.'s artistic integrity

Though R.E.M.'s albums ensured the group's commercial success during the

R.E.M. Tours

R.E.M. began touring extensively during the 1980s to support their album releases. They also recorded while on the road. While there have been some great times, overall traveling has been hard on the band. Initially, touring went well, with some inspiring moments. In 1984, for example, Roger McGuinn of the Byrds—a group that, along with Patti Smith and Bob Dylan, greatly influenced the band—joined R.E.M. on stage to sing "So You Want to Be a Rock'n'Roll Star." Then in 1987, R.E.M. enjoyed a successful U.S. tour promoting Life's Rich Pageant.

R.E.M.'s world tour in 1989 to promote Green established the group as arena performers, but it marked the beginning of a series of terrible ordeals due to the group's health problems while performing abroad.

During the Green tour, drummer Bill Berry contracted a bronchial infection, which has also been reported in some sources as Rocky Mountain spotted fever. His illness resulted in R.E.M.'s canceling tour dates in Germany. After that, R.E.M. shied away from touring until 1992 when it performed throughout Europe, including Germany, Italy, Spain, Holland, France, and Sweden.

It would be three years before the next world tour, and that one for Monster in 1995 seemed particularly jinxed. The ambitious tour was to start in Australia, then move to Europe, then to the United States. But the tour stalled when Berry left the stage with a migraine one March night in Switzerland, leaving the others to perform acoustic numbers until a replacement drummer arrived. Berry's migraine was actually a ruptured aneurysm that required emergency brain surgery. Of course, R.E.M. again canceled its European performances.

Upon Berry's recovery, the tour began again in May, with the band returning to Europe in June. More medical emergencies, however, ensued in short order. In July Mike Mills needed abdominal surgery to remove a tumor in his intestines. Again, six European performances were canceled. Just one month later, Michael Stipe was diagnosed with a hernia in Czechoslovakia, so he returned home for surgery. The Monster tour ended in November in Atlanta. Ironically, it won the Rolling Stone Reader's Poll Award as the best tour of 1995. Not surprisingly, R.E.M. planned no tours to promote its 1996 release New Adventures in Hi-Fi.

Throughout the last ten years, R.E.M.'s misfortunes during tours have undoubtedly left many fans disappointed by cancelled shows. The band still performs to sellout audiences wherever it plays, and leaves many happy fans in its wake.

Parents Aren't Supposed to Like It

1980s, at no time did group members sacrifice their artistic integrity for mass appeal. Their philosophy in 1984, according to Peter Buck, was "in the long run, if we keep plugging at it, we'll get to the level of popularity we deserve." "It may take longer," he told *Guitar World,* "but it'll be worth it."

In 1988, after several years with the independent label IRS, R.E.M. signed a ten million dollar contract for five albums with Warner Bros. Records. Superstar status followed. R.E.M. soon appeared on the cover of *Rolling Stone* as America's best rock band, and the group won its first major industry award in 1989 when its "Orange Crush" video won the MTV Video Music Award in the best post-modern video category.

The second decade

Bolstered by the success of the albums from the previous decade, R.E.M. started the 1990s at the height of their popularity. The band's 1991 certified gold release *Out of Time* was the first album by a rock band to reach number one on the U.S. music charts, including the Billboard 200, since 1989. The album featured the Grammy-award winning megahit, "Losing My Religion," which the *Los Angeles Times* called "a masterful expression of anxiety and self-doubt." The album, the single, and the accompanying video garnered R.E.M. seven Grammy nominations and three Grammy awards.

The next year's R.E.M. release, *Automatic for the People,* opened at number two on the Billboard 200. With a soft,

acoustic sound and a dark but beautiful vision, *Automatic for the People* featured slow, brooding songs such as Southern gothic ballads about the loss of innocence and torch songs. The double platinum album sold 218,500 copies in the first week of its release, eventually selling more than three million copies worldwide.

R.E.M.'s 1994 release, *Monster,* reflected the continued artistic evolution of the band. The album's music was clearly bolder than *Automatic for the People.* Its songs were loud and sexy, yet offering intelligent and deep explorations of isolation and identity. Aggressive rhythms and amps replaced the strings and mandolins of earlier albums. *Monster* reached the number one spot on the Billboard 200 and sold well throughout the world. In fact, the album sold more than three million copies in non-English-speaking markets from July 1994 to January 1996.

"The influence that I'd like to think we have is that people saw that there's a way to go about doing this on your own terms. The thing is, you have to not worry about success."

R.E.M. created a "spectacular anti-spectacle" for its *Monster* tour. The band designed a 360-degree stage, with a variety of unusual films and visual images projected on translucent screens during performances. Definitely not high-tech, the visuals were intended to keep performances focused on the music instead of theatrical glitz.

Moving rock forward

R.E.M. recorded its twelfth and most ambitious album during the band's *Monster* tour. *Adventures in Hi-Fi,* featured thoughtful, well-constructed songs focused on freedom and liberation. Recording the album while on the road gave it a sense of spontaneity. The album's first single, "E-Bow the Letter," for example, "seems to have been written on the spot," observed Jeremy Helligar of *People.* Featuring rock legend Patti Smith, the song made a definite impact on modern and mainstream rock charts. "Thanks in part to the meandering quality of singer-songwriter Michael Stipe's delivery and his now-legendary elliptical lyricism," Helligar continued, "it starts to make sense only after multiple listens."

New Adventures in Hi-Fi, as indicated by the title, was a progressive yet retrospective work. Although reminiscent of R.E.M.'s earlier recordings, *New Adventures in Hi-Fi* offered a new, dynamic mix and sequencing of songs that encompassed the band's sixteen-year career, including—in addition to typically abstract lyrics—college-dance-party rhythms, gentle mandolins, and some serious rock music. Overall, *New Adventures in Hi-Fi* peaked at number two on Billboard's 200, indicating listeners were still eager for more.

The groundbreaking continues

Despite nearly twenty years of recording and performing together, R.E.M. continues to influence the music industry. "Rock 'n' roll eats its old," wrote Farley in *Time.* "Bands like Green Day,

Hootie and the Blowfish and Pearl Jam are built up, and then, when they become successful, trashed by the very same tastemakers and trendmeisters who declared these acts worthwhile to begin with. Only a few bands like U2 and R.E.M. manage to escape the ritual slaughter and mature with grace."

It is a source of pride for the group that they have succeeded in their own way. "The influence that I'd like to think we have is that people saw that there's a way to go about doing this on your own terms," Buck explained to *Rolling Stone.* "The thing is, you have to not worry about success."

Still, R.E.M. has been wildly successful. They began in relative obscurity with a sound unlike any other to achieve status as one of the best rock bands in history. Once considered avant-garde, R.E.M.'s albums have become classics. In 1996 the band renewed its contract with Warner Bros. for somewhere around eighty million dollars. Having achieved popular and commercial appeal, R.E.M. nevertheless maintained their artistic integrity. Thus, as *Billboard*'s Paul Verna noted, the band earned its reputation as a rock group "that consistently gambles and consistently wins."

Selected Awards

Village Voice, Best Independent Single of the Year Award for "Radio Free Europe," 1981.

MTV Music Video Awards, Best Post-Modern Video Award for "Orange Crush," 1989.

Billboard Music Awards, Modern Rock Artist and Top World Album Awards, 1991.

Parents Aren't Supposed to Like It

MTV Music Video Awards, Best Video, Best Group Video, Best Art Direction, Best Editing, Best Direction, and Breakthrough Video Awards for "Losing My Religion," 1991.

BRIT Awards, Best International Group Award, 1992, 1993, and 1995.

Grammy Awards, Best Pop Performance by a Duo or Group (with Vocals) Award for "Losing My Religion," Best Alternative Music Album Award for *Out of Time,* Best Music Video (short form) Award for "Losing My Religion," 1992.

Rolling Stone Music Critics' Picks, Best Album Award for *Automatic for the People,* Best Band Award, and Best Male Singer Award for Michael Stipe, 1993.

MTV Video Music Awards, Best Editing, Best Cinematography, and Best Breakthrough Video Awards for "Everybody Hurts," 1994.

MTV Video Music Awards, Lifetime Achievement Video Vanguard Honor, 1995.

Rolling Stone Music Critics' Picks, Best Band Award, 1995.

Rolling Stone Readers' Critics' Picks, Best Band and Best Tour Awards, 1995.

Selected Discography

Chronic Town (IRS), 1981.
Murmur (IRS), 1983.
Reckoning (IRS), 1984.

Fables of the Reconstruction (IRS), 1985.
Life's Rich Pageant (IRS), 1986.
Dead Letter Office (IRS), 1987.
Document (IRS), 1987.
Eponyms (IRS), 1988.
Green (Warner Brothers), 1988.
Out of Time (Warner Brothers), 1988.
Automatic for the People (Warner Brothers), 1994.
Monster (Warner Brothers), 1994.
New Adventures in Hi-Fi (Warner Brothers), 1996.

Further Reading

Farley, Christopher John, "R.E.M.: New Adventures in Hi-Fi," *Time,* September 2, 1996, p. 64.

Fricke, David, "Monster on the Loose (R.E.M. Opens Tour in Australia)," *Rolling Stone,* March 23, 1995, p. 27+.

Helligar, Jeremy, "New Adventures in Hi-Fi," *People,* September 16, 1996, p. 31.

Verna, Paul, "R.E.M.: New Adventures in Hi-Fi," *Billboard,* September 21, 1996, p. 63.

Contact Information

Warner Brothers Records
3300 Warner Blvd.
Burbank, CA 91510

Web Site

http://www.wbr.com/rem

SiLVERCHaiR

Australian alternative pop/rock band

Formed in Newscastle, Australia, in 1992

Reporters writing about Silverchair have made a special point to notice all the band's juvenile behavior. In the United States, a *Rolling Stone* reporter said the three members "belch, fart, swear, inhale their meals, bum quarters off their dads for video games and as yet have few cultural interests other than music." The focus of the media is due to the age of band members. When Silverchair first became known to the rock world, each member was only fifteen years old. In 1997, with their second record "Freak Show" out, the band's average age was only seventeen. Age is a sore spot with the band. "It sucks," said bassist Chris Joannou, to Australian *Rolling Stone*. "It should just be about the music, not age."

The ages of Silverchair certainly aren't hurting them career-wise. Their debut *Frogstomp* went double platinum and, a couple weeks after coming out, *Freak Show* went gold.

The Cinderella story

Silverchair actually started their first band when the guys were twelve. Growing up in Newcastle, Australia, an industrial city, the three surfer kids decided to start a garage band. They used equipment their parents bought them and called themselves Short Elvis, then the Innocent Criminals. "We just wanted to be a garage band," said singer and guitarist Daniel Johns in *Rolling Stone*. "We started playing Black Sabbath and Zeppelin covers because we had nothing to do. We never expected to do anything."

"It stops you from getting a big head if you know like millions and millions of people hate you."

But Johns's neighbor told him about a national demo tape contest called Pick Me, run by *Nomad,* a pop music TV show. They entered their song "Tomorrow" and won first prize, beating out over 800 other entries. The prize was a day in the recording studio of Australia's national alternative radio station 2JJJ-FM. The band re-recorded "Tomorrow" and gave the tape to the station. When the station added the record, listener response was so high that the song made it to heavy rotation. Soon, they had a number one single in Australia.

After an EP that went to number one in Australia, Silverchair went to the studio to record a full-length record. They recorded *Frogstomp* in nine days. It entered the Australia charts at number one and they scored an American record deal. Although some critics considered the band to be a grunge rip-off band and dubbed the band "Nirvana in Pajamas and Sound(kinder)garden," Silverchair had a hit in the United States.

Being young and in a band

The Silverchair parents have had to pitch in to deal with the band's sudden fame. The Silverchair moms managed the band (now the band has hired a regular manager) and the Silverchair dads have been taking leaves from their businesses to help out with the band's touring. School life has also been changed by all the touring. The principal at their high school, Newcastle High, has changed the band's school requirements so that the members can get special credits in music. "It's really great because one of the requirements of this course is to give them a recorded piece of music," said drummer Ben Gillies in *Rolling Stone*. "So we can just give 'em the CD and go, 'Thank you very much!'"

No sophomore slump

In 1997 Silverchair set out to prove that *Frogstomp* hadn't been a fluke and came out with *Freak Show*. According to *Rolling Stone*, the new record is "more diverse, with bursts of guitar blending easily with strings, acoustic moments and quasi-Indian elements." *Freak Show* looks like it will follow in the footsteps of *Frogstomp,* selling a bunch of records and getting trounced by the critics.

That's fine with the members of Silverchair, who claim not to be bothered by the criticism. "We don't care. It's good in some ways. It stops you from getting a big head if you know like millions and millions of people hate you," said Johns in Australian *Rolling Stone*. "And if people hate you, it makes you want to keep going, 'cause you want to prove them wrong."

Selected Awards

Frogstomp, double platinum.

Freak Show,, gold record.

Selected Discography

Freak Show, (Epic) 1997.

Frogstomp, (Epic) 1995.

Further Reading

Eliezer, Christie, "Silverchair Aims to Leapfrog across the Pacific on Epic," *Billboard*, July 1, 1995, p. 12.

Fricke, David, "Boys' Life," *Rolling Stone*, February 22, 1996, p. 44.

Hendrickson, Matt, "Silverchair Let Their Freak Flay Fly," *Rolling Stone*, February 6, 1997, p. 17.

Kot, Greg, "The Cradle Will Rock," *Rolling Stone*, August 24, 1995, p. 31.

Sinclair, Tom, "The Kid Is Uptight," *Entertainment Weekly*, February 7, 1997, p. 67.

Contact Information

Epic Records
2100 Colorado Ave.
Santa Monica, CA 90404

Web Site

http://www.soundworld.hl.com.au/swsilv.html

SMASHING PUMPKINS

American alternative pop/rock band
Formed in Chicago, Illinois, in 1989

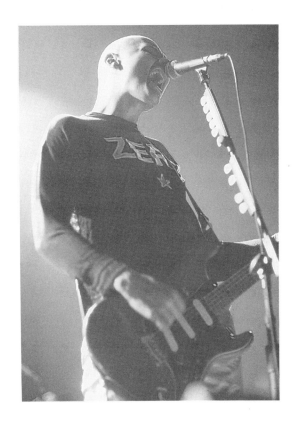

I want the power and emotional content to be so overwhelming it's almost hard to watch. Because when I go see other bands, I want them to take my breath away," said Smashing Pumpkins frontman Billy Corgan in *Details*. No one can accuse Corgan of not having big goals. Even when the first Smashing Pumpkins' record *Gish* came out in 1991, Corgan was thinking big. Instead of taking one of the many major label deals offered to the band, Corgan chose to sign with the tiny independent label Caroline Records. "What this band does is so specific that we couldn't dilute it in any way," said a then-twenty-four-year-old Corgan to *Rolling Stone* in 1991. *Rolling Stone* called *Gish* "awe-inspiring." It sold over 500,000 copies.

Throughout the band's fast rise Corgan has remained just as bold and sure about what he wants for the band. In 1995, he followed up the smash hit *Siamese Dream* with what many thought was a pretentious and stupid move. He put out a two-hour, two-CD set called *Mellon Collie and the Infinite Sadness* and said he wanted it to be to "this generation what Pink Floyd's *The Wall* was

"In a weird kind of way, music has afforded me an idealism and perfectionism that I could never attain as me." —Billy Corgan, Smashing Pumpkins frontman

Billy Corgan

Smashing Pumpkins, clockwise from top left: James Iha, Jimmy Chamberlin, D'Arcy, Billy Corgan

for kids in 1979," reported *Details*. "My whole thinking is to try to get everything about life in," he said in a press release for *Mellon Collie*. Corgan's faith in his own ideas have paid off. *Time* called *Siamese Dream* "an emotional declaration of independence." It has sold over five million copies. And Corgan's gamble, *Mellon Collie and the Infinite Sadness,* sold over eight million copies.

Mellon Collie baby

Billy Corgan did not enjoy his childhood. His parents divorced when he was very young and Corgan was bounced around to different homes. He spent most of his time with his stepmother while his father, a guitar player, toured with different bands. "There are still a lot of issues from that time that are unresolved," said Corgan in *Rolling Stone*. "My parents were nowhere to be found, there's no getting around that."

Corgan was taller than other kids and spent most of his time collecting baseball cards. Although his father played guitar, Corgan didn't think about playing himself until later. "I saw my friend playing in his basement, and that was it. Saved up all my birthday money, bought a guitar. The first day I got it I practiced for four hours," he remembered in *Rolling Stone*.

Corgan learned about music working in record stores and considered himself to be an intense, "overly dramatic" teen. "If you can imagine, I was more emotional than I am now—with nowhere to put it. Imagine that same kind of twisted heart locked in this eigh-teen-year-old body with nothing to do. It wasn't pretty," he said in *Rolling Stone*.

Marked

Before the Pumpkins, Corgan was in a goth-rock band in Florida called—with typical Corgan drama—Marked, so named because he and another member had birthmarks. When he moved to Chicago, Illinois, he met James Iha and started Smashing Pumpkins as a duo. "I was working in a used record store, living with my dad and basically being the four-track-cassette-making geek," he said in *Rolling Stone*. "That's basically how it started—me, James and a drum machine. We played a show at this bad Chicago Polish bar and here we were playing this geeky, gloomy art rock with a drum machine and me on bass."

D'Arcy (Wretzky) became the third member of the Pumpkins after Corgan met her in a parking lot after a show. The two argued and Corgan invited her to audition for the band. Corgan said that when D'Arcy auditioned, she was so nervous that she couldn't even play. "Her hands were shaking so bad, she couldn't hold the instrument. But I thought she was nice and such an interesting person that, hey, we'll worry about the rest later," he told *Rolling Stone*.

When Jimmy Chamberlin joined as drummer, he helped change the band's sound. Corgan and Iha had grown up on alternative music like British new wave bands the Cure and Bauhaus, but Chamberlin was into hard rock bands like Led Zeppelin and Deep Purple. "We were still playing this kind of dark pop, and it

The Pumpkins vs. Pavement

Pavement put down the Pumpkins in the song "Range Life" with the lyrics "Out on tour with the Smashing Pumpkins ... They don't have no function." Then there was a rumor that Pavement told people that Corgan kicked them off of Lollapalooza. Billy Corgan said in a Rolling Stone interview that he has "no problem" with Pavement, but added: "There's always been flak we've gotten from certain bands—the Mudhoneys and Pavements of this world—that somehow we cheated our way to the top, that we deceived the public to get where we're at," said Corgan. "It's like high school all over again. You have the football team, except the football team is the guys in Pavement and Mudhoney. And they're all patting themselves on the back for how cool they are instead of healthily challenging themselves to greater heights."

chaos," adding "the band thrashes around in waves of feedback and beautifully distorted melodies—swirling energy that conjures up visions of Jimi Hendrix sitting in with the Stooges." It sold a surprising amount of records for an independent release, partially because the band toured so heavily in support of it.

> "Before *Gish* came out, the most we'd been together on the road was ten days. And suddenly we're on the road for four months. We were pinching pennies, arguing about who was going to order what at breakfast because it was expensive."

Touring so heavily put a strain on the band. Iha and D'Arcy broke up as a couple and Chamberlin began to use more drugs. The band went to record *Siamese Dream* and Corgan had an experience that he later called a nervous breakdown. "I was a twenty-four-year-old man under tremendous pressure, not only from the world of music but in my own mind," said Corgan in *Details*.

Corgan tried to handle his problems by taking control in the studio. He took over the bass and guitar parts from D'Arcy and Iha and played them himself. Corgan says he now regrets the decision but says he did it because the band had been suddenly thrust together and was not getting along. "Before *Gish* came out, the most we'd been together on the road was ten days. And suddenly we're on the road for four months. We were pinching pennies, arguing about who was going to order what at breakfast because it was

wasn't really putting a dent in anybody. But if you want other people to pay attention to you, you have to have some other thing going on. And for us, it was power," said Corgan in *Details*. When the band mixed alternative and hard rock, things happened fast.

The fast rise

The Smashing Pumpkins had found their sound. "Our fourth show, we opened for Jane's Addiction. We went from nobody to somebody," said Corgan in *Rolling Stone*. They got a record deal and put out *Gish*. The album got rave reviews. *Rolling Stone* called it "meticulously calculated

expensive. It was really down to dumb, dumb (stuff)," he said in *Rolling Stone*.

Success

Regardless of the method they used to come up with it, *Siamese Dream* was a huge success for the band. *Guitar Player* praised its "deep focus production, beatific pop melodies (and) pulse-pummeling ultra-Zep dynamics." *Time* said: "It's an album of contrasts, going from fuzzed-out guitar bursts one moment to tender piano the next."

Mellon Collie and the Infinite Sadness was the ambitious follow-up—too ambitious, according to many critics. But Corgan and the other Pumpkins proved them wrong. The record was the best selling double CD of the 1990s. *Details* called the record "an amazing double CD of bone-rattling nihilism and gentle, nostalgic love songs" and said "the music—impossibly passionate, wet and epic—overwhelms the senses."

Tragedy

In 1996, just when the band was at the peak of their success, Jimmy Melvoin, a keyboardist touring with the band, overdosed on drugs and died. He had been doing drugs with Chamberlin. Chamberlin was kicked out of the band. The Pumpkins decided to hire new musicians and go back on tour. "We're not turning a blind eye to tragedy, but who are we punishing by not continuing the tour? Ourselves and our fans. And that seemed to just make the tragedy even worse," said Corgan in *Details*.

The Pumpkins came back with a show in Las Vegas. *Rolling Stone* gave it a good review, saying "the band has managed to transform its recent mishaps into catalysts for musical growth." They followed up the tour with a boxed set of B-sides and covers called *The Aeroplane Flies High*.

Whatever the band does on its next record is sure to be something big. And with Corgan in control, it's safe to say that every note on the record will be exactly as Corgan wants. "Sonically, we want to create a perfect picture so people will be drawn into it," he explained in *Guitar Player*. "When you're a scummy, awful human being, there's a lot of attraction in having a chance to make beautiful music and leave a little postcard of yourself."

Awards

Mellon Collie and the Infinite Sadness certified eight times platinum.

Siamese Dream certified five times platinum.

The Aeroplane Flies High certified platinum.

Gish certified gold.

Grammy Award, Best Hard Rock Performance, "Bullet with Butterfly Wings," 1997.

MTV Video Music Awards: 1) "Tonight, Tonight" (Best Video of the Year, Breakthrough Video), and 2) "1979" (Best Alternative Music Video), 1996.

American Music Awards, Favorite Alternative Artist, 1997.

Selected Discography

Siamese Dream, (Virgin), 1993.

Gish, (Caroline), 1991 and (Virgin), 1994.

The Aeroplane Flies High, (Virgin), 1996.

Pisces Iscariot, (Virgin), 1994.

Mellon Collie and the Infinite Sadness, (Virgin), 1995.

Further Reading

Blashill, Pat, "Out on a Limb," *Details,* October, 1996, p. 148.

Farley, Christopher John, "Smashing Pumpkins: Mellon Collie and the Infinite Sadness," *Time,* November 13, 1995, p. 146.

Fricke, David, "Billy Corgan Talks," *Rolling Stone,* September 19, 1996, p. 26.

Fricke, David, "Smashing Pumpkins: The Rolling Stone Interview with Billy Corgan," *Rolling Stone,* November 16, 1995, p. 50.

Rogers, Ray, "Smashing Pumpkins," *Interview,*, February, 1996, p. 76.

Schoemer, Karen, "Germ Warfare," *Newsweek,* October 14, 1996, p. 72.

Contact Information

Fan club:

P.O. Box 578010
Chicago, IL 60657

Record company:

Virgin Records
338 N. Foothill Rd.
Beverly Hills, CA 90210

Web Site

http://www.virginrecords.com/pumpkins/home.html

SOUL ASYLUM

American alternative pop/rock band
Formed in Minneapolis, Minnesota, in 1981

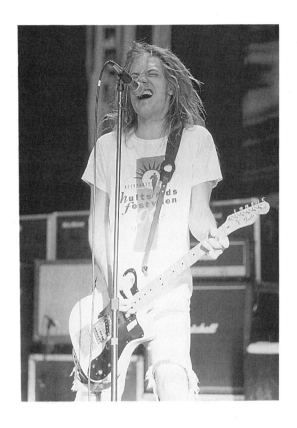

Grave Dancers Union, the record that made Soul Asylum famous, almost didn't get made. Right before it, Soul Asylum was in their worst period ever. They had been making records for eight years and, still, nothing was happening. By 1991 they had left their label, A&M, feeling that their previous record *And the Horse They Rode In On* hadn't been promoted enough. Soul Asylum owed the label $200,000 to break the contract. They didn't have that kind of money. The guys in the band were either back at their day jobs or thinking about going back.

Then the dejected singer and guitarist Dave Pirner saw Oliver Stone's rock and roll movie *The Doors*. "I was like, 'That's right. I was in a band that had a chance to be something,'" said Pirner in *Rolling Stone*. The movie inspired Pirner to re-form the band. Soul Asylum signed with Columbia and headed to the studio to work on the record *Grave Dancers Union*. A few months later their single "Runaway Train" was all over MTV, Pirner was dating actress Winona Ryder and Soul Asylum had their biggest hit ever.

> "I would like to have the coup of just having been in a great rock band that nobody cares about anymore." —Dave Pirner in *Rolling Stone*.

David Pirner

169

The early years

Dave Pirner was an athlete who played hockey for twelve years as a kid and football in high school. His mother insisted that he take up an instrument, so he chose the trumpet over the piano, thinking because it had fewer buttons, it would be easier to play. In middle school he played trumpet for the jazz band. He was inspired to write lyrics by his high school English teacher. "She was the meanest, hardest teacher and everybody thought I was a total square for taking her class," said Pirner in *Rolling Stone*. He was especially affected when the teacher told a passionate story about a porch swing. "She got teary—and she's like this sixty-five-year-old woman. It just made me understand why she was so hard on her students, because she was trying to make them understand the power of the English language and poetry."

Meanwhile, Daniel Murphy (guitar, vocals) and Karl Mueller (bass, vocals) were attending high school together. After school they got an apartment together and formed a band, Loud Fast Rules. They recruited Pirner to play drums at first, then Pirner switched to vocals. Grant Young joined as drummer, and they changed their name to Soul Asylum. In 1983, they signed with Twin/Tone, the Minneapolis label that also had Husker Du and the Replacements.

Obscurity

Soul Asylum put out several Twin/Tone records in the 1980s, like *Made to Be Broken, While You Were Out,* and the EP *Clam Dip and Other Delights* to general-ly good reviews, but no widespread success. Of *Made To Be Broken, Rolling Stone* said: "punk and pop play tug of war with folky ballads on one side, thrashing noise on the other and Pirner's hoarse, edgy voice smack dab in the middle."

Soul Asylum scored a major label deal with A&M and put out *Hang Time* in 1988, which some critics consider their best record ever. The band was also getting a lot of attention for its energetic live show. Several newspapers, including the *Village Voice* called them "the best live band in America." Things seemed good for the band so they released their next record *And the Horse They Rode In On* with high expectations. They waited for record buyers to discover Soul Asylum. It didn't happen. That's when Soul Asylum almost quit.

A second chance

They replaced Grant Young with Sterling Campbell and Soul Asylum set to work on *Grave Dancers Union*. "We stayed real focused on the songs—what they were about, what they need," said Pirner in *Pulse!*. "The idea was to make them come across in as crystallized a fashion as possible." It worked. Songs like the gentle ballad "Runaway Train," "Black Gold," and the punkier "Somebody to Shove" struck a chord with listeners and made the record a huge hit. The reviews were good, too. *Entertainment Weekly* gave it an "A." *BAM Magazine* complimented the record's "innate tunefulness" and "consummate styling."

The band denied feeling any kind of pressure for their follow-up record.

"We've been doing this for a while now, so all we really wanted to do was the same thing we've always done: make a good record," said Murphy in press materials for 1995's *Let Your Dim Light Shine*. Whether they did or not depends on who you ask. *Billboard* called it "a work of rare depth and brilliance." *Mademoiselle* called it a "pop masterpiece." But record buyers weren't so kind. The song "Misery," about a bad romance, was a hit, but sales-wise the record was no *Grave Dancers Union*.

But whatever record sales are, Pirner won't give up music again. "If I lost everything, if my girlfriend dumped me and the band got rid of me, you know what I'd do? I'd just travel around like Woody Guthrie, doing solo concerts," he told *Rolling Stone*. "And in the middle of a show, I'd ask if anyone had a place to stay, and even if there were forty people there, some fifty-year-old guy or some sixteen-year-old girl would take me in."

Selected Awards

Let Your Dim Light Shine, platinum record.

Grave Dancers Union, double platinum status.

Selected Discography

Made to Be Broken (Twin/Tone), 1986.

Hang Time (Twin/Tone/ A&M), 1988.

Clam Dip & Other Delights (Twin/Tone), 1989 (EP).

Soul Asylum and the Horse They Rode In On (Twin/Tone/ A&M), 1990.

Grave Dancers Union (Columbia), 1993.

Let Your Dim Light Shine (Columbia), 1995.

Further Reading

Dunn, Jancee, "Soul Asylum," *Rolling Stone*, November 17, 1994, p. 55.

Sanz, Cynthia, "Soul Asylum: Runaway Train," *People*, October 4, 1993, p. 143.

Schoemer, Karen, "Been There, Heard That," *Newsweek*, July 3, 1995, p.57.

Stenger, Wif, "Soul Asylum," *Seventeen*, October 1992, p. 90.

Strauss, Neil, "A Hard Dazed Night," *Rolling Stone*, June 29, 1995, p. 28.

Contact Information

Columbia Records
2100 Colorado Ave.
Santa Monica, CA 90404

Web Site

http://www.music.sony.com/Music/
ArtistInfo/SoulAsylum/

SOUNDGARDEN

American grunge/heavy metal band

Formed 1984 in Seattle, Washington; disbanded early 1997

A short announcement issued by the members of Soundgarden read: "After 12 years, the members of Soundgarden have amicably and mutually decided to disband to pursue other interests." With that statement, it seemed that the era of Seattle grunge finally and definitely ended. It had been five records with 20 million sold since Soundgarden became what *Interview* declared in 1994 "the founding fathers of a trendy regional style: a Black Flag/Black Sabbath punk-metal fusion, which has set the aural standard for juggernauts like Nirvana, Pearl Jam and Alice In Chains."

Soundgarden saw other bands like **Nirvana** (see entry) and **Pearl Jam** (see entry) rise to huge levels of fame, while for years, Soundgarden remained comparatively unknown. At times, Soundgarden was even accused of imitating the other Seattle bands. "We were sometimes perceived as this band who was sort of copying the Sub Pop trend, even though we had the second release on the label," said lead singer Chris Cornell to *Spin*. But by sticking with it for so long and putting out records like *Superunk-*

Chris Cornell

nown, with its monster summer hit "Black Hole Sun," Soundgarden finally became just as famous as the others. Not that fame was what the band was after in the first place. Like any good Seattle band, the members of Soundgarden think fame is just a bit silly. "It can be pretty embarrassing. It's something I don't feel worthy of," said drummer Matt Cameron on the *Superunknown* tour in *Rolling Stone*.

Pre-grunge

When flannel was just a cheap way to dress and before grunge was a music term, Soundgarden singer Chris Cornell was a kid growing up in an Irish-Catholic neighborhood in Seattle and getting into trouble. He was one of six kids and his parents broke up when he was fourteen. After that, he dropped out of high school and started working full-time as a cook to help pay the family's bills. He also played in a few bands, but was discouraged by other musicians who would play Top 40 songs just to make a few extra dollars. "They weren't musicians at all—they were just dish-washers with guitars. So I learned early on that I wasn't going to allow music to be this thing I used to pay the rent. It was mine and more sacred than that," he said in *Pulse!*

Guitarist Kim Thayil grew up in Park Forest, Illinois. His parents were emigrants from India; his mother was a music school teacher. But Thayil doesn't think that's what got him into music. "Sorry, Mom, I know you were a music teacher for twenty years, but I got my

musical education from locking myself in my room as a teenager and listening to Kiss," he said in *Spin*. Thayil went to high school with Sub Pop founder Bruce Pavitt and the original Soundgarden bassist Hiro Yamamoto. After school, the three all moved to Washington. Thayil (who was studying philosophy at the University of Washington) and Yamamoto ended up in Seattle and Yamamoto moved in with Cornell. The three formed a trio in 1984, naming the band for a sculpture in Seattle. At the time, Cornell sang and played drums.

Early records and bad timing

With new drummer Scott Sundquist, the band contributed a few songs to a 1986 compilation called *Deep Six*, which was regarded as the beginning of the grunge phenomenon (or what the *Rolling Stone* called "the Great Seattle A & R Stampede," in which record labels were in a frenzy to sign the up-and-coming grunge rockers in Seattle). Sundquist quit the band, and they chose Matt Cameron to replace him. Cameron, who had played with Skin Yard, had been drumming since he was 11. Soundgarden was his favorite band. "It still dawns on me—'Wow, I'm in Soundgarden,'" he said in *Details*.

The band had bad timing on labels. They released two EPs on Sub Pop, *Screaming Life* and *Fopp*, but just as the label started getting popular, they switched to SST Records for *Ultramega OK*. About the record, *Rolling Stone* said: "A pastiche of psychedelia, blistering hardcore and

Soundgarden, from left: Matt Cameron, Chris Cornell, Kim Thayil, Ben Shepherd

wrecking ball blooze wrapped up with odd tunings and time signatures."

Major label, more bad timing

Soundgarden had bad timing again when their grunge record *Louder Than Love* came out on A & M, a year before "alternative" marketing existed. Soundgarden was classified as a heavy metal band. "While Soundgarden's Seattle contemporaries in Nirvana and Pearl Jam were busy cultivating the neuroses that would later make them household names, Soundgarden was touring with [heavy metal bands] Skid Row, Danzig, and Guns 'N Roses," reported *Spin*.

Signing to a major label had been a big decision. At first Soundgarden was "horrified," according to *Details*, that A & M thought their music could be commercial. "We thought there was something wrong with us. Like for some reason we were wimpier or lamer than these other bands that we liked," said Cornell.

"Every single person in Seattle started looking like me, all the young white boys with long curly brown hair and facial hair."

In 1991, bassist Ben Shepherd joined the band. Like Cameron, he had been a big Soundgarden fan. "When I was asked to join the band, I felt like

Charlie Bucket (of 'Charlie and the Chocolate Factory') getting the golden ticket to go to the chocolate factory," he said in *Spin*. It was quite a time to join the band because, also in 1991, the world was figuring out what this new kind of music called grunge was. Whatever it was, Soundgarden's 1991's *Badmotorfinger* had it. On that record, "a distinctive Garden sound emerged: heavy, hypnotic, with assaultive riffs underscoring distorted guitars that could sound like sitars or giant mosquitoes," explained *Details*.

Seattle hype

By the early 1990's Nirvana had broken through with "Smells Like Teen Spirit," the movie *Singles* came out, and everyone knew about the Seattle scene. "Seattle—as a fashion scene and musical movement—has been bought packaged and mass-marketed to the point where department stores are selling pre-ripped flannel shirts," reported *Pulse!* Seattle bands were shocked to see people around the world copying their style, or anti-style. One day, fed up, Cornell cut his hair. "Every single person in Seattle started looking like me, all the young white boys with long curly brown hair and facial hair," said Cornell in *Pulse!*

It wasn't just the style hype that irked the bands, it was being lumped together with all the other Seattle bands, regardless of how different the bands sounded. "It's not like Pearl Jam is doing the same thing as us. I mean 'Jeremy' doesn't sound like anything we've ever done. They're as different from us as Nir-

---

The proper way for a Seattle rock star to behave in the early 1990s

Pearl Jam's Eddie Vedder avoids videos and hates doing interviews. Nirvana's Kurt Cobain distrusted the press and wore a "Corporate Magazines Still Suck" t-shirt to a Rolling Stone photo shoot. Those bands became famous for their reluctance to play "rock star" for the public and Soundgarden members were no different. Interview pointed out Soundgarden's "anti-star attitude" and described them as "genuinely gawky, overly sensitive, punk-weaned professionals." Details reported: "They're too aloof to party down with the metal fraternity; they'd rather play chess than entertain groupies." Cornell explained the Seattle phenomena of down-to-earth, unassuming rock stars to Interview in 1994: "Right now it's turned around the other way. It's like, 'I like him because he's the type of person I can sit and talk to,'as opposed to being attracted to a band because they're better looking than you and have more women around them and really nice cars and motorcycles."

---

vana is from us. What seems unusual to me is that the whole scene punched a hole in this L.A. commercial rock scene," said Cornell in *Rolling Stone*.

Getting their dues

Cornell "may have the only voice in rock that bears relation to the great operatic divas," reported *Spin*. On *Superunknown*, fans got a better chance to hear Cornell's voice because instead of using his high, screaming/singing style of earlier records, he sings in a lower, more emotional voice. "Eddie Vedder, eat your heart out," said *Pulse!* Cornell explained: "The reason it seems like it's better is because, rather than being up against the wall all the time like usual, I'm being mellow and flying under the radar, so the points when (my voice) shoots up will seem more aggressive."

With the hit "Black Hole Sun," leading the way, *Superunknown,* brought Soundgarden mainstream success and critical acclaim. *Details* called it "very heavy and very trippy." *Melody Maker* said it was "a heroic attempt to mark a change in direction" and "a brilliant, brilliant album." *Rolling Stone* praised it as "easily the most cohesive record the band has ever made—from the first sassy opening riff of 'Let Me Drown' to the low-slung, plodding swing of 'Fell on Black Days.'"

Gloomy lyrics

Even though the band was finding success, their lyrics remained gloomy. "Soundgarden have never been especially restrained when it comes to spewing out great clouds of woe, and the songs on *Superunknown* continued in that tradition," said *Rolling Stone.* An example of Cornell's non-cheeriness: "In my disgrace/boiling heat/summer stench/'neath the black/the sky looks dead," from "Black Hole Sun."

Why all the dark lyrics? "It's probably a combination of being used to writing when I'm in that frame of mind and the fact that I'm in a darker frame of

mind more often than other people," said Cornell in *Rolling Stone.*

Soundgarden live

Although quiet off-stage, the members of Soundgarden came alive onstage. *Pulse!* commented on Cornell's "star quality": "Cornell anchors the band from center stage, legs splayed, long hair whip-cracking in time to each riff, voice skyrocketing into glass shattering crescendos." *Rolling Stone* described a 1994 performance of "Face Pollution": "They're wringing wet and exuberant: Shepherd caught up in his usual spastic contortions, lurching all over the stage, his bass nearly dragging on the ground; Cornell leaning over the barricade to high-five a few delirious fans; Thayil indulging in a few tongue-in-cheek rock-god poses; and Cameron ... bashing the cymbals with a big goofy smile."

Down On the Upside

In 1996 Soundgarden put out *Down On the Upside.* It was a return to their rawer, more hard-rocking sound of the past. *Rolling Stone* gave it an average rating calling it "the same ol' metal machine music." It turned out to be Soundgarden's last record. In 1997 they suddenly and abruptly announced that they were breaking up.

Even though the band broke up, they left behind the thing that they always considered most important, the music. "It's like the only thing that's really yours. Relationships are never yours. Property is never yours. Your body isn't even yours. Music is something that actually is. It's forever in a way," said Cornell to *Details* in 1994. In a 1994 interview in *Interview*, Kim Thayil said how he would want people to remember Soundgarden: "In twenty years I'd like to see young musicians discovering our records and being influenced by them, just like people were yelling about the Stooges five years ago. I wouldn't want to be a blurb."

Awards

Badmotorfinger certified platinum.

Superunknown certified five times platinum.

1994 MTV Music Awards, Best Metal/Hard Rock Video for "Black Hole Sun."

1995 Grammy Award for Best Hard Rock Performance for "Black Hole Sun," Best Metal Performance for "Spoonman."

1995 Rolling Stone Music Awards, Best Metal Band (both readers and critics' picks).

Selected Discography

Ultramega OK, (SST), 1988.

Louder Than Love, (A&M), 1989.

Screaming Life/Fopp, (Sub Pop), reissued 1990.

Badmotorfinger, (A&M), 1991.

Superunknown, (A&M), 1994.

Down on the Upside, (A&M), 1996.

Further Reading

Blush, Steven, "Soundgarden," *Interview,* March 1994, p. 82.

Gold, Jonathan, "Hammer of the Gods," *Spin,*, April 1994, p. 36.

Lanham, Tom, "Soundgarden: In Search of the Monster Riff," *Pulse!* March 1994, p. 40.

Myers, Caren, "Garden of Earthly Delights," *Details,* April 1994, p. 150.

Neely, Kim, "Into the Unknown," *Rolling Stone,* June 16, 1994, p. 46.

Strauss, Neil, "Soundgarden: Down on the Upside," *New York Times,* May 19, 1996, p. 28, section 2.

Contact Information

Fan club:
P.O. Box 61275
Seattle, WA 98121

Web Site

http://www.imusic.com/soundgarden/
menu2.html

Stone Temple Pilots

Alternative pop/rock band

Formed in 1990 in San Diego, California

Although Stone Temple Pilots did most of their dues-paying in California, they are often spoken of in the same breath as Seattle's grunge and metal bands such as **Pearl Jam** (see entry), **Alice in Chains** (see entry), and **Soundgarden** (see entry). In spite of critics downplaying the band for those similarities, fans have shown their love for and support of the Stone Temple Pilots by buying more than a million copies of each of the band's three albums.

Mighty Joe Young

Stone Temple Pilot's beginnings can be traced to a 1987 Black Flag concert in Long Beach, California, where Scott Weiland met Robert DeLeo. "It was one of those weird things. You get into a heavy discussion with a total stranger, and you discover that both of you are seeing the same girl." When the girl left town, Weiland and DeLeo moved into her vacated apartment. Immediately, Weiland and DeLeo formed a band, calling it Mighty Joe Young. It combined Weiland's punk rock inclinations and DeLeo's hard

Scott Weiland and Robert DeLeo

rock aspirations. Seeing the band's potential, Eric Krez, a drummer, joined the band. Soon after, Robert DeLeo's brother, Dean DeLeo, decided to play guitar in the band, completing the quartet. The band performed in San Diego under another name before settling on Stone Temple Pilots in 1990.

Core

Stone Temple Pilots built a fan base in San Diego bars in order to steer clear of the Los Angeles corporate music scene and build up their technique and following in the clubs. In 1992, Stone Temple Pilots signed with Atlantic Records. Their first album, *Core,* was released in September of same year. Although the album contained such diverse and popular songs as "Sex Type Thing," "Plush," and "Creep," critics condemned Stone Temple Pilots as rip-off artists whose greatest ability lay in copying other grunge bands such as Pearl Jam, Alice In Chains, and Soundgarden.

This linkage is understandable, as Stone Temple Pilots do sound like their grunge contemporaries, even listing the same 1970's punk influences as the bands to which they are constantly compared. But it would be impossible for Stone Temple Pilots to have stolen from any contemporary band, as they were playing San Diego, not Seattle, and the band pre-dates any releases by the bands with whom they are constantly compared. The similarities between Stone Temple Pilots and other grunge band were caused more by sharing common influences than by copying one another.

In spite of the critics, Stone Temple Pilots continued to gain fans. Bringing their music to the people, they toured for four weeks opening for **Rage Against the Machine** (see entry), then played a forty-date tour supporting heavy metal band **Megadeth** (see entry).

1993 brought continued success on the road, with the band headlining a two-and-a-half-month U.S. tour. Playing live shows allowed the band to display both a playful and socially conscious side. Two sold-out shows in New York's Roseland Ballroom featured Stone Temple Pilots in good-humored full Kiss make-up (causing at least one critic who missed the point to dismiss the band as glam-rockers), in honor of their childhood heroes. While the song "Sex Type Thing" was about date rape, Stone Temple Pilots offered proof that the band's activism went beyond the voicing of opinions straight into action, by performing at benefits for pro-choice organizations.

Fans vs. critics, or dubious honor bestowed

The loyalty of the band's fans and the animosity of its critics came to a head in January 1994 when the band was simultaneously voted Best New Band by *Rolling Stone's* readers and Worst New Band by the magazine's music critics. The tie was broken the next month, when Stone Temple Pilots won Favorite Pop/Rock New Artist and Heavy Metal/Hard Rock New Artist at the American Music awards. On March 1, at the Grammy Award ceremonies, *Plush* won

Scott Weiland in performance

weeks of recording session work had to be scrapped in February, and in May Weiland was arrested for possession of heroin and cocaine in Pasadena, California, when police found the illegal drugs in his wallet. Facing up to three years in prison, Weiland pled not guilty, and a trial date was set the next year.

Following Weiland's arrest, the Pilots separated. Weiland formed a temporary side unit called the Magnificent Bastards, which contributed a song to the movie soundtrack of *Tank Girl* and a cover song to a John Lennon tribute album. By October 1994, though, the band regrouped with Weiland to begin recording its third album.

the band its first Grammy Award for Best Hard Rock Performance with Vocal.

Purple

In the spring of 1994 Stone Temple Pilots returned to the studio to work on their second album, *Purple.* Completed in less than a month, *Purple* debuted at number one in the United States upon its release in June. The radio-friendly "Interstate Love Song" quickly became a hard rock classic, spending a record-setting fifteen weeks atop the album rock tracks chart. By October, just four months after its release, *Purple* had sold three million copies. Stone Temple Pilots had achieved across-the-boards popularity.

Success and struggle

Although the band's success continued into 1995, it would not be a good year for the Stone Temple Pilots. Two

Tiny Music

The Stone Temple Pilots released their third album, *Tiny Music: Songs from the Vatican Gift Shop,* in April 1996. Fans again showed their support of the band when the album debuted at number four on the U.S. charts. Although the album contains songs done in different styles, the critics continued to carp. David Browne of *Entertainment Weekly* claimed, "None of it ... has a distinct personality." On a more positive note, *Rolling Stone* was surprised at "the clattering, upbeat character of the music" given Weiland's much-publicized run-ins with drugs and the law.

However, Weiland's drug addiction again became a serious obstacle to the band's success. The band was unable to launch a tour to promote the album and even had to cancel previously announced dates. Following the release of *Tiny Music,* the band issued a statement saying that Weiland "has become unable to rehearse or appear for these shows due to his dependency on drugs. He is currently under a doctor's care in a medical facility."

Weiland's entry into a drug rehabilitation program was not voluntary. In April 1996 he was ordered by a Pasadena judge to spend up to six months under round-the-clock medical supervision. After Weiland completed five months in a drug treatment program, the charges of cocaine and heroin possession were dropped in October 1996. Unfortunately, Weiland's 1996 stay in a rehabilitation center proved useless. In January 1997 he checked himself into another drug treatment center. Once again, a tour was cancelled.

Despite their fans' loyalty, the band's patience with Weiland came to an apparent end. *Guitar Magazine* reported in May 1997 that the Stone Temple Pilots will honor their five-album recording contract, but they expect the next album to be recorded without Weiland, with a new sound and a new name.

Selected Awards

"Plush," MTV Video Music Award for Best New Artist, 1993.

Billboard Music Award for: 1) Top Modern Rock Act of the Year, and 2) Top Rock Track for "Plush," 1993.

Voted Best New Band in the Reader's Pick, *Rolling Stone's* 1994 Music Awards, January 1994.

Voted Worst New Band by the Music Critics, *Rolling Stone's* 1994 Music Awards, January 1994.

American Music Awards for 1) Favorite Pop/Rock New Artist, and 2) Heavy Metal/Hard Rock New Artist, 1994.

"Plush," Grammy Award for Best Hard Rock Performance with Vocal, 1994.

Selected Discography

Core (Atlantic), 1992.

Purple (Atlantic), 1994.

Tiny Music: Songs From The Vatican Gift Shop (Atlantic), 1996.

Further Reading

Culley, Erin, "Breaking Silence: Scott Weiland of Stone Temple Pilots Opens Up and Gets Busy," *Rolling Stone,* June 15, 1995, p. 21.

"Downed Pilot: Drug Problems Ground Rocker Scott Weiland," *People Weekly,* May 13, 1996, p. 101.

Fricke, David, "Stop Beaking Down," *Rolling Stone,* February 6, 1997, p. 28.

Fricke, David, "Tiny Music: Songs from the Vatican Gift Shop," *Rolling Stone,* December 26, 1996, p. 186.

Contact Information

Atlantic Records
75 Rockefeller Plaza
New York, NY, 10019

Web Sites

http://www.stonetemplepilots.com

http://www.fyi.net/~asciiman/stp/index.html

http://www.mlode.com/~guzzetta/stp/stp.html

SUBLIME

American alternative pop/rock band

Formed in Long Beach, California, in 1988; ended 1996

"What I really want to say is there's just one way back, and I'll make it, but my soul will have to wait." —from "Santeria."

It started with a riot and ended with a death. In between those two bookends, Sublime energized the California music scene, invented a new blend of punk/ska/reggae, and released three crucial records.

The riot was set off by Sublime's first-ever show, back in 1988, in their hometown of Long Beach, California. The show took place a couple of weeks after singer Brad Nowell, drummer Bud Gaugh, and bassist Eric Wilson decided to stop talking about how cool it would be to have a band and actually formed one.

It's no surprise the crowd went wild, because the band was creating a musical style totally new and totally cool. Around the beach towns of Southern California, Sublime quickly became the hottest band around.

At first Sublime's detractors dismissed them as a below-average, good-time punk band, the kind of group you'd want playing at your birthday party, but not one you'd pay to see. Raucous and ramshackle they may well have been, but that wasn't the point. Their sense of fun, manic music, and genre-crashing style was the draw for the fans that followed them everywhere.

40 oz. to freedom

As no label was willing to sign them, Sublime formed their own label, Skunk Records, in 1992, and released their first album, *40 oz. to Freedom.* "Hurtling hardcore punk passages are just the punctuation, not the entire grammar, of a band that also took significant cues from the reggae of Bob Marley," wrote the *Los Angeles Times.* What that reviewer was trying to say was that Sublime was more than just your typical melodic punk band. Not only did they mix reggae and rocksteady into their music, they also crossed their sound with hip-hop. It was brilliant. And just to further muddy the waters, not only did *40 oz. to Freedom* include a cover of a Grateful Dead song, but one of an old Bad Religion song as well. Even more surprising, the whole album was made for less than $1000.

Robbin' the hood

Their next record, 1994's *Robbin' the Hood,* was virtually a bedroom recording. Working on a four track (most albums are recorded onto twenty-four tracks, and sometimes even forty-eight or seventy-two tracks) mostly in living rooms and squats, this record came closest to capturing Sublime's chaotic live shows. Within the album, the band jumps from machine gun delivered raps to hardcore punk, from reggae to rock,

and everything in between. *Robbin' the Hood* was much more experimental and daring than *40 oz. to Freedom.* Sublime mixed in dialogue from movies, played with electronic effects, and blended different styles of music together in mind-shattering ways.

This time around they did a reggae cover of Peter Tosh's classic "Steppin' Razor." "I'm like a steppin' razor, you better watch my sides, I'm dangerous," Brad Nowell sang. And indeed Sublime was. They were totally reinventing punk, pulling it back to its original roots. Along the way, they reminded listeners that although punk could and should be hard and fast, it was also fun, even though the songs often had important things to say.

But Old School Punk bands were also very open to other kinds of music; the Clash was one of several bands that had done reggae covers or utilized reggae rhythms. And Sublime were determined to retie the knot between punk and reggae, while reaching out to new influences like hip-hop and electronics as well. On songs like "Saw Red," with **No Doubt**'s (see entry) Gwen Stefani on guest vocals, they managed to twist rock, reggae, punk, and dub into one great skein of sound.

Get Ready

In 1995, Sublime played the Warp tour, their biggest shows yet, and were also invited to play Board Aid III, which took place outside of Los Angeles. By then, Sublime was more than ready for the big time, and they signed to MCA.

Ska: A Brief History

In the 1950s and early 1960s reggae and ska developed when Jamaican musicians began to copy popular American songs, with an island twist. They had an energetic and powerful sound of their own, which many brought with them to Britain, where they sought better jobs. Britain developed an early underground following of Jamaican rhythms and instrumentation. Then, in 1964, a young woman named Millie Small had an international hit with "My Boy Lollipop," now a classic. In Britain a whole generation of kids became hooked on ska. This era of ska is often referred to as Blue Beat, after the famous ska label of the same name.

Ska was evolving, first into rocksteady, then into reggae. Rocksteady was an early form of reggae that downplayed the ska-style horns and emphasized a booming bass, solo vocals, and a more assertive guitar rhythm. Early reggae hits began reaching American audiences in 1969, and by the early 1970s, the great reggae artists like Bob Marley and Peter Tosh, both of whom started in the ska scene, began reaching wider audiences. By the end of the 1960s, ska didn't really exist anymore. People preferred the slower, more assertive rhythms of reggae. Ska was brash, fast, and punchy and didn't really fit the big, overblown rock sound so popular in the 1970s.

By the end of the 1970s the punk era was underway, with its own short, brash, fast, and punchy songs. Ska and punk combined well, and new bands formed in this union. Their bands were later called Two-Tone, because one of the groups, The Specials, started their own label called 2-Tone, and most of the new ska bands were signed on the label. The label called itself 2-Tone because most of the bands had both black and white members. The label's logo was black and white as well, and a black and white checkerboard often appeared on album sleeves. The checkerboard became an emblem for ska.

Four of the 2-Tone bands—The Specials, The Selecter, English Beat, and Madness—went on to have many British hits. Although each had their own sound, the groups all shared some things in common. They all had horn sections, a keyboardist, and at least two singers. Each of the new bands had their own style. Madness were from London (not from North England, like the rest), the members were all white, and they had a wacky sense of humor. The English Beat were the truest of the new British groups to original ska, which they blended with 1960s pop style. The Selecter, meanwhile, featured a female and a male vocalist, and were more rock-based than the other bands. At the same time, they included some ska covers in their set, and sometimes they borrowed from old ska songs. The Specials also borrowed or covered old hits. Their music was the darkest of all the groups. All the Two Tone bands wrote about politics and social problems, but the Specials were the hardest hitting.

The ska audience was growing, but in Britain, many ska shows were ruined by fights among the crowds. There were also internal problems at the 2-Tone label. By

1982, almost all the bands had broken up or changed so much in sound they couldn't be called ska.

A few years later, a ska revival began in the United States, led by the British bands Bad Manners, General Public, and the Special Beat. By then, American ska groups were popping up, including hard-working, ever-touring bands like New York City's The Toasters and Boston's Bim Skala Bim. Ska scenes were springing up in big cities and college towns throughout the nation. The groups had no chance of being signed by a major label, but they kept ska's flame alight in the musical underground. Through the rest of the 1980s, ska quietly picked up steam. Unfortunately no one outside the scene itself seemed to notice.

In 1985 Moon Records was founded, initially to release The Toasters' albums, but as the decade progressed, so did Moon's catalogue. Over the coming decade they signed scores of bands and distributed many more. They were the only ska label in the United States.

As the 1980s came to a close, new bands, fanzines, and radio shows popped up. And just as had happened in Britain, ska changed again as it was blended with American influences. Operation Ivy (see entry on **Rancid**), for example, didn't have horns, but in their two years of existence, the band had a powerful impact. They had all the right ingredients: loads of energy, a sense of humor, catchy songs, and hardcore attitude. When they broke up, the Mighty Mighty Bosstones stepped in with their ska-core combination of hardcore lyrics and ska-based music.

Other bands in the mainstream have continued to bring ska to wider audiences. **The Offspring's** (see entry) Smash album sported a ska song. Rancid's ...And Out Come the Wolves had three. NOFX had been including ska songs on their albums and live sets for years. The 1990s band **No Doubt** (see entry) were ska veterans, having formed back in the 1980s. But they shed most of their ska sound by the time they made it big. Sublime's music had irresistable reggae and ska rhythms.

With grunge music giving way in the late 1990s, the sound of horns and upbeat rhythms are once again making the airwaves dance. Ska's influence on pop music today is apparent whenever we listen to the radio.

Perhaps that's why their final album, *Sublime*, sounds a bit muted in comparison to their more anarchic earlier records. But it was very successful. "Sublime offers up a sound that is fresh and potent," *Time* said.

Certainly there weren't as many jokes as the past. Sublime were great practical jokesters with their music. Take a song like "I Don't Care Too Much for Reggae Dub," which in reality is a perfect reggae dub song. Then there was the final track on *40 oz to Freedom*. Over a perfect rocksteady beat and melody, Nowell not only thanked everyone he knew (and some people he didn't), but also included personal messages to friends, with explanations on the side for the listeners.

In contrast, *Sublime's* songs were filled with sadness, violence, and apologies. From a riot in Miami, to rape, to child abuse, the album drowned in depression. Nowell had a few solutions; falling in love, getting drunk, and getting high. In the end, none would work for him.

By the time Sublime had signed to MCA, ska was finally gaining attention in the national magazines, and Sublime with it. Suddenly the trio were being touted as a possibility for the next big breakthrough band. Their new album could have made them stars, unfortunately it was already too late.

What happened

Early on May 25, 1996, Nowell tried to convince Wilson to take a walk on the beach, near Sublime's San Francisco hotel room. "It's a beautiful day out there," Nowell begged. The bassist just pretended to be asleep. A few hours later, Gaugh walked into Nowell's room and found the singer dead of a heroin overdose. He left behind an eleven-month-old son and his bride of one week, Troy. Sublime died with him.

Yet their music lived on, and three months later the hit album *Sublime* was released.

Nowell wrote in the song, "Santeria," "What I really want to say is there's just one way back, and I'll make it, but my soul will have to wait."

Selected Discography

40 oz. to Freedom (Skunk Records), 1992.

Robbin' the Hood (Skunk Records), 1994.

Sublime (MCA), 1996.

Further Reading

Farley, Christopher John, "When the Music's Over," *Time*, August 12, 1996, p. 62.

Hendrickson, Matt, "Drugs Claim Sublime's Singer," *Rolling Stone*, July 11, 1996, p20.

Higgins, Jamie, "Sublime," *Mean Street*, May 1994.

Contact Information

MCA Records
100 Universal City Plaza
Universal City, CA 91608

Web Site

http://www.hallucinet.com/sublime/

Urge Overkill

American alternative pop/rock band

Formed in Evanston, Illinois, in 1986

We all wish show business was a bit more suave. It's just too tacky these days. I don't think it has the cool element it once had," said Urge Overkill drummer Blackie Onassis (aka John Rowan, Blackie O) in *Pulse!*. To counteract the lack of cool in show business, Urge Overkill has taken it upon themselves to adopy a high level of suave. To do this, the band unashamedly focuses on their image. They drive fancy cars, wear fancy clothes, and make sure they look good on record covers. "Man, I'd always stare at album covers and look at what they were wearing, how they stood," said Onassis in *Alternative Press*. *Guitar World* called them the "most dapper band in the world."

Besides being known as the most suave band around, Urge Overkill has become most famous for a song they did not write. Quentin Tarantino picked their cover of the Neil Diamond song "Girl, You'll Be a Woman Soon," for the soundtrack of his hit film *Pulp Fiction*. The record was a hit and propelled Urge Overkill into the spotlight. The success of the cover has made the band surer about their routine of hitting the studio first, then figuring

"It's showbiz."—Nash Kato, Urge Overkill singer and guitarist

out the songs. "'Girl, You'll Be a Woman Soon' was recorded and mixed in about an hour—like LensCrafters," said singer/guitarist Nash Kato (aka Nathan Katruud) in *Guitar World*.

Early urge

Growing up in Minneapolis, Minnesota, Kato always liked music and pop culture. "When I was a kid, I wanted to live in the Monkees' house," he said in *Guitar World*. As the next best thing, he took some guitar lessons from "some hippie down the street."

In the early 1980s, Kato moved to the Chicago area to go to school at Northwestern University and met Ed Roeser, also from Minnesota. The two formed Urge Overkill, naming it for lyrics in a Parliament song. They picked Blackie Onassis, one of their fans, as their third member. The band went for style and wore things like embossed dinner jackets and gold necklaces. "When we started doing this, we were really reacting to Chicago's prevailing hardcore aesthetic," said Roeser in *Guitar World*.

The indie years

Urge Overkill put out several records on the independent Chicago label Touch & Go—*Jesus Urge Superstar, Americruiser* and *The Supersonic Storybook*—and started racking up critical acclaim. *Detour* called the Urge sound of these years "guitar-driven albums sauteed with screechy, sometimes off-key vocals." Said *Spin* about *Americruiser*: "The band has become a powerful road machine, spewing out boogie riffs and guttural bluesman grunts from the exhaust pipe."

The big time—sort of

In 1993 Urge Overkill put out their first major label release *Saturation* on Geffen Records. They hired hitmaking production team the Butcher Brothers (Kris Kross, Cypress Hill) to give it a big, commercial sound. "Toothsome, witty pop songcraft wedded to atom-smashing guitar world," said *Musician*, calling the record "almost absurdly terrific."

Still, the band didn't get widespread attention until their cover of "Girl, You'll Be A Woman Soon" in *Pulp Fiction*. Seeing what they considered to be a rough version of "Girl" become popular encouraged them to return to their old, less polished, one-take approach. "[On 'Girl']) my pitch is way off and I kept screwing up this acoustic guitar part that's on the original. People always point that out: 'I love that guitar that comes in at the end,'" said Kato in *Guitar World*.

When Urge Overkill released *Exit The Dragon* in 1995, *Entertainment Weekly* praised its "effortless hooks and gear-grinder guitars," adding that on the record, the band members "completely drop any alternative rock pretenses and become what they've always aspired to be—successors to Grand Funk, the Guess Who, and other wonderfully cheese-ball AM-radio classic rock bands."

New label and what next?

Exit The Dragon wasn't the huge success that the band has hoped for and in 1996, they left Geffen and signed with

Sony 550, another major label. They have tentative plans for a new record and are putting songs through the rigorous Urge filtering process. "You have to go home at night and ask yourself, does this rock?" explained Roeser in *Alternative Press*. Added Kato: "If it doesn't rock, it doesn't make the grade."

Selected Discography

Exit the Dragon, (Geffen), 1995.

Saturation, (Geffen), 1993.

Supersonic Storybook, (Touch & Go), 1991.

Americruiser, (Touch & Go), 1990.

Jesus Urge Superstar, (Touch & Go), 1989.

Strange, I, (Ruthless), 1986.

Further Reading

Beaujour, Tom, "The House That Urge Built," *Guitar World,* September, 1995, p. 82

Elliott, Cyndi, "Urge Overkill," *Alternative Press,* July 1995, p. 64

Greer, Jim, "Urge Overkill," *Spin,* June 1995, p. 78

Mundy, Chris, "Urge Overkill: Exit the Dragon," *Rolling Stone,* September 7, 1995, p. 69

Rubiner, Michael, "Urge Overkill Indoors," *Rolling Stone,* August 11, 1994, p. 22

Contact Information

Sony 550 Music
2100 Colorado Ave.
Santa Monica, CA 90404

Fan club:

U.R.G.E. Secret Society Internationale
P.O. Box 354
Kulpsville, PA 19443

Web Site

http://www.fanbase.com/urgeoverkill/

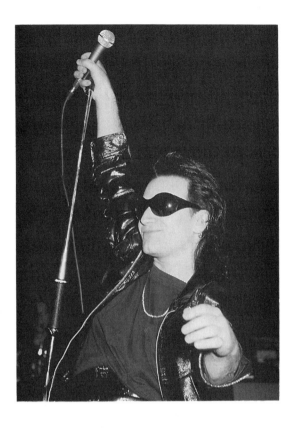

U2

Irish alternative pop/rock band

Formed in Dublin, Ireland, in 1976

"Musicians, painters, whatever, they have no choice but to describe where they live."

—Bono, lead singer and songwriter

Rising from the remains of the post-punk era and starting somewhere this side of the big arena sound of the Who, U2 has led a generation of searchers over the past two decades, remarkably maintaining their position at the top of the ever-changing pop music scene. U2 has always felt that there was something to discover, that a journey was underway.

Starting out

U2 started out as a schoolboy band in Dublin, Ireland, in 1976. Singer Bono (Paul Hewson), guitarist The Edge (Dave Evans), and bassist Adam Clayton responded to a note tacked on the bulletin board at Mount Temple High. Drummer Larry Mullen, Jr., was looking to form a band. The four immediately meshed and called themselves Feedback. Their first gigs were playing local pubs doing mainly cover songs. Unhappy with the name Feedback, the four searched for something less defining and came up with U2, which could mean you too, you two, the boat, the plane, or the submarine. The rest, as they say, is rock'n'roll history.

Bono

Far from an overnight sensation, U2 plugged away with talent competitions, recordings, and tours. The band's first recording, U2:3 (CBS Ireland), topped the Irish charts. From there, U2 built a strong home following and regularly played to sold out crowds. With their eyes on the prize, U2 headed for England. Their first British appearance was in 1979 at a London club, where they played before a handful of fans. Undaunted, U2 released "Another Day," and were spotted by a talent scout who signed them to the Island Label.

Political expression

Their first single on Island, "11 o'-clock Tick Tock," failed to make the British charts. They followed with two albums: *Boy* (1980), and *October* (1981). Raw and troubled, full of religious imagery and strong political messages, these albums hit home with Irish youth and were described by VH1 as "youthful explorations in hope." But no one outside of Ireland seemed especially interested. U2's first American tour in 1981 hit the major cities but was limited to smaller venues.

"Sunday, Bloody Sunday," from the album *War* (1983), changed all that. Played for the first time at a concert in Belfast, Northern Ireland, both sides of the Atlantic suddenly took notice. Following the release of *War* with a twenty-seven-date tour of the UK, and a two month arena tour of the States, U2 was finally tasting success on the strength of its politically involved songs.

These early albums emphasize, according to *Much Music Online,* "Irish, hu-

Biographical Information:

Paul Hewson "Bono," vocals, born May 10, 1960, Dublin, Ireland.

David Evans "The Edge," guitar, born August 8, 1961, Wales.

Adam Clayton, bass, born March 13, 1960, Chinnor, Oxon.

Larry Mullen Jr., drums, born October 31, 1961, Dublin, Ireland.

man, and global struggles with an apocalyptic edge." Set against the shallowness that seemed standard for the 1980s, where greed was supposed to be good and where synth/pop was music, U2's sound was praised as "fresh, full, honest and exhilarating."

The band of the 1980s

U2 began 1984 with a new world tour, then released *The Unforgettable Fire* in October. Described as softer and more complex, richer in its layers, *The Unforgettable Fire* showed the influence of new producer, Brian Eno. A single from the album, "Pride (In the Name of Love)," was a tribute to the late civil rights leader, Dr. Martin Luther King, Jr.; it became their biggest hit to date. Shows were now routinely sold out. U2 also participated in musical relief efforts such as Band Aid and Live Aid, events that raised money for worthy causes.

In 1985, *Rolling Stone* declared U2 "The Band of the Eighties." Continuing to demonstrate their social and political involvement, the four lads from Dublin

U2, announcing their Pop Mart Tour, 1997, from left to right: The Edge, Larry Mullen, Bono, Adam Clayton

next headlined on Amnesty International's Conspiracy of Hope Tour. Playing with music legends Lou Reed, Joan Baez, and Miles Davis as well as with rockers Brian Adams, Peter Gabriel, and Sting, U2 was hitting rock stardom in full stride.

International fame

In February 1987, U2 began a 110-date world tour, coinciding with the March release of *The Joshua Tree*. Wildly successful, both critically and commercially, it came in at number one on the British charts and went platinum in 48 hours, selling over one million copies. It reached number one in the United States and stayed there for nine weeks. *Time*

featured them on their cover, proclaiming U2 "Rock's Hottest Ticket." Two singles: "I Still Haven't Found What I'm Looking For," and "With or Without You," became number one U.S. hits. U2 couldn't go much higher.

"[I] would hate to think everybody was into U2 for 'deep' and 'meaningful' reasons. We're a noisy rock'n'roll band."

Rolling Stone called *The Joshua Tree*, U2's "defining moment of megastardom," and described the band as "four Dublin boys against the world, about to conquer it." Critics praised U2 as being at their musical best. Some went so far

Parents Aren't Supposed to Like It

as to claim U2 as saviors of rock'n'roll, emphasizing that the band had done it "their way," an important element in the increasingly commercial and compromising world of rock music. Other critics described the album as combining the personal and the political, poetic as well as perceptive.

They're green

U2 regularly supported a variety of causes, from saving the environment to helping the unemployed in Ireland. Though they were identified for their social awareness, Bono told *Time*'s Jay Cocks that he "would hate to think everybody was into U2 for 'deep' and 'meaningful' reasons. We're a noisy rock-'n'roll band." However, U2 as a force in contemporary consciousness was one of the main reasons, according to Christopher Connelly of *Rolling Stone*, that U2 "has become one of the handful of artists in rock (and) history ... that people are eager to identify themselves with."

Something new

U2 was becoming an international rock phenomenon, and they knew it. Ready to try something outside the political awareness arena, they released *Rattle and Hum* in October 1988. A film by the same name coincided with the release of the album. Suddenly, critics who had gushed over *The Joshua Tree* found U2 taking themselves too seriously. Described as simple, loud and brash, Jon Pareles in the *New York Times* called it "A dead end," and an "awkward emulation of American blues and soul."

Nevertheless, it was number one in several countries.

On December 31, 1990, U2 did a live New Year's Eve broadcast from Dublin, Ireland. Following the show, Bono told much of Europe that the band would "go away and dream it all up again ..." True to their word, U2 released *Achtung Baby* in November 1991. Described as dark, trashy, open, and honest, the album preserved U2's image as a cutting-edge band. As Island Records executive, Hooman Majd explained on *Much Music Online,* U2 has the ability to "look around at what's going on" and "be affected and influenced by exciting new things." *Achtung Baby* was hugely successful as U2 shifted to new themes concerning love and relationships. Also, the band was one of the first big acts to request that distribution for *Achtung Baby* be in environmentally friendly packaging.

Technology baby

U2 began their grandly theatrical Zoo TV Tour in February 1992. Using satellite dishes, huge multimedia images, and strange stage characters, the sold-out tour hit nearly every arena and stadium in the United States and Europe. During the first twelve months of the tour, U2 met presidential candidate, Bill Clinton, played New York's Yankee Stadium (only Billy Joel had played there previously), and ordered 10,000 pizzas at the Palace of Auburn Hills in Michigan. (About a 100 were actually delivered an hour later.)

The finale of each show on the Zoo TV Tour featured Bono placing phone calls from the stage, dressed in a gold suit, painted white face and devil's horns, and calling himself "Mr. Macphisto, the Last Rock Star." *VH1 Online* reported: "The flashy multimedia circus was a sharp contrast to the simplicity of previous tours. Nevertheless, fans flocked to the shows." Hugely successful, the first year of the tour brought in $67 million and reached nearly five million people.

U2 recorded *Zooropa* and released it in July 1993. Characterized as U2's most chaotic and scattered effort, it entered the British charts at number one. In yet another departure from their previous works, *Zooropa* features the techno-rap "Numb" and country music legend Johnny Cash singing "The Wanderer."

PopMart kitsch

It took U2 nine months to record *Pop*, released in March 1997. Described by Bono to Jon Pareles of *New York Times* as "a mixed-up kind of a record," the album received mostly positive critical reviews. Barney Hoskyns in *Rolling Stone* wrote, "What we can say immediately is that *Pop* sounds absolutely magnificent." Karen Schoemer, in *Newsweek,* declared that while the "new" U2 is not nearly as new as they would have us believe, the material, like most U2 material has "has been working pretty well for years." Hoskyns review essentially agreed; what you find in *Pop*, he said, "is a whole arsenal of sound effects, tape manipulations, distortions and treatments designed to mask the fact that U2 are essentially a four-piece male rock band."

U2 kicked off their extravagant PopMart world tour in Las Vegas, Nevada, on April 25, 1997. And in keeping with the "kitsch-rich ... cheesing of America" approach, as Anna Holmes described it in *Entertainment Weekly,* U2 held a press conference to announce the tour in a Manhattan KMart store.

Most critics agree that U2 is as effective a band today as they were twenty years ago. Hoskyns goes on to say that *Pop* "may turn out to be a make or break album for U2. Alone among the giants of the `80s, they have a chance to carry their musical vision into the 21st century while still selling a ton of records."

Staying power

Remarkably, no member has ever left U2, they've never changed record labels, and they remain with their original manager, Paul McGuinness. They work together in a democratic consensus. Each member, drawing on his own unique Irish roots, contributes. Jon Pareles reported in the *New York Times:* "For a band like U2, making an album is essentially a slow-motion improvisation in which ideas are seized and refined while the tapes roll."

As their many albums show, U2 is a band always intent on artistic renewal. Says Bono, near the end of John Waters' book, *Race of Angels:* "Part of what we do, part of what any artist does, is illusion: you suggest rather than spell out. I think it's very important to keep that flirtatousness, to write trashy pop songs set in these worlds. So we say things, and then dance back from them and run like hell."

Parents Aren't Supposed to Like It

Selected Awards

Band Of The 80's, *Rolling Stone,* 1985.

MTV Video Music Awards, Viewers Choice, "With or Without You," 1987.

BRIT Awards, Best International Group, 1988, 1989, 1990.

Grammy Awards, Album of the Year, and Best Rock Performance by a Duo or Group, *The Joshua Tree,* 1988.

Grammy Awards, Best Rock Performance by a Duo or Group with Vocal, "Desire," and Best Performance Music Video, "Where the Streets Have No Name," 1989.

MTV Video Music Award, Best Video From Film, "When Loves Comes to Town," (U2 and BB King shared the award), 1989.

MTV Video Music Awards, Best Group Video and Best Special Effects, "Even Better Than the Real Thing," 1992.

Billboard Music Awards, Top Album Rock Tracks Artists, Top Album Rock Tracks, Top Modern Rock Tracks Artists, Top Modern Rock Tracks, *Achtung Baby,* 1992.

BRIT Awards, Best Live Act, 1993.

Grammy Award, Best Rock Performance by a Duo Or Group with a Vocal, *Achtung Baby,* 1993.

Juno Awards, International Entertainer of the Year, 1993.

Grammy Award, Best Alternative Music Album, *Zooropa,* 1994.

Grammy Award, Best Music Video, Longform, "Zoo TV—Live from Sidney," directed by David Mallet, 1995.

Selected Discography

Boy (Island), 1980.

October (Island), 1981.

War (Island), 1983.

The Unforgettable Fire (Island), 1984.

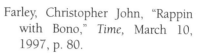

The Joshua Tree (Island), 1987.

Rattle and Hum (Island), 1988.

Achtung Baby (Island), 1991.

Zooropa (Island), 1993.

Pop (Island), 1997.

Further Reading

Periodicals

Farley, Christopher John, "Rappin with Bono," *Time,* March 10, 1997, p. 80.

Flick, Larry, "U2 Gets Down with Dance-Land In 'Discotheque,'" *Billboard,* January 1, 1997, p. 34.

Fricke, David, "Scratching the Surface," *Rolling Stone,* March, 6, 1997, p. 21.

Holmes, Anna, "Arch Deluxe," *Entertainment Weekly,* March 28, 1997, p. 12.

Hoskyns, Barney, "Disco Inferno," *Rolling Stone,* March 20, 1997, p. 81.

Shoemer, Karen, "Pop," *Newsweek,* March 10, 1997, p. 68.

Books:

Stokes, Niall, *Into the Heart: The Stories Behind Every U2 Song,* Thundermouth Press, 1996.

Waters, John, *Race of Angels: The Genesis of U2,* Fourth Estate Limited, 1994.

Contact Information

Island Records
825 Eighth Ave.
New York, NY 10019

Web Sites

http://www.island.co.uk/

http://www.med.virginia.edu

http://alt.fan.u2

http://alt.music.u2

veruca salt

American alternative pop/rock band

Formed in Chicago, Illinois, in 1992

"I love coed rock. I think it's part of the solution."—Veruca Salt's Louise Post in *Rolling Stone.*

In 1995, Veruca Salt was the band that small bands and indie labels everywhere were using as a source of inspiration. The band released a catchy single, "Seether," on the small Chicago label Minty Fresh and, by the next month, were the subject of a major label bidding war. Geffen won the war and Veruca Salt and Minty Fresh got lots of money. Just a couple months later "Seether" was in MTV's Buzz Bin and the band's debut *American Thighs* was going up the charts. Veruca Salt had hit the indie jackpot.

The band's rise was fast and the fallout from the rise was fast, too. Veruca Salt's sudden popularity created some problems, especially from rival bands and people who thought any kind of mass popularity was completely uncool. "A backlash of sorts has begun among insiders—before most people have even heard of the group," reported *Rolling Stone* when *American Thighs* first came out. But even though Veruca lost some "indie cred" that year, they were still the best Cinderella story of the 1995 music world.

From left, clockwise: Stacy Jones, Steve Lack, Louise Post, Nina Gordon

Veruca Salt and the Chocolate Factory

Guitarist and singer Nina Gordon first picked up a guitar when she was seven and learned a few chords, but she gave it up out of boredom. She didn't pick it up again until 1991 when she was lonely and depressed, living in Chicago and felt the impulse to write songs. Gordon learned the chords from different songs over the phone from her brother. "I still really don't even know the names of the chords I play—I know them as 'the third chord in the chorus of 'Photograph' by Def Leppard or the first chord in 'We Got the Beat,'" she said in a press release for *American Thighs*.

Meanwhile, guitarist and singer Louise Post, who had grown up in St. Louis, Missouri, came to Chicago to start a band. She and Gordon were introduced at a New Year's Eve party by a friend who thought they would hit it off. They did. A year and a half later, they enlisted Steve Lack on bass and Gordon's older brother Jim Shapiro on drums. They named themselves after the greedy girl who gets thrown down the garbage chute in "Charlie & the Chocolate Factory."

Every member of Veruca Salt has divorced parents. "Much of their mordantly cynical sense of humor, anger, insecurity and even their love for 70's pop was forged when their families fell apart," analyzed *Rolling Stone*.

The whirlwind rise

Veruca Salt recorded *American Thighs* with producer Brad Wood, the man who also did **Liz Phair's** (see entry) *Exile in Guyville*. The record immediately started making waves, based almost entirely on the single "Seether." Gordon wrote the song after discovering an angry side of herself. "I was talking to someone and I felt myself seething," she said in *Rolling Stone*. "I had this vision of scraping this person's face on the sidewalk. I was so shocked I wanted to do that." In a review for the record, *Rolling Stone* said the band has "come up with some melodies that lodge themselves in your brain and resonate." *Time* called the music "both disturbingly dysfunctional and thoroughly enjoyable," saying "the band's lyrics are downbeat, fuzzy and weird while the tunes are upbeat and full of melodic guitar bravado."

Follow-up

After a 1996 EP that didn't do much, Veruca Salt returned in 1997 with a new full-length record *Eight Arms to Hold You*. Reviews have been mixed. *Rolling Stone Online* called it "an uninspired offering." But the people over at *Details* thought the record was "the best music they've ever made—twitchy, powerful ... sexy."

Selected Awards

Gold status for *American Thighs*.

Selected Discography

Eight Arms to Hold You, (Outpost) 1997.

Blow It Out Your A—, It's Veruca Salt EP (DGC), 1996.

American Thighs (Minty Fresh/DGC), 1994.

Further Reading

Ahearn, Kim, "Veruca Salt: American Thighs," *Rolling Stone,* November 3, 1994, p. 100.

Farley, Christopher John, "Veruca Salt: American Thighs," *Time,* October 24, 1994.

Fine, Jason, "Veruca Salt Flex Newfound Muscle on 'Eight Arms,'" *Rolling Stone,* January 23, 1997.

Raphael, Amy, *GRRRLS: Viva Rock Divas,* St. Martin's Griffin, 1996. (Contains a chapter on Nina Gordon and Louise Post.)

Weisel, Al, "Saline Solution," *Rolling Stone,* January 26, 1995, p. 19.

Contact Information

Outpost Records
8932 Keith Ave.
Los Angeles, CA 90069

Web Site

http://www.outpostrec.com/verucasalt/

Wallflowers

American alternative pop/rock band
Formed in 1990 in Los Angeles, California

Having a famous father probably has helped Jakob Dylan with his music career, but only to a certain extent. The rest has been up to him. For example, in 1992 it looked like Jakob Dylan and his band the Wallflowers were finished. The band had put out their self-titled debut and ... nothing. The record was a stiff. The Wallflowers left their label. "In that situation, I think my dad worked against me," said Dylan, the son of 1960s musician Bob Dylan, in *People*. "It looks like I was dropped by the label and I was Bob's son. People thought, 'Gee, he must be bad.'"

After three years of trying to get attention for his band, Dylan finally came back with a new band, a new record label and a new record, *Bringing Down the Horse*. Now with several hit singles like "6th Avenue Heartache," "One Headlight," and "The Difference," Dylan and the Wallflowers are suddenly hot.

"Essentially, we're doing the same thing we were doing three years ago, when I played 'Sixth Avenue Heartache' every night, but nobody would come down to see us. It's kind of absurd, actually," Dylan told the *New York Times*.

"The truth is, yeah, it was weird. Relatively interesting, but weird. I could write a book. But I'm not going to." —Jakob Dylan on his childhood

Jakob Dylan

Son of a Bob

Jakob grew up in Los Angeles, the youngest of five children. His father, Bob Dylan, and his mother Sara Lowndes Dylan, a model, went through a harsh divorce when he was six. His mother got custody. Dylan doesn't like to talk about his father or what it's like to be Bob Dylan's son. "It's certainly an unsurmountable expectation for anybody to have to deal with, so I don't feel that there's any reason that I should pay attention to it," he said to the *New York Times*.

Dylan grew up listening to his older brothers' records and became a fan of bands like the Clash. At thirteen, he took up the guitar. At eighteen, he started writing songs, but didn't want to become a songwriter because he didn't want to deal with all the comparisons to his father. Instead, he went to art school in New York for a short time, then tried drumming and playing guitar in bands. Finally he just gave in and started writing songs. "It was something I felt compelled to do, so I just started. Everybody lives under shadows. I obviously have one but I don't pretend it's any worse than anyone else's," he said in *Newsweek*.

The germination of the Wallflowers

Dylan put together his band—Barrie Maguire (bass), Rami Jaffee (piano, organ), Peter Yanowitz (drums) and Tobi Miller (guitar). They started playing weekly Tuesday gigs at the "Kibitz Room," a kitschy spot in an old time restaurant/deli in West Hollywood. The gigs weren't an instant success. "We'd beg our friends to come to a show, which is always embarrassing. You look out into the audience and recognize everybody and it's like 'Why didn't I just invite you all over to my living room?'" said Dylan in *Interview*.

The shows got more popular and eventually helped the band land a record deal with Virgin Records. In 1992, they released their first record *The Wallflowers*. But even with a video for "Ashes to Ashes," directed by Dylan's brother Jesse, the record didn't sell well. "We couldn't even get an A&R guy's secretary to come to a gig," remembers Dylan in *Interview*.

"It's sick: You've got the same demo tape, you've got the same show, but suddenly you're completely fascinating to people."

The band's contact at the record company left and the Wallflowers became unhappy with the label. "We didn't feel like anyone was behind the band. They all [said] 'We're in it for the long haul, we're all behind you.' We learned the hard way it wasn't true," said Dylan in *The Salt Lake Tribune*. The band asked to be released from their contract and gained a reputation for being a difficult band.

The lean years

When the band stepped back to regroup, the line-up changed. Dylan and Jaffee stayed, and they added Greg Richling (bass), Michael Ward (guitar), and Mario Calire (drums). It was a discouraging time. "You try not to put a lot of value in the opinions of people in the business, but at the same time, when you're not getting any credit and people aren't interested, it makes you feel like you're not good at what you do. At some points, I wondered whether I wanted to be part of it anymore," said Dylan in the *New York Times*.

They stuck with it though. "For about a year nobody would come down and listen to us. Then one day we were getting telephone calls from people driving Porsches, saying 'You write the deal. It's all yours!' It's sick: You've got the same demo tape, you've got the same show, but suddenly you're completely fascinating to people," said Dylan in *Interview*.

Back in the saddle again

The Wallflowers released *Bringing Down the Horse* on a new label in 1996. Helped by a guest appearance by the Counting Crows' Adam Duritz on "6th Avenue Heartache," the record became a hit. "The single ... typifies all that is good about the Wallflowers," said *Interview*. "It's catchy, honest, simple, familiar, earthy." *Newsweek* called the record "wildly derivative" but "so comfortably, soulfully *right* that you won't care."

About one show, *Rolling Stone* said: "Jakob Dylan is a young man of a certain passion, singing his own words with a shy, fitful intensity that seems, sometimes to take him out and above this big, hot room. It's not the raspy unremarkable voice so much as the delivery that draws them, some strain of the ageless troubadour DNA...."

There have been some comparisons with the elder Dylan, but more about looks and personality than songwriting.

The *New York Times* described the younger Dylan as looking "vaguely like a leaner, handsomer version of his father." *Newsweek* called him *"the 90s Dylan: a young, handsome, sincere, singer-songwriter who's willing to wear his heart on his sleeve and who doesn't act so damn ornery all the time."*

Dylan seems to understand the comparisons and just deals with them by not talking about his father in interviews and ignoring the Bob Dylan fanatics who come to the Wallflowers' shows. "If somebody's not wearing my t-shirt (and) they're wearing somebody else's that looks familiar to me, I've got a good idea why they're there," he said to the *New York Times*. "I'm glad they spent money on the show, but I don't really want to talk to them."

Dylan's achieved enough on his own that no one now thinks he got his career by riding on his father's coattails. "The baggage doesn't disappear," he said in a record company biography. "But you can't create and still think about that kind of thing. You do the best you can."

Selected Awards

Double platinum status for *Bringing Down the Horse.*

Selected Discography

Bringing Down the Horse (Interscope), 1996.

Wallflowers (Virgin), 1992.

Further Reading

Ehrlich, Dimitri, "Jakob Dylan," *Interview,* October, 1996, p. 90.

Evans, Paul, "Wallflowers," *Rolling Stone*, November 26, 1992, p. 74.

Hirshey, Gerri, "Jakob's Ladder," *Rolling Stone*, June 12, 1997, p. 50.

Pond, Steve, "… Another Goes His Own Way," *New York Times,* October 6, 1996. p. 42 (section 2).

Powers, Ann, "The Wallflowers," *Rolling Stone,* January 23, 1997, p. 32.

Schoemer, Karen, "The Kid's All Right," *Newsweek,* September 2, 1996, p. 68.

Contact Information

Interscope Records
10900 Wilshire Blvd., Suite 1230
Los Angeles, CA 90024

Web Site

http://www.interscoperecords.com/lrwallbio.html

Parents Aren't Supposed to Like It

neil young

Influential rock musician

Born November 12, 1945, Toronto, Canada

In over three decades working on the frontlines of rock, Neil Young has acquired more names than he has released new albums—which, for someone who has never been content to simply sit back and wait for his last disc to stop selling, is quite an accomplishment. From the Prophet of Doom of the mid 1970s, to the Prince of the Punks at the end of the decade; from the Techno Savage of the 1980s and onto the Godfather of Grunge in the 1990s, Neil Young has never stood in the same place for long. And when he does, it is only for as long as it takes for the rest of the world to catch up with him.

"I just play what I feel like playing ... and every once in a while I'll wake up and feel like playing something else."

—Neil Young

Early days

The Canadian-born Young is the son of a sports reporter and local television personality. Surviving childhood battles with diabetes, polio, and epilepsy, he moved to Winnipeg with his mother following his parents' divorce, and it was there that he made his first musical efforts, learning the ukulele, then switching to guitar in his early teens. By 1963, he was already a veteran of the local music scene, and in September of that year, his latest band, the folk-rocking Squires, released its first and only single, "The Sultan." Another early Young band, the Mynah Birds, was signed briefly to the Motown label.

In 1965, at a bar in a small Ontario town, Young met Stephen Stills, an American musician who would become one of his most regular collaborators over the next decade. They met again the following year, when Young and fellow Mynah Bird Bruce Palmer bought a hearse, filled it with everything they owned, and drove to California. There, stuck in a Los Angeles traffic jam, Stills spotted the vehicle and recognized the Canadians.

The short life of the Buffalo Springfield

Young, Stills, and Palmer, joined by Richie Furay and Dewey Martin, formed the Buffalo Springfield in 1966. Making politically aware music that was perfectly in keeping with the psychedelic mood of the era, the group was an immediate success and released three albums. But the speed with which they won fame was difficult for the still-youthful musicians. Squabbles and temporary departures rocked the group's entire existence, and in May 1968, Buffalo Springfield disbanded, leaving Young free to record his first solo album.

The loner

Neil Young was released in January 1969, an uncertain collection of songs for which Young himself has little liking. Uncertain about his own voice, he

buried it in the mix. But still, the album introduced his own style of singing and songwriting to a public which had only known him as one of several talents fronting Buffalo Springfield. The album also includes several of Young's best loved songs, such as "The Loner" and "The Old Laughing Lady."

In the years since then, Neil Young has never allowed his audience to guess what he will do next, or even what he will sound like. This was certainly the case with his next album, *Everybody Knows This Is Nowhere,* his first with what would become his regular backing band, Crazy Horse—Billy Talbot (bass), Ralph Molina (drums), and Danny Whitten (guitar). Characterized again by Young's thoughtful songwriting, the album was highlighted by the pair of lengthy guitar workouts that dominate it: "Down By the River" and "Cowgirl in the Sand." Along with the opening "Cinnamon Girl," these songs are still part of Young's live show.

Superstardom and retreat

Young reunited with Stills in a new band, Crosby, Stills, Nash, and Young, in the summer of 1969, and together the act played the Woodstock Festival that August. The following year, their first album was released. *Deja Vu,* like the live *Four Way Street* album which came out a year later, features only a handful of Young songs, although his songs ("Helpless" on the first album, "Ohio" on the second) are considered by many to be the best on the records.

The enormous success CSN&Y won during their short year together was inherited by Young after the quartet disbanded. Both *After the Gold Rush* (1970) and *Harvest* (1972) were enormous sellers, with *Harvest* even giving Young a #1 single, the gentle "Heart of Gold." Young, however, was not too pleased about that. Writing in the liner notes to 1977's *Decade* compilation, he complained, "this song put me in the middle of the road. Travelling there soon became a bore, so I headed for the ditch. A rougher ride, but I saw more interesting people there." His next project, the rough and raw live album, *Time Fades Away,* marked the first steps of this new journey.

Tonight's the night

The success of *Harvest* was further spoiled when Crazy Horse guitarist Whitten died from a drug overdose in August 1972. This tragedy was the inspiration behind *Tonight's the Night,* the album Young planned as the follow-up to *Harvest.* Unfortunately, his record label refused to release it for another two years. "When I handed it in to Warners, they hated it," Young told *Newsweek.* "We played it ten times as loud as they usually play things, and it was awful. It was a story of death and dope. It was about a sleazy, burned-out rock star just about to go, about what fame and crowds do to you. I had to exorcise those feelings. I felt like it was the only chance I had to stay alive."

While he waited for the release of *Tonight's the Night,* Young completed a movie, the sprawling *Journey Through the Past,* and an equally sprawling sound-track album. Vital listening for anybody wanting to learn how Young's mind works, the album includes some great live recordings, together with a twenty-minute-plus version of "Words," one of the loveliest songs on *Harvest.*

He also recorded yet another new album, *On the Beach.* Once again, the record had little in common with the gentle moods of *Harvest.* It took its title from a movie about what might happen after a nuclear war and was loaded with songs like "Vampire Blues" and "Ambulance Blues." But the best song on *On the Beach* was "Revolution Blues," about an army of outlaws who descend upon the superstars living around Hollywood and slaughter them in their sleep. Once again, Young was showing his dislike for fame, yet he was still not totally against it. The year 1974 also saw him rejoin Crosby, Stills & Nash for an unbelievably successful reunion tour. He would later work with Stills alone in 1976, and there would be a third CSN&Y reunion in 1989.

Like a hurricane

Less than six months after *Tonight's the Night* was finally released, Young had another new album ready to go, *Zuma.* No less epic than *On the Beach,* reflected Young's fascination with America's history before, and right after, the white man arrived, a story best told by the lengthy "Cortez the Killer." This song was banned in Spain, where Cortez is as well-loved as is President Lincoln in the United States.

Retaining his love for very long songs with lots of guitar solos, Young's next hit was "Like A Hurricane," a song he had been playing live since 1975, but did not record until 1977's *American Stars 'n Bars*. Once again he was on the edge of massive success, and once again he backed down, following this album with the gentle, country flavored *Comes a Time*. "Folk music can be as authentic as rock-'n'roll," Young said at the time. "It's soul and depth which matter most." Yet he hated the way the album turned out, finally persuading his record label to sell him the entire pressing for $200,000 ($1 per disc), and let him remix it.

It's better to burn out than fade away

Despite such problems, *Comes A Time* became Young's biggest hit since *Harvest,* again prompting hopes that he might follow it up in similar style. Of course he didn't. *Rust Never Sleeps,* in 1979, returned him to a harder rocking sound, with the title track a mass of heavy guitar and cracking vocals. "Hey hey my my, rock'n'roll will never die," Young sang, before dedicating the song to Sex Pistols vocalist Johnny Rotten. Fifteen years later, Nirvana's Kurt Cobain would borrow another line from the song, "it's better to burn out than fade away," for his suicide note. It was a choice that prompted Young, in turn, to write a song for Cobain himself, the title track to Young's 1994 album *Sleeps with Angels*.

Rust Never Sleeps, both the album and the massive tour that followed, did more than return Young to the upper half of the chart. It also established him as one of the few older rock stars who

had not been dissed by the birth of punk rock. Other musicians of Young's age were being described by the punks as "boring old farts." Young, with his latest album, proved that it was the punks who were boring. He was taking bigger risks than they ever would.

He continued to prove this through the 1980s, a decade that confused his fans and really upset his record company. Young signed with Geffen at the beginning of the decade; by its end, the label was threatening to sue him for not delivering any hit albums!

Sample and hold

Yet two of his next three albums count among the best he ever recorded. Exhausted by the massive *Rust* tour, 1980's *Hawks and Doves* was a disappointment. But 1981's *Re.Ac.Tor* was tremendous, one of the noisiest records ever made, and one of Young's most relaxed. Then came *Trans* in 1983, which saw him playing with cutting edge computer technology, and even getting into a bit of dance music. One track, "Sample and Hold," was released as a dance mix. It was all very new, and it is sad that Young's audience, who should have been used to his constant changes by now, seemed to hate this new direction.

Young retaliated by moving away from the future, and losing himself in the past. Forming a new band, the Shocking Pinks, 1983's *Everybody's Rockin'* saw him go back to modern rock's roots in rockabilly music. Then came another country album, *Old Ways,* and by the time Young was invited to play the 1986 Live Aid festival, he was fronting another group, the International Harvesters, and having a hoedown onstage.

An EP recorded with this group was never released; instead, Young returned to a hard rock edge with 1986's *Landing On Water* before reuniting Crazy Horse for the first time since *Re.Ac.Tor* and blasting out *Life*. Neither album was particularly good, but it was some time before the world became aware of why Young had apparently lost his edge.

After being dropped by Geffen and signing with Reprise Records, Young came back to the musical limelight with *This Note's for You* in 1989, a bluesy, big-band album he made with a backing band called the Bluenotes. The title song attacked the use of classic rock tunes in advertisements selling everything from beer to sneakers, and the modern need to win sponsorship contracts with companies like Coca Cola, Budweiser, and McDonalds to finance expensive tours. Young's video for the title song was banned by MTV, but the network eventually relented, and "This Note's For You" ended up being voted best video of the year.

Rocking in the free world

Young and Crazy Horse went back to the world of hard rock with 1989's *Freedom*, an album that mirrored *Rust Never Sleeps* in that it was divided equally by acoustic and electric numbers, and opened and closed with different versions of the same song, the anthem "Rockin' in the Free World."

Freedom and Young's next albums, *Ragged Glory* (which *Rolling Stone* called

Building the bridge

Neil Young's first son, Zeke, with actress Carrie Snodgrass, was born with cerebral palsy. His second child, Ben, also had the condition. In a 1988 Rolling Stone interview, Young explained that Ben was quadriplegic and unable to speak, and described his attempts to develop his son's communication skills through games and computer technology, which in turn helped inspire the Trans album.

"This was hard to deal with," Young admitted, but he and his wife Pegi "have learned to turn it around into a positive thing and to keep on going." When Pegi became involved in setting up a Bay Area school for disabled children called the Bridge School, Young began arranging an annual fundraising benefit, calling in superstars from all corners of the rock world to play along with him.

The Bridge was not Young's only long-running charitable cause. He also heads Farm Aid, a benefit for the small American farmers who are being forced out of work by big business and industry, and again, he has never had a problem filling the annual bill. Some of the biggest stars in rock have given their time to the cause.

"a classic Crazy Horse album"), and the live *Weld/Arc* re-established Young in both the commercial and critical world. With a new generation of rockers, the grunge superstars of **Nirvana** (see entry), **Pearl Jam** (see entry), Sonic Youth and so on, breaking through, Young suddenly found himself acclaimed a major influence by artists who'd barely been born when he first started recording. It was an honor that means more than any of the other awards he has received through his career, because it proves that people were really listening to him. At a time when so much pop music gets thrown away with yesterday's newspapers, Young's music had a passion that not only bridged generations (many of his oldest fans are now into their 50s and beyond), but spanned the years, too.

Young's next move was the release of a follow-up to his hit of twenty years before, *Harvest*, 1992's stripped back *Harvest Moon*. It was a beautiful record; *Rolling Stone* called it "a chronicle of survival, focusing on loss and compromise and the ultimate triumphs of being a married father approaching fifty." Young himself added to this mood with his triumphant appearance on MTV's *Unplugged* later in the year.

In contrast to his earlier 1990s albums, 1994's *Sleeps with Angels*, dominated by the Kurt Cobain-inspired title track, and the following year's *Mirror Ball* collaboration with Seattle Grunge band **Pearl Jam** (see entry), were very weak. But of course Young bounced back in 1996, with *Broken Arrow,* a big wall of guitar that divided critics as much as any of Young's other, more essential, albums: *Re.Ac.Tor* and *Trans* from the 1980s, *On The Beach*, *Tonight's The Night* and *Journey Through The Past* from the 1970s.

Still the greatest

But you can understand their confusion. The closing track, a cover of a song Elvis Presley helped make famous, "Baby What You Want Me To Do," sounds like it was recorded from the back of the room on a Walkman. Yet that is how the best rock'n'roll should sound. As Young himself said, it's not the style of music that matters, it's the soul and the depth. As he moves through his fifth decade, Neil Young has soul and depth to spare.

Selected Awards

Long May You Run certified gold, 1977.

Rust Never Sleeps certified platinum, 1980.

After the Gold Rush certified double platinum, 1986.

Everybody Knows This is Nowhere certified platinum, 1986.

Decade certified platinum, 1986.

Live Rust certified platinum, 1988.

"This Note's for You," Best Video of the Year, MTV Video Music Awards, 1989.

Freedom named 1989 Critics' Choice for Best Album, *Rolling Stone,* 1990.

Harvest Moon, Outstanding Album, Bay Area Music Awards, 1993.

Unplugged certified gold, 1993.

"Philadelphia," Academy Award nomination for Best Song from a Motion Picture, 1994.

Harvest Moon, Album of the Year, Juno Awards, 1994.

Harvest Moon certified quadruple platinum, 1994.

Inducted into the Rock and Roll Hall of Fame, 1995.

Mirror Ball certified gold, 1995.

Selected Discography

Solo and with Crazy Horse (unless otherwise noted)

Everybody Knows This Is Nowhere (Reprise), 1969.

After the Gold Rush (Reprise), 1970.

Harvest (Warner Bros.), 1972.

Journey through the Past (Reprise), 1973.

On the Beach (Reprise), 1974.

Tonight's the Night (Reprise), 1975.

Decade (Reprise), 1977.

Rust Never Sleeps (Reprise), 1979.

Live Rust (Reprise), 1979.

Reactor (Reprise), 1981.

Trans (Geffen), 1982.

Freedom (Reprise), 1989.

Ragged Glory (Reprise), 1990.

Weld/Arc (Reprise), 1991.

Harvest Moon (Reprise), 1992.

Sleeps with Angels (Reprise), 1994.

Mirror Ball (Reprise), 1995, with Pearl Jam.

Broken Arrow (Reprise), 1996

With Buffalo Springfield

Retrospective (Atco), 1969.

With Crosby, Stills, Nash & Young

So Far (Atlantic), 1974.

With the Stills-Young Band

Long May You Run (Reprise), 1976.

Further Reading

Farley, Christopher John, "Mirror Ball," *Time,* July 3, 1995, p. 56.

Goodman, Fred, "MTV Nixes Neil Young's Acerbic 'This Note's for You'," *Rolling Stone,* August 11, 1988, p. 25.

Heatley, Michael, *Neil Young: His Life and Music,* Hamlyn, 1994.

Henke, James, "Back in the Saddle Again," *Rolling Stone,* October 4, 1990, p. 44.

Light, Alan "Forever Young," *Rolling Stone,* January 21, 1993, p. 34.

O'Connor, Rob, "Broken Arrow," *Rolling Stone,* August 8, 1996, p. 58.

Santoro, Gene, "Rockin's in the Free World," *Nation,* March 11, 1991, p. 318.

Contact Information

Record company:

Reprise Records
3300 Warner Blvd.
Burbank, CA 91505-4694

Fan club:

Neil Young Appreciation Society
2A Llynfi St.
Bridgend Mid Glamorgan
CF31 1SY, Wales

Web Sites

http://www.RepriseRec.com/

http://ourworld.compuserve.com/homepage/nyas (homepage of the Neil Young Appreciation Society)

INDEX

Italic type indicates volume numbers;
boldface type indicates featured entries and their page numbers;
(ill.) indicates photographs.

Anderson, Brett 2: 222, 254, 270-272
Anderson, Kevin 2: 419
Anderson, Laurie 3: 656
...And Out Come the Wolves 1: 147
Androgyny 2: 222, 232, 270, 271
Anselmo, Philip 3: 490, 491
Anthrax 2: 395
Antifolk movement 1: 25
Anti-Semitism 2: 363
Appel, Mike 3: 598, 599
Apple, Fiona 3: 613
Araya, Tom 3: 493 (ill.), 494
Arista 3: 456
Arm, Mark 1: 118
Armstrong, Billy Joe 1: 60 (ill.), 61 (ill.), 62-64, 146
Armstrong, Tim 1: 145 (ill.)
Arrested Development 2: 307, **312 (ill.)**, **313**, **314 (ill.)**, **315-316**
Art-rock 1: 123, 165; 3: 654
Arthurs, Paul "Bonehead" 2: 266
Artist Formerly Known As Prince (see Prince)
Asuo, Kewsi 2: 315
Athens, Georgia 1: 4, 154
Atlantic Records 3: 553, 573, 618
The Attractions 2: 243, 245, 246
Australia 1: 160
Autobahn 2: 278, 288
Automatic Dlamini 2: 257
Automatic for the People 1: 157
Avant-garde music 2: 221, 222, 231; 3: 655
Avery, Eric 1: 76
AWOL 2: 292
Azor, Hurby "Luvbug" 2: 411

B

Babes in Toyland 1: 5, **16 (ill.)**, **17-19**
Babes in Toyland: The Making and Selling of a Rock and Roll Band 1: 18
Babyface 2: 277; 3: 503, **506 (ill.)** **507-510**, 517, 536
Bacharach, Burt 2: 220, 245
Backbeat (film) 1: 49
Bad Boy Records 2: 310, 427, 428
Badmotorfinger 1: 175

Bad Radio 1: 116, 117
Baez, Joan 3: 439, 440
Ballard, Glen 3: 613, 640
Ballew, Chris 1: 127
Bambaataa, Afrika 2: 304, 308
Bamonte, Perry 2: 250
The Band 3: 603
Band Aid 1: 191
The Barenaked Ladies 1: **20 (ill.)**, **21-23**
Barnwell, Timothy 2: 313
Barrett, Dickie 1: 5
Barron, Chris 3: 594-596
Bartos, Karl 2: 288
Bayyan, Khalis 2: 345
B-Boy DJs 2: 304, 306
B-Boy label 2: 318
The Beastie Boys 1: 26; 2: 309
The Beatles 2: 220, 221, 237, 239,266, 267, 275; 3: 540, 613
Beauford, Carter 3: 585
Beautiful South 2: **223 (ill.)** **224 (ill.)** **225-226**
Beavis and Butt-head 1:16, 18, 132
Beck 1: 3, **24 (ill.)**, **25-26**, **27 (ill.)**, **28-29**; 3: 550
Bedford-Stuyvesant, New York 2: 387; 3: 631
Bee Gees 2: 276
Behler, Chuck 3: 483
Bell, Frank 2: 250
Bell, Marc 1: 141
Bell, Ricky 3: 517
Bellmark 3: 532
Ben Folds Five 3: 613
Bennett, Tony 2: 244
Bennett, William 1: 79
Benson, Al 3: 502
Benson, Brendan 3: 613
Berlin, Germany 1: 72; 2: 232
Berlin, Steve 3: 580
Berry, Bill 1: 154, 156
Berry, Chuck 2: 244, 275; 3: 539 (ill.), 540, 541
Bettie Serveert 1: **30 (ill.)**, **31-32**
Beverly Hills 90210 1: 58
B52s 2: 292
Big Bank Hank (Henry Jackson) 2: 306
Big Daddy Kane 2: 307
Big Head Todd and the Monsters 3: 550
Biggie Smalls (see The Notorious B.I.G.)

Bill and Ted's Bogus Journey (film) 3: 483
Bim Skala Bim 1: 185
Bin Hassan, Umar 2: 305
Bittan, Roy 3: 598, 601
Bivins, Michael 3: 517, 519
Bjelland, Kat 1: 16 (ill.), 17-19
Bjork 2: 222, 300; 3: 613, **621 (ill.)**, **622 (ill.)**, **623-625**
Black-on-black violence 2: 318, 372
Black Crowes 3: 541, 542, **545 (ill.)**, **546 (ill.)**, **547**, 550
"Black Hole Sun" 1: 176
Black Love 1: 9
Black Panthers 2: 393, 425
Black Rock Coalition 3: 480
Black Sabbath 3: 465, 466
Blackie O 1: 187
Blades, Ruben 2: 245
The Blasters 3: 580
Bleach 1: 95
Blige, Mary J. 2: 307
Blondie 1: 139; 2: 277, 308
Blood of Abraham 2: 341
Blow, Kurtis 2: 309, 404
Blue Beat 1: 184
Blue Cheer 3: 466
Blue Flames 3: 502
Blues 2: 304
Blues Band 3: 549
Blues Traveler 3: 541, 542, **548 (ill.)**, **549-551**
Blur 2: 221, 222, **227 (ill.)**, **228 (ill.)**, **229**, 255, 268
BMI New Music Showcase 3: 557
Boarder Baby Project 3: 509
Body Count 2: 366, 369, 370
Bolan, Marc 2: 272
Bones Thugs-N-Harmony 2: 307
Bonet, Lisa 3: 630-632
Bono 1: 190 (ill.) 191-195
Booga Basement 2: 345
Boogie Down Productions 2: 309, **317 (ill.)** **318-320**, 399, 407
Booker T. and the MGs 2: 276
Boquist, Dave 3: 592
Boquist, Jim 3: 592
Bostaph, Paul 3: 495
Bottrell, Bill 3: 628
Bowie, David 1: 6, 71, 72, 91; 2: 219 (ill.), 222, **230 (ill.)**,

222   Parents Aren't Supposed to Like It